CW00927295

TALES

from the

TOWER OF

LONDON

TALES
from the
TOWER OF
LONDON

DANIEL DIEHL & MARK P. DONNELLY

SUTTON PUBLISHING

First published in the United Kingdom in 2004 by
Sutton Publishing Limited · Phoenix Mill
Thrupp · Stroud · Gloucestershire · GL5 2BU

British Library Cataloguing in Publication Data
A catalogue record for this book is available from the British Library.

ISBN 0-7509-3496-4

Typeset in Photina MT 10.5/15 pt.
Typesetting and origination by
Sutton Publishing Limited.
Printed and bound in England by
J.H. Haynes & Co. Ltd, Sparkford.

CONTENTS

INTRODUCTION

There are only a handful of buildings in the world that are universally recognisable by both their name and location. The Eiffel Tower, the Colosseum, Britain's Houses of Parliament (and their accompanying clock, Big Ben), China's Great Wall, the White House (thanks primarily to television news), the pyramids and their neighbouring Sphinx, the Empire State Building, Notre Dame, the Taj Mahal and the Tower of London. Even the great temple complex at Ankor Wat and Moscow's Kremlin are only partially recognisable; the first by its distinctive architecture, but not by location (Cambodia) and the second only by the presence of the magnificent cathedral of St Basil. Of all these wonderful monuments to architectural creativity the Tower of London is unquestionably the most drawn, painted and photographed. No occupied building in the world is, or has been, more often represented on paper.

Amazingly, as universally popular as medieval castles are with the public, of all the buildings listed above only the Tower of London is a castle and, with the exception of the White House, the only one ever used as a private residence. Having been in constant use since the 1080s, the Tower can also lay claim to being the oldest living community in Europe, if not the world. These factors alone qualify it as a site worth studying.

Building of the Tower of London was begun in 1078 by command of William the Conqueror, but its initial form was a far cry from that which we see today. The only original buildings still remaining are the White Tower, which dominates the complex, and a few sections of the old Roman city wall that remain embedded in the curtain wall and scattered around the inner yard. The rest of the original buildings, and their surrounding fortification, were constructed of wood and have long since disappeared.

Through most of its nine and a half centuries, the Tower was a place where the monarchs of England could house their private army, seek refuge in times of trouble and use as a base of operations. More than one of these periods of strife are dealt with in depth in this book. Curiously, the Tower was not originally intended to protect the city of London, but rather to protect the occupying Normans from what William the Conqueror called 'the vast and furious population' of England. The idea was to build a castle so massive and so terrifying that the indigenous Anglo-Saxons would think twice before challenging their Norman overlords. To that end, it worked magnificently.

In the centuries since the Normans first began construction of the Tower, it has undergone massive (and until the mid-nineteenth century) almost constant change. Old buildings and towers were routinely torn down and new ones erected in their place. Sometimes these changes were brought about by purely practical needs and other times to repair the destruction brought about by the occasional fire, siege, or bombing (both during the Second World War and during 1970s terrorist attacks). Existing buildings were also frequently converted from one use to another to suit changing social demands and political reality. As one monarch after another remodelled the complex to suit their individual needs, the names of some existing towers and buildings also changed. What is now known as the Bloody Tower was originally called the Garden Tower because of its proximity to the complex's kitchen garden. We have tried to reflect these changes in the text of our stories.

The Tower has alternately, and often simultaneously, been used as a royal palace, a fortress, a zoo, a military garrison, the Royal Treasury, an arsenal, the Royal Mint, a state office building, a museum and the repository of the Crown Jewels. As late as the reign of Queen Elizabeth I, John Stow commented on the Tower's multiple uses, stating that it was 'a citadel to defend or command the city, a royal palace for assemblies or treaties, a prison of state for the most dangerous offenders; the only place of coinage for all England. . . . The armoury for warlike provision; the treasury of the ornaments and jewels of the crown; and general conserver of the records of the Queen's courts of justice.'

The Tower complex's architectural make-up as we see it today is, to a great extent, the result of Victorian 'remodelling', to make it more accessible to the public and appear more 'appropriately medieval'. Since Queen Victoria first opened the Tower to tourists in 1837, the general public has come to think of it primarily as an awe-inspiring museum. While 'wowing' the tourists may only recently have become one of the Tower's official functions, it has had that effect on visiting dignitaries since the Middle Ages. After all, as London's most visible symbol of the monarchy it was the Tower's job to impress, and impress it does.

The Tower of London is, quite literally, a town in a stone envelope tucked in the heart of London. Deep inside massive walls, the streets and alleys of the Tower complex twist, turn and double back on themselves like some bizarre stone maze. Nearly everything here, from the looming White Tower to the enclosure walls, road surfaces, walkways and smallest public toilet, are made of stone – the only relief is the occasional blank stare of a window or the narrow ribbon of sky appearing over the outer curtain walls.

Popular though they are, neither photograph nor drawing can impart the sheer mass of the place. Unless visitors constantly remind themselves that this is not some perfectly preserved medieval town, but a very real military base, the most thrilling aspect of the Tower experience will be lost amid the tourist-friendly splash.

As spectacular as the Tower is architecturally, chronicling its physical development is not the primary concern of this book. For nearly two centuries there have been dozens, if not hundreds, of books written about the tower's physical history. Nearly all of them, from the simplest guidebook to the most lavish 'coffee table' volume, have attempted to give an overview of the old fortress' development, changing uses, important prisoners and gory tortures that have all contributed to the rich tapestry of its history. Instead of reploughing this well-trodden field, we have limited ourselves to telling the stories of the lives, and too often the deaths, of a few of the individuals who have passed through the gates of the Tower over the centuries. Most of the people whose stories are told here are at least briefly mentioned in many of these earlier books, giving us tantalising glimpses into their lives, but seldom, if ever, telling their whole story as it relates to their time at the Tower. It is the stories of these individuals, stories of bravery, greed, lust, heroism and ambition that we endeavour to bring to light in this volume.

Some of the people you will meet in the following pages will be at least slightly familiar. Wat Tyler and the Peasants' Revolt of 1381, the disappearance of the Princes in the Tower, Henry VIII's ill-fated fifth wife, Katherine Howard, and others, will be familiar, but hopefully we will add to your understanding of them. Others such as the foolhardy Colonel Blood, the tragic Alice Tankerville and the Nazi spy Josef Jakobs may well take you into unfamiliar territory.

The vast catalogue of adventures and adversities that people have faced in connection with the Tower of London is almost endless and it would be impossible to recount all, or even most, of them in a single volume. Practical limitations have forced us to omit many worthwhile, and often familiar, incidents of Tower history. Anne Boleyn, Sir Walter Raleigh and Scots patriot William Wallace are only a few of the people whose stories might have been told here, but space forced us to leave them out. But take heart dear reader; hopefully we will cover them in a future book.

We have approached each chapter in *Tales from the Tower* as a complete work in itself, capable of being read on its own and in no particular order. If you prefer not to read them in the chronological order in which they are presented, by all means do so. There are instances, however, where this might cause you to miss some revealing insights. In the chapter on Katherine Howard, you will find a seemingly benign mention of Bishop Edmond Bonner who performed the marriage ceremony between Katherine and Henry VIII. In the following chapter you will meet Bonner again, but in a far less pleasant capacity. However you choose to approach this book, rest assured that each chapter has been provided with sufficient background material to give you a sound historical 'feel' for the story, its characters and its setting in time and place.

Our book is not designed to be a weighty academic tome. We have tried to make every chapter an exciting, enjoyable read, free of excessive and superfluous detail. There are no footnotes or obscure references to bog you down. At the same time, we have gone to extraordinary lengths to ensure the historical accuracy of every name, date, place and incident you will come across in these pages. Often, in our research, we uncovered conflicting and contradicting accounts of individual incidents, or dates, or other information, and have checked and cross-checked to make certain our accounts are the most accurate version of the story possible. For instance, in the story of Lord and Lady Nithsdale, we found several different descriptions of the cloaks worn by Lady Nithsdale and her friends on their visit to the Tower. One account said they wore bright cloaks in a variety of different colours, while another insisted they all wore similar, brown cloaks. It was only when we discovered that one of the cloaks survived in the collection of the current Duchess of Norfolk that we could verify its colour; it is brown. This may seem a small detail, but we hope that knowing the information you uncover in these pages is not only enjoyable, but also historically accurate, will add to your reading pleasure.

We hope you enjoy reading these stories as much as we enjoyed writing them, and should you ever be lucky enough to visit the Tower of London, we sincerely hope your experience there is happier than that of most of the people you will meet in the following pages.

PLANS OF THE TOWER OF LONDON, TWELFTH TO TWENTIETH CENTURY

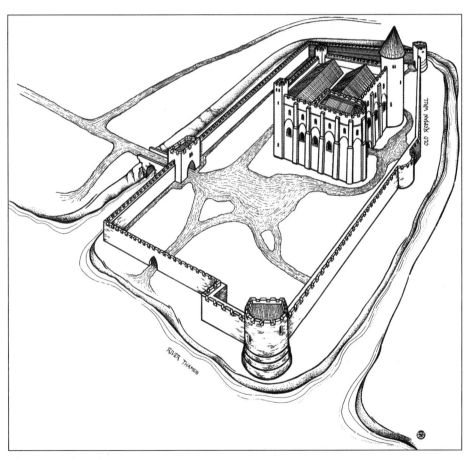

The Tower of London, *c.* 1100.

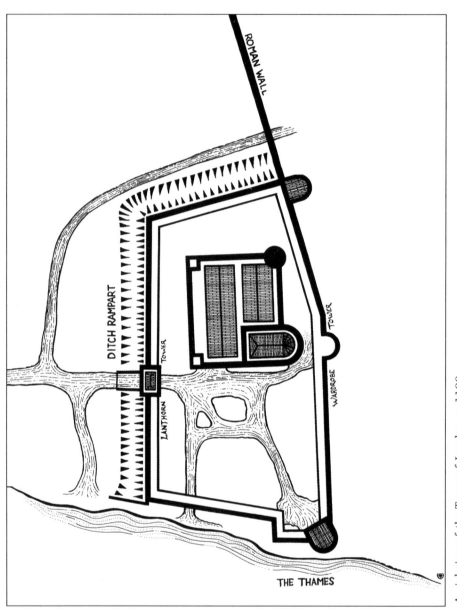

ROMAN WALL

DITCH RAMPART

TOWER

LANTHORN

WARDROBE TOWER

THE THAMES

Aerial view of the Tower of London, c. 1100.

Interior of the White Tower, *c.* 1100.

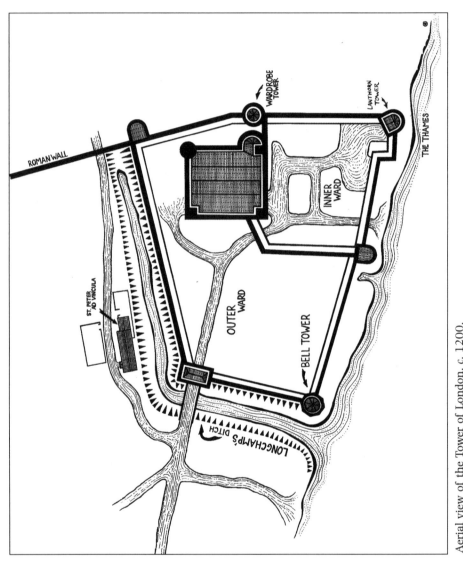

Aerial view of the Tower of London, c. 1200.

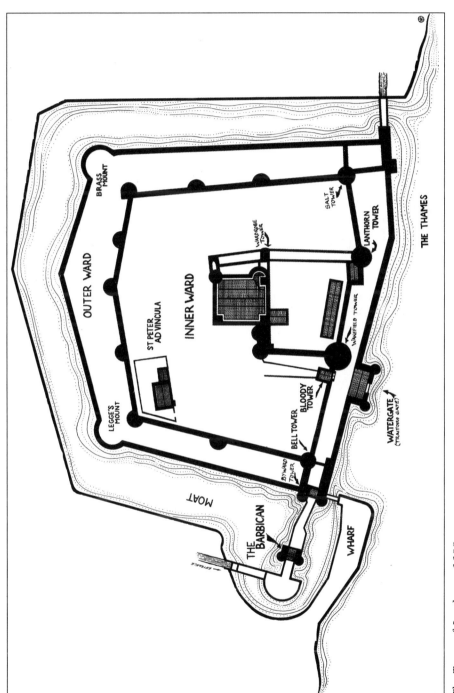

The Tower of London, c. 1300.

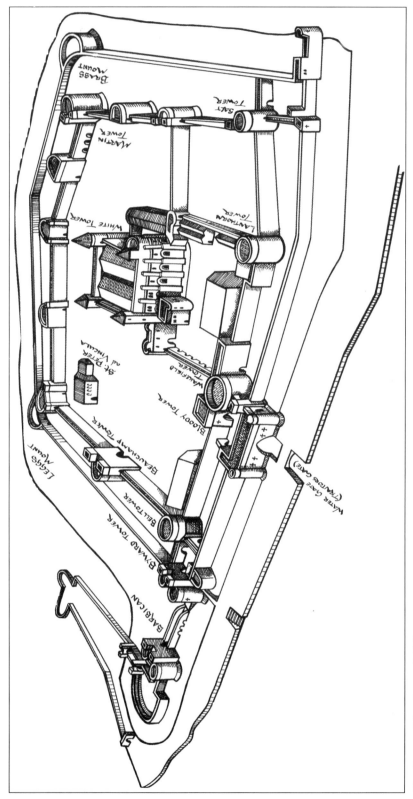

The Tower of London, c. 1490.

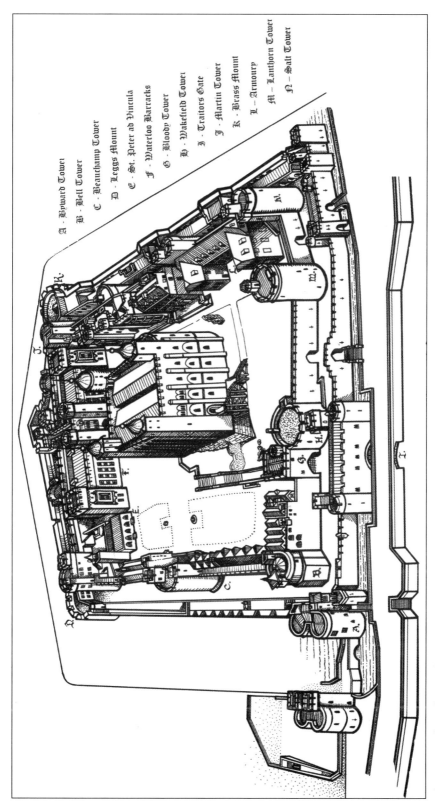

A - Byward Tower
B - Bell Tower
C - Beauchamp Tower
D - Leggs Mount
E - St. Peter ad Vincula
F - Waterloo Barracks
G - Bloody Tower
H - Wakefield Tower
I - Traitors Gate
J - Martin Tower
K - Brass Mount
L - Armoury
M - Lanthorn Tower
N - Salt Tower

The Tower of London in the nineteenth and twentieth centuries.

PART I
Building a Castle and a Kingdom

One

THE AXE, THE ARROW AND
THE WAILING MONK

William the Conqueror and Brother Gundulf
1066–80

King Edward, the great-great-great-grandson of King Alfred the Great, had reigned over Anglo-Saxon England for nearly a quarter of a century. With the exception of paying a massive annual tribute to the Viking Danes who controlled the northern half of England his reign had been a relatively peaceful one. The English channel had always been so effective at preventing any large-scale invasion of England that Edward had confidently devoted much of his later years to building churches and cathedrals rather than the massive stone fortresses which were appearing all over continental Europe.

The king was perceived as being so gentle and pious that his people respectfully dubbed him Edward the Confessor. The grandest monument to Edward's earnest faith in God was the massive new church, the Abbey of Westminster, which stood just yards beyond Edward's palace near London's west gate. By the end of December 1065 the Abbey Minster was nearly finished, but so was Edward the Confessor. On 27 December the 63-year-old monarch suffered a stroke and drifted in and out of consciousness for days. Confused and near death, the king clutched at his bedclothes, mumbling incoherently about 'devils that shall come through all the land with fire and sword and the havoc of war'.

For all his piety the dying king had good reason to worry about the future. He was leaving behind a kingdom with no direct heir to the throne, which amounted to a disaster of monumental proportions in the turbulent eleventh century. Over the years he had probably dangled the promise of the throne in front of many friends and enemies as a means of keeping them on his side. Now there was no time left to play politics. On 5 January, just hours before he died, Edward named his young brother-in-law, Harold Godwinson, Earl of

Wessex, as his heir and successor. Even if there had been other legitimate contenders for the throne, in Anglo-Saxon England a deathbed request from the monarch had the strength of law. The following day, 6 January 1066, King Edward was laid to rest in his new cathedral at Westminster and Harold was crowned King of England.

If the coronation seemed rushed, there was more than ample reason for haste. The noblemen of England may have supported Edward's choice of Harold, but there were others across the Channel who were less than pleased. Harold was not the late king's only brother-in-law. Like his brother Harold, Tostig was also a brother of Edward's widow Queen Edith – giving him equal claim to the crown. The fact that he had been stripped of his title as Earl of Northumbria and sent into exile only the year before didn't seem to matter to Tostig.

Then there was Harald III Hardrada, King of Norway. As ruler of the Viking Confederation Harald had clawed his way to the throne through pure brute force. He now ruled Norway, Sweden and Denmark, and commanded vast portions of northern England known as the Danelaw. With no legitimate heir to the English throne, there was no reason why the rest of England should not come under Viking rule. And Harald had an ally. Tostig knew he was not strong enough to seize the country alone, and so had thrown in his lot with that of Harald. Their combined armies posed a serious threat to the security of the British Isles.

Finally, there was William, 'the bastard' Duke of Normandy, who, at forty years of age, was as hard and strong as a younger man and a brutally determined master of military strategy. Not only did England and Normandy have strong political and blood ties, William insisted that he had personally been promised the throne of England. Depending on which story you believe, Edward the Confessor may indeed have promised it to William and then changed his mind shortly before he died. If he had promised the crown to William, it is also possible he had sent his brother-in-law Harold Godwinson (now King Harold) to Normandy with verbal confirmation of this promise. Or Harold may have been taken prisoner on the continent, been rescued by Duke William and, in a fit of gratitude, offered to lay aside all claim to the throne and support William when the time came. William insisted that one or more of these stories were the truth. Conversely, Harold argued that it was all rubbish and that even if it were not, the king's deathbed request legally superseded all previous agreements.

Whatever the claims, whatever the truth, Tostig was unhappy, Harald
Hardrada of Norway was unhappy, William of Normandy was unhappy and
King Harold was in deep and immediate trouble.

Comprehending the full scope of the threat facing him and his kingdom,
Harold immediately began assembling an army. The nobles were instructed to
call into service every able-bodied man, and the navy was made ready for
war. Then, just before Easter 1066, a strange and frightening omen appeared
in the skies over northern Europe. Day and night a blazing ball of light ripped
through the sky for more than a week. The cyclical nature of Haley's Comet
was not yet understood and its appearance seemed an ominous portent. The
more superstitious spread tales about hails of fire and strange and unnatural
births as rumours of impending disaster rumbled through England.
Disregarding the fears of his credulous people, King Harold continued to
prepare for war.

By midsummer the English army was, according to the Anglo-Saxon
Chronicles: 'larger than any king had assembled before in the country'.
Because the English Channel had been storm-tossed since early spring, Harold
knew the first wave of invasions would come from the north, sweeping
southward through the Danelaw, towards free England. Accordingly, late in
August he began moving his army north towards York.

About 15 September the 200 Viking longboats carrying Harald
Hardrada's invasion force landed on the north-east coast of England.
Thousands of warriors slipped ashore to meet up with the forces of Tostig,
who had fought their way across the length of England. The confederates
then marched on York where they slaughtered the local militia and laid
down terms of surrender to the city, retreating about 10 miles eastward to
the village of Stamford Bridge to make camp and await an answer from the
city fathers of York.

On 25 September, even before the Vikings had established a defensible camp,
the English army appeared, seemingly out of nowhere, and fell on the invaders
with a vengeance. Hour after hour the two sides hacked at each other with
swords, spears and vicious long-handled axes that could split a man from
collarbone to pelvis with a single blow. By the end of the day, thousands lay
dead or dying on the blood-soaked field. Among the dead were both Hardrada
and Tostig. The first threat to Anglo-Saxon England was over, and centuries of
terror at the hands of Viking raiders were effectively ended. Having lost more
than a quarter of his army in that single day, King Harold moved the survivors

to York to rest and regroup. But as the clouds of battle still hung over Stamford Bridge, the weather cleared over the English Channel.

Just three days after the disastrous defeat of the Vikings at Stamford Bridge, William of Normandy landed on the Pevensey coast of southern England near Hastings. With him were seven thousand men, more than two thousand horses and five portable wooden forts. It did not take long for word of this second invasion to reach the English army.

To King Harold's credit, after weeks of marching and intense fighting, the remains of his army was still largely intact. Hurriedly, he reassembled his men and sent out messengers to plead for more volunteers to join him in London. In a feat of incredible stamina the already beleaguered army marched the 250 miles between York and London in just eighteen days. Pausing only five days in London to collect his volunteers and supply his forces, Harold then pressed on southward towards Hastings, 40 miles away. As impressive as the feat was, before they encountered the Normans the English were exhausted from their long ordeal.

Even before the English had arrived in London, a messenger in the employ of one of William's relatives in England reached the Norman camp with news that the English king had: 'given battle to his brother and the king of Norway, killing both of them and destroyed their mighty armies. He now hastens towards you. . . .' Duke William's commanders urged him to set up defensive positions and wait for the English. Confident in his cause and his men, William refused: 'I have no desire to protect myself behind any rampart, but intend to give battle to Harold as soon as possible.'

In a clever ploy to deprive his adversary of food, shelter and any hiding place, William began laying waste to the farms, forests and villages north of Hastings. He also sent out messengers to make contact with the English king. When a Norman envoy caught up with the English army south of London, he offered Harold an opportunity to surrender his crown and kingdom. King Harold's sentiments were much the same as William's had been when advised to dig in. According to one chronicler, he replied, 'We march at once, we march to battle. May the Lord decide this day between William and me, and may He pronounce which of us is right.' The stage had been set for the most pivotal battle of the early Middle Ages.

Just after nine o'clock in the morning on 14 October, the two sides came within sight of each other about 7 miles north-west of the town of Hastings. Hurriedly positioning themselves near the top of a low rise, the

English took up battle formation. What the Normans were doing seemed to make no sense.

Like most armies of the day, many of the English rode to battle on horseback, but before taking up attack formation they dismounted. A man could not swing a war axe from horseback and horses were too awkward, and too valuable, to be ridden into battle. The Normans did not seem to understand this. Fascinated with all the latest technology and tactics of warfare, William of Normandy had long since incorporated the use of stirrups to enable mounted cavalry to hold their position in the saddle while fighting. He had also picked up the concept of using massed contingents of archers as a force separate from either cavalry or infantry. In his drive to make his army the most modern and efficient in western Europe, William had also incorporated a new weapon called a crossbow into his archery units.

The Norman archers stood in units at the front of their battle lines; the infantry positioned behind them, while the cavalry waited at the rear. The English arrayed themselves in the accepted manner of the period, with warrior nobility at the centre of the line flanked by units of levied commoners on either side, with a few archers scattered randomly among the ranks.

Norman archers opened the battle by unleashing volley after volley of arrows and crossbow bolts into the English line – the deadly missiles slamming through the shield wall protecting the front ranks of soldiers. To their credit, despite this horrific punishment the English line held. Next, William ordered a massive infantry charge. If the English could be kept too confused to regroup, the Norman cavalry could move in and destroy them before a counter-attack could be organised. But the English stood their ground and mowed down the Norman infantry with a hail of spears. The few survivors were then cut to pieces with swords and long axes. According to the Anglo-Saxon Chronicle, the battle was so terrible that 'the noise of the shouting could barely be heard over the clash of weapons and the groans of the dying'. William of Normandy now saw that the English would not collapse as easily as he had hoped. To urge his men forward in the face of this punishing defence, William and some of his cavalry rode into the thick of battle, shouting and exhorting his men to greater effort.

Somehow, in all the confusion, William's horse was killed. Word spread among the Normans that Duke William himself had been slain. Confused and apparently leaderless, the Norman line began to falter and fall back. Seizing their advantage, the English pushed forward, heedless of the safety of maintaining a solid defensive line, driving the frightened Normans before them.

Realising what had happened, William tore off his helmet, grabbed another mount, raised himself up in his saddle and shouted that he was unharmed. In a desperate attempt to regroup the cavalry for a concerted charge, William and his mounted knights withdrew slightly. Thinking a rout was in progress, the English drove deeper into the sea of Normans. There was no longer any order on the field. When the Norman cavalry had reassembled, they rode headlong into the midst of the enemy. Only minutes before the cavalry engaged the English, Norman archers unleashed a final, massed volley of arrows. In less than two hours the hopes for a free Anglo-Saxon England were shattered.

Nearly all the English nobility lay dead, including two of the king's brothers and the king himself; his body was so horribly mangled that his men could not identify him. Leaderless and defeated, the Anglo-Saxons surrendered to William of Normandy, now the Conqueror of England.

After the battle, King Harold's mother and his mistress, the beautiful Edith Swansneck, managed to identify the king by sorting through the mountain of corpses one at a time. Among his many other wounds, it is likely that King Harold had been shot through the eye with an arrow during the final volley from the Norman archers. Despite the women's pleas, and the queen mother's offer of gold equal in weight to her son's body, William would not give them the dead king for a decent Christian burial. There would be no martyrs to stand between William and the throne of England.

William, Duke of Normandy, may have become William I, Conqueror and King of England, but he had made no friends in his new realm and he knew it. His next job was to 'pacify' the land and control what William referred to as 'the fickleness of the vast and furious population'. But William understood the art of domination as thoroughly as battlefield tactics. Like most early medieval princes, he ruled essentially by terror. To consolidate his power, he devastated the land of anyone who might even conceivably put up resistance, systematically destroying the ancient Anglo-Saxon kingdoms and duchies and wiping out remaining Viking strongholds in the Danelaw, so recently freed by King Harold's victory at Stamford Bridge. Anglo-Saxon noblemen were stripped of their titles and nearly all land was confiscated to be divided among the Norman lords.

Rather than waste time and resources trying to take London in a straight assault, he simply devastated the surrounding land for miles in every direction and sat down to wait for the city to capitulate. His tactics were so brutal, even by the standards of the day, that one of his closest supporters, Ordericus, was appalled by the devastation: 'William in the fullness of his wrath ordered that the corn and cattle, with all the farming implements and provisions, to be collected on heaps and set on fire.' For months, the Normans laid waste to such vast tracts of land that the resultant famine would not subside in some areas for seventeen years. The compiler of the Anglo-Saxon Chronicle prayed 'may God will an end to this oppression'.

If all this were not enough, to make certain his new subjects did not forget who controlled their country, William began a programme of castle building that would last for the rest of his life. Most of these early castles were little more than one or two wooden buildings inside a series of wooden palisade walls, which could serve as supply depots and redoubts for army patrols. Thanks to all the free Saxon labour he now commanded and an average construction time of only three to four months apiece, within a few years there were somewhere in the neighbourhood of eighty castles dotting the English countryside.

But above all, William knew, as had the Romans and Anglo-Saxons before him, that the key to controlling England was controlling London. It not only guarded the mouth of the Thames estuary, but major roads from every point on the island converged on the capital. London alone boasted three of the new wooden fortresses. William chose the best situated of these London strongholds as his base of operations.

When the Romans moved into Britain in the first century AD they made London, which they called Londinium, the administrative centre of the province. Surrounding the city with more than 3 miles of stone wall 8 feet thick and 20 feet high, they constructed a massive fortress in the south-east corner to protect the town and the Thames harbour. Although the Romans abandoned Britain in the fourth century, many of their fortifications remained and William set about repairing the surviving sections of wall around London, building his timber castle on the foundations of the ancient fortress.

In 1077, more than a decade after the Norman invasion, London was devastated by a fire, which destroyed hundreds of homes and businesses. Whether the king's castle itself was burned remains unknown, but the fire was enough to prompt William to rebuild the fortress in a style befitting the conqueror of England. A new, stone castle would dominate the town and be large enough to serve as a royal palace, military garrison for the king's household troops and administrative centre for the kingdom. It was a monumental undertaking that required the services of the best architect available, and William knew just the man for the job.

When Prior Lanfranc was sent from Normandy to England by the Pope in 1067 to become the new Archbishop of Canterbury, he brought with him his loyal clerk, Gundulf. Gundulf had already developed a reputation as an architectural genius on the continent, having designed numerous churches and military fortifications in a career that spanned more than three decades. He also had a reputation of being more than a little eccentric. Pious and emotional, Gundulf was subject to outbursts of weeping, sulking, fervent prayer and depression at the slightest provocation. His odd behaviour had earned him the none-too-flattering nickname of 'the wailing monk'.

More concerned with Gundulf's abilities than his personal problems, the king summoned the monk to the royal presence and offered him the job of designing the new castle. Gundulf refused. He was a man of God and had no desire, at his advanced age, to build any more fortresses. He wanted to dedicate his few remaining years to designing churches and would be pleased to offer his services to William in that capacity.

Not to be denied, the king happily offered Gundulf the commission to build a new cathedral at Rochester, 40 miles east of London. To sweeten the deal, he would guarantee that Gundulf became Bishop of Rochester. Gundulf jumped at the offer, breaking into a fit of tears, praising the king's wisdom and generosity. Obviously, Gundulf had never dealt with William the Conqueror. He would have the bishopric, and his cathedral, but first he would build the king's fortress in London. Whining and haggling, the two finally struck a deal. Gundulf would first be appointed bishop, then build the new castle and finally he could retire to build his cathedral. Reluctantly, the old monk agreed. Within months he was made Bishop of Rochester and in the following year, 1078, began work on William's castle.

After the wooden castle was torn down, the Roman foundations were repaired and strengthened while Gundulf designed the new building. Incorporating the many uses the building would have to serve into a single, massive tower, the designs revealed a gigantic, cube-like structure more than 100 feet square and nearly as high. The only entrance would be situated on the west front of the building, facing the town, but the entry gate would be concealed and protected by an outer wall. The entrance itself would be located one floor above ground, and the ground floor would have neither windows nor doors to prevent attackers from breaking into the building. The entry stairs were probably made of wood so they could be destroyed or burned if the tower came under siege. No one would get into the great tower unless the king wanted them in. Protected on one side by the old Roman wall, on another by the River Thames and fortified with 15 foot-thick walls, the new castle would be unassailable.

The ground floor, without windows or doors, would contain barracks for the king's personal troops, beneath which were cells, dungeons and a specially constructed room with a vaulted ceiling and a massive oak door. This was the royal treasury. On the floor above the barracks would be the banqueting hall, armoury and chapel. Above these were the royal council chambers and on the top floor were the royal apartments. With the exception of the chapel, which projected from the south-east corner, the building was no more than a massive square box. The few windows were mostly limited to tall, narrow arrow slits, allowing the entire building to become a bunker should the occasion require it. The building had no adornment of the type found in the great churches and cathedrals; there were no unnecessary frills. This was not a building to be loved; it was designed only to protect the king and inspire fear and awe in both his subjects and enemies. The Anglo-Saxon Chronicles lamented: 'He built him a castle as a place to annoy his enemies from. . . . And they oppressed the people greatly with castle building.' So it would seem that the king's subjects were every bit as 'annoyed' by the project as his enemies.

Carrying out this monumental project required hundreds of workmen. Not merely masons and carpenters, but quarrymen to mine the stone as well as carters and boatmen to move it from the quarry to the building site. When Gundulf agonised over the amount of manpower needed, the king simply sent out his soldiers to commandeer London's labour force. When this proved insufficient, farmers and craftsmen from the surrounding villages were rounded up as well. This was, in part, legitimate. Every subject under the feudal system owed forty days' service a year to his or her lord, but partly it was pure punishment for having lost a war to the Duke of Normandy.

To his credit, this distressed Gundulf greatly. He insisted that forced labour did not make good workers, and convinced the king that everyone above the rank of common labourer should be imported from Normandy. William undoubtedly hated to spend the extra money on skilled (and more importantly voluntary) labourers, but Gundulf would not be moved. Along with the imported labour force came thousands of tons of limestone slabs from Norman quarries. The local ragstone, which the king provided as the building material, did not please Gundulf. He finally agreed it would work for the large areas of wall, but the corners and levelling courses between floors had to be good Norman limestone. Each block of limestone had to be quarried, carted to a long-ship, transported across the English Channel and then up the Thames to the castle site. As with so many government and military projects throughout history, budget was obviously not a serious issue.

No matter how impossible Gundulf must have been to work for, the results of his labours were rather impressive. After barely three years the tower was finished. With foundation dimensions of 118 by 107 feet, the battlements of the massive fortress soared more than 90 feet into the air. Higher still were four sleek towers, three of which were square and one round.

Shortly after the tower's completion the entire outside of the building was whitewashed. Not only did this make it seem even larger and more ominous, looming over the thatched houses and huts of London, but should an enemy attack, the massive white walls would act like a mirror, reflecting the sun into their eyes. In reality, however, it simply made the entire fortress appear stark and alien on the landscape. Which, in truth, is what it was.

Although many European castles had names, there seemed no sense in giving a name to the only stone castle in England. It was just 'The Tower' and once painted, its gleaming walls added another dimension to the name. William the Conqueror's castle was simply 'The White Tower'.

William was true to his word. When Bishop Gundulf finished his work late in 1080, he was released to Rochester where he immediately began work on his beloved cathedral. Although it would not be finished until 1130, nearly three decades after his death, the wailing monk lived long enough to see substantial portions of the work completed. It would seem that he lived to be nearly eighty-four years old. William the Conqueror was not, however, so lucky. In 1087, only nine years after commissioning the construction of the White Tower, William I of England died, leaving his kingdom, his throne and his fortress to his son, William II, known as William Rufus (the red) because of his bright red hair. While the English may have understandably hated his father, Rufus was equally despised by his own Norman lords, but he did carry out substantial work on the White Tower and persuaded Gundulf, the wailing monk, to build one last castle in his bishopric of Rochester.

DANGEROUS LIAISONS

Wat Tyler and the Peasants' Revolt
1381

Fourteenth-century England was a place of unprecedented social and economic turmoil. By mid-century the Black Death combined with the endless military campaigns of the Hundred Years' War had reduced the workforce by nearly half and bled the Royal Treasury dry. Add to these disasters a series of bad laws, bad administration and pure bad luck and the result was the most devastating urban riot in the nation's history. Fortunately the entire incident was recorded not only by numerous court chroniclers, but also by the greatest chronicler of the age, Jean de Froissart, and a young clerk named Geoffrey Chaucer.

When the beloved heir to the throne, Edward the Black Prince, died in 1376, his ageing father, Edward III, was left with a dilemma. Should the crown pass to his younger son, John of Gaunt, Duke of Lancaster, or the Black Prince's son Richard? Adhering to a strict interpretation of the succession laws, Edward left the crown to his nine-year-old grandson and appointed the massively unpopular Gaunt as head of the government and regent until Richard reached the age of majority. Gaunt, who had been appointed head of the English army in France on his brother's death, was not pleased with his father's choice of heir. Within a year of making these arrangements Edward III was dead, the new king was a ten-year-old child and John of Gaunt, though not king himself, was responsible for the management and welfare of England as well as the ongoing Hundred Years' War with France.

The day after his grandfather's death, Prince Richard was escorted to the Tower where he would be sequestered for his own safety until final plans for his coronation could be made. Three weeks later, the streets of London were festooned with banners and tapestries and lined with cheering crowds to welcome their new king as he rode to Westminster Cathedral and his coronation. It was a grand and awesome spectacle and, by all accounts,

Richard II lived up to everyone's expectations. He was an extraordinarily beautiful child; pale and aesthetic looking, with wavy golden locks that glistened like a halo in the sun ringing his delicate face. Dressed entirely in white for his investiture, the new king was, according to the chronicler Holinshed, 'as beautiful as an arch-angel'. But beneath the fine medieval pageantry lurked a social cancer that had been eating away at English society for two generations.

Between 1348 and 1353 the Black Death had swept through England, taking the lives of nearly one-third of the population. To add to the devastation, more than a decade before the plague struck, England had begun a series of wars with France that had, by the time of Richard's coronation in 1377, reduced the male population by another 25 per cent. This massive drop in the labour force left huge tracts of once-productive farmland untended and entire towns and villages deserted. The scarcity of farm labour brought about an acute shortage of food and an accompanying rise in prices as workers demanded higher wages, or simply left their farms in search of better paying jobs elsewhere. Understandably, landowners were desperate to keep their peasants (many of whom were serfs and legally tied to their manor) on the land and working. To make matters worse for everyone, as the economy imploded, taxes crept higher and higher to maintain government services and to fund the ongoing French wars.

As early as 1351 the government attempted to address the problem by imposing a wage and price freeze known as the Statute of Labourers. Among the provisions of the statute were the following:

All labourers under the age of thirty-six must work for the same wage as they received prior to 1348.

Any worker or servant who leaves his lord's service without cause or licence would be imprisoned.

Any man who pays his servant more than their pre-1348 wage will be fined twice the amount of that labourer's wage.

Anyone giving alms to the poor or gifts to beggars will be imprisoned.

This last clause was to make certain that everyone physically able to work did so. Despite the Statute of Labourers, serfs continued to steal away from their land, prices continued to rise and each new round of taxes became a heavier burden on everyone. By the time the young Richard II came to the throne, England was physically exhausted, nearing bankruptcy, and the people were growing increasingly restive. Only the natural human tendency to grumble rather than fight kept the nation from unravelling.

But John of Gaunt, Richard's uncle and regent, was more concerned with making war on the French than bureaucratic details or public welfare. Much that could have been done to redress the problems was ignored or grossly mishandled. What taxes could be collected were promptly funnelled into the military rather than the projects for which they had been earmarked. At Gaunt's urging, in November 1380 the new Chancellor (Archbishop of Canterbury Simon Sudbury) and the king's sergeant-at-arms (John Legge, a member of the privy council) came up with a new, single-levy poll tax set at 3 groats (the equivalent of 1 shilling) to be paid by every person over the age of fifteen. For skilled tradesmen this was the equivalent of a week's wages; for serfs who seldom even saw hard currency, it was nothing short of disastrous. Worse still, the 1380 levy was the third such tax to be passed in four years.

The tax collectors were resisted everywhere they went. Taxmen were run out of towns and villages while thousands of people temporarily disappeared. When the tax boxes returned to London, they contained less than two-thirds of what had been expected. To make up for the loss in revenue, in the spring of 1381 the tax men were sent out to collect the tax again – from everyone, whether they had paid the previous tax or not. Riots broke out wherever the taxman showed his face.

Anywhere people congregated, in churches, in public squares and at town markets, agitators were there inciting them to resist the extortionate tax. Among the most virulent opponents of government policy was a defrocked priest from Maidstone, Kent, named John Ball. He not only advocated refusing to pay the tax, but called for massive social changes including stripping the nobility of its power to impose such taxes. Ball was repeatedly arrested and thrown into jail. As soon as he was released, he returned to his personal crusade.

With the economy collapsing at an ever-increasing rate and people simply running away from their homes to escape the taxmen and the 'enforcers' who now accompanied them, by late spring thousands of starving, homeless peasants wandered England. In early June 1381, nearly twenty thousand dispossessed men and women from the county of Kent chose an ex-soldier and highwayman named Wat (or Walter) Tyler to be their leader, though it is equally possible that Tyler elected himself. In either case, he seems to have been a mesmerising speaker whose military experience provided him with a basic understanding of organisation and crowd control.

In a matter of days, Tyler began formulating an agenda. He and his motley band of followers marched along the River Medway. Their first stop was Maidstone, where they ransacked the local jail, freed all the prisoners and invited them to join the crusade. Among those who accepted the invitation was John Ball. Between Ball's fiery rhetoric and Tyler's organisational skills, the group quickly became a formidable force. Moving east from Maidstone, their next stop was Canterbury, where they gathered so many additional recruits that Froissart said 'they departed [there] and all the people of Canterbury with them. . . . And in their going they beat down and robbed houses . . . and had mercy of none.'

Now turning back to the west, the mob moved slowly towards London, solidifying their plans. The only person to whom they would pay allegiance was King Richard. Everyone else in the ruling class, from the greatest nobleman to the humblest lawyer, was to be forced out of office and put on trial. Halfway along the 40-mile stretch between Canterbury and the capital lies the town of Rochester, and here the rebels seized the castle, ransacked it and took the family of Sir John Newton, the constable, prisoner. Newton himself was sent to London with a message for the king: Richard would meet with the rebels at Blackheath in three days to hear their demands. If Newton failed to deliver the message, or if the army was called out, his family would be killed. Over the next two days, Tyler's army plodded steadily westward. Unknown to them, another rebel army even larger than their own was also converging on London from Essex, north-east of the capital.

For some reason, word of the rebels' approach took the King's Council and the government completely by surprise; certainly they should have been aware of the level of discontent in the country, and the tax riots could hardly have escaped their attention. Possibly, it was the sheer size of the uprising that overwhelmed them. The combined force of Tyler's army and the Essex men has been estimated at more than one hundred thousand – nearly twice the population of London itself and three times the size of the largest medieval army ever assembled. Certainly it did not help matters that the government's driving force and chief military mind, John of Gaunt, was in Scotland at the time.

Trying to come to grips with an unprecedented situation, the Council sent messengers to Windsor to bring King Richard to the safety provided by the

Tower and the 1,200 troops stationed there. The Queen Mother, Joan (known as the Fair Maid of Kent), was also rushed to the Tower where she and her son were joined by virtually everyone in the government. The king's uncle, the Earl of Buckingham, along with the Earls of Suffolk, Kent, Salisbury and Warwick were there, along with Sir Robert Hales, the Lord Treasurer, John Legge, who had devised the poll tax, and Simon Sudbury the Archbishop of Canterbury and Chancellor of England. With them was Willian Walworth, a successful fishmonger serving as that year's Lord Mayor of London. Everyone had their own idea of how to deal with the mob, but the king insisted that the only right thing to do was to meet them and hear their demands.

On 12 June 1381, the king and his ministers left the Tower by barge, sailing eastward to Greenwich, where they planned to disembark and walk the mile and a half to Blackheath. Even before they approached the mooring site, they could hear the shouting multitude. Tyler and the Kent contingent had come to Greenwich to meet them. Despite the king's efforts to land and open a dialogue, the crowd only screamed and taunted him and his ministers. According to Froissart, 'And when they saw the king's barge coming, they began to shout, and made such a cry, as though the devils of hell had been among them. . . . And when the king and his lords saw the demeanour of the people, the best assured of them were in dread.'

In fact, Richard tried repeatedly to speak with the mob, shouting 'I have come to speak with you – tell me what you want', but his words were drowned out by shouts and insults. Left to his own devices, Richard might have continued his efforts, but Chancellor Sudbury, Warwick and Suffolk all knew they were in serious personal danger and urged the king to return to London and the safety of the Tower. Reluctantly, Richard agreed. But when the barges turned to leave, the action enticed the crowd to follow.

Moving faster than the rebels, the royal barges made it to the Tower before the mob hit the city walls where, as luck would have it, nearly sixty thousand screaming peasants from Essex joined them. When the guards at London Bridge refused to open the gates to Tyler and his followers, they threatened to burn down the surrounding suburbs and take the city by storm. To prove how serious they were, they rampaged through ultra-fashionable Fleet Street, which lay just outside the safety of the city walls, looting and burning the shops and homes of the merchants.

Whether this incident alone was sufficient cause for the gates of the city to be opened to the howling mob is unknown. What we do know is that thousands of apprentices, day labourers and servants in the city supported the rebels and it may have been their rearguard attack on London Bridge that finally opened the gates and unleashed a wave of discontent that engulfed the city. By the time the swarm from Kent crossed London Bridge, the Essex men had successfully stormed the gate at Aldgate. Simultaneously, nearly one hundred thousand angry, hungry peasants surged through the narrow streets and lanes of London, sacking and burning everything they could not eat or steal in an orgy of looting, murder and destruction.

Desperate to save their lives, homes and property, terrified Londoners offered them food, beer and wine. But the more the mob drank, the more uncontrollable they became. Froissart wrote that the rebels 'rush[ed] into the houses that were the best provisioned . . . [where] they fell on the food and drink that they found. In the hope of appeasing them, nothing was refused them . . . and in their going they beat down abbeys and . . . diverse fair houses.' Any home that suggested a prosperous owner was subjected to the same treatment. In their rampage, the mob attacked and destroyed the Fleet and Marshalsea prisons, setting the prisoners free and inviting them to join in wreaking vengeance on the city.

In the New Temple, the district housing the law courts and residences of most of the city's lawyers and judges, they sacked and burned everything they could get their hands on, including the home of the hated Lord Treasurer, Sir Robert Hales. Everywhere, books, tapestries and clothes were torn to shreds, tossed from windows and set alight in the streets. When a house was completely vandalised, it too was either pulled down or torched. At Lambeth Palace, London home of the Archbishop of Canterbury, several of the buildings were burnt and all the tax records from the Chancery Office were thrown into the fire. Froissart records that a similar fate was meted out to John of Gaunt's Savoy Palace: 'And when they entered [Gaunt's house] they slew the keepers thereof and robbed and pill[ag]ed the house, and when they had so done, they set fire on it and clean destroyed and burnt it. And when they had done that outrage, they . . . went straight to the fair hospital of the [Knights of] Rhodes, called St John's, and there they burnt house, hospital, Minster and all.'

Their anger spent and the day waning, the mobs converged on the Tower at Tower Hill and St Catherine's Square. Here, they took up the less strenuous sports of hard drinking and taunting the young king and his ministers who they knew were trapped inside. They screamed alternately for the Chancellor, the Lord Treasurer, or anyone else involved in levying the hated poll tax, all the while insisting that, as Froissart put it '. . . they would never depart thence till they had the king at their pleasure'.

Now prisoners in their own fortress, Richard and his council gathered on the parapets of the Tower more than 100 feet above the seething, drunken mob. From there, in the eerie, orange half-light of more than thirty fires burning out of control across the city, the fourteen-year-old king and his frightened ministers looked down on a scene that could have been snatched straight from the mouth of hell. The resilient Tower was completely cut off from the outside world; the rioters had all the supplies of London to sustain them and the rioting continued into the night, punctuated by a chorus of cries and screams as hundreds of innocent citizens were murdered or roasted alive in their burning houses.

The sense of fear that had clutched at the ministers for two days was now replaced by galloping panic. Earlier that morning, while Richard and his ministers tried to talk to Tyler's people at Greenwich, a messenger had arrived at the Tower with news that the rebellion was spreading through every county south and east of London. There were also reports of riots in Cambridgeshire and Huntingdonshire. In some areas the rebels were in effective control of entire cities. If something was not done soon, the country would collapse. Lord Mayor Walworth and the more resolute members of council insisted they would make a fight of it. In the Tower alone there were more than six hundred men at arms and at least as many archers. Sir Robert Knollys had about one hundred men at his fortified manor and nearly four hundred of John of Gaunt's soldiers were still somewhere in the city. With luck a complement of nearly two thousand men could be raised and, although they were outnumbered nearly fifty to one, only a tiny fraction of the mob was armed, all of them were exhausted and most were now too drunk to stand. A well-trained force should be able to kill them off like flies.

The Earl of Salisbury, the oldest and most experienced of Richard's councillors adamantly disagreed, advising the king, 'Sir, if you appease the mob with fair words, that would be better; grant them all they ask, for if we begin something we cannot finish, nothing will ever be recovered, for us or for our heirs, and England will be a desert.' It would take a lot more courage to face Wat Tyler and his screaming cut-throats than to turn the army loose on them, but even at fourteen years of age, Richard knew it was the wisest course of action. The trick was to arrange a meeting in such a way that it would draw the rebels out of London and provide Archbishop Sudbury, Treasurer Hales and John Legge a chance to escape from the Tower before they were torn to pieces.

The next morning, 14 June, both King Richard and Wat Tyler were ready. When, according to Froissart 'on the Friday in the morning the people . . . began to . . . cry and shout, and said, without the king would come out and speak with them, they would assail the Tower and take it by force, and slay all them that were within', Richard was ready to put his plan into action. Shouting down from the parapets he told the crowd he would meet with them and discuss their grievances if they would then disperse peacefully. As insurance against reprisals, the king signed a blanket pardon, there on the Tower wall, and sealed it in full sight of the mob. Handing it to two of his knights, he ordered it to be taken to the gates of the Tower and read aloud in public. The offer fell short of its mark; many of the rebels shouted down the heralds and went back to drinking and looting. Most, including Tyler, a few of his followers from Kent and the majority of the Essex men, agreed to meet the king at the place he suggested, a meadow known as Mile End, located well outside the city walls.

Later that day, accompanied only by a few dozen bodyguards, pages and the Lord Mayor, young Richard II rode out to confront more than sixty thousand of his angry subjects. It was his hope that with so much of the rabble drawn out of the city, the ministers would be able to escape by barge down the Thames. Proceeding out of London through Bulwark Gate, Richard and his party met the rebels at Mile End – near the site of the burned-out Hospital of St John – at the appointed time. Amazingly, for all their ferocity of the previous days, the mob greeted the king with respect, kneeling and swearing that they respected him both as their king and as the son of their hero, Edward the Black Prince. With this apparent gesture of goodwill, Richard agreed to rescind the poll tax and work towards the abolition of serfdom. Serfs would become tenant farmers, free to stay on their land, or leave, as they chose. He also reiterated his promise of a full pardon, saying, according to Froissart '"and also I pardon everything that ye have done hitherto, so that ye . . . return to your houses [immediately]" . . . and then the king ordained more than thirty clerks the same Friday, to write with all diligence letters patent and sealed with the king's seal.'

Tyler now insisted that those to whom he referred as 'traitors', meaning the Archbishop, Legge, Hales and others complicit in devising the poll tax be put on trial. Although Richard promised to look into the matter and deal with the men 'as could be provided by law', it did not satisfy Tyler. While Richard remained immersed in negotiations and attempts to placate the crowd, Wat Tyler slipped away and headed back to the city and the more than forty thousand rebels, mostly his Kentish contingent, who were still there.

While Richard and the rebels had been working through their differences, the Archbishop, Chancellor Hales and John Legge had attempted to row out of the Tower's watergate and slip downriver. It was a good plan, but it didn't work. As soon as their boat emerged from the Tower gate the crowd on Tower Hill recognised the men. Within minutes they were forced back to the Tower. By the time Wat Tyler returned to his followers, they had surrounded the Tower and were howling for the council's blood. Thoroughly convinced that he could bend the king to his will, Tyler whipped his men into a fury, saying that if they could get rid of the hated ministers they would control all England within a week.

Exactly how the Kentish rebels got through the gates of the Tower will probably never be known. One gate may have been knocked down, it may have been opened by an 'inside man' or simply unlocked by a terrified guard. What is certain is that once inside the Tower complex, the mob poured through alleyways, halls and passages destroying everything they could find; scattering ministers, servants, soldiers and courtiers in all directions. In the royal armouries they grabbed weapons of every description to facilitate their rampage. The Queen Mother was caught in her bedroom where her ladies-in-waiting tried desperately to protect her as the rioters tore down bed hangings and tapestries and ripped them to shreds. Although Queen Joan escaped with no more than a few forced kisses, one of her ladies was brutally raped in front of her terrified companions. As the mob moved off in search of new plunder, the queen was rescued by her pages who disguised her as a servant and hustled her to the watergate, commandeered a small boat and rowed her to the safety of Baynard's Castle a few miles down the Thames.

When the rioters smashed through the doors of St John's Chapel, they found what they had been looking for. With a grim sense of fatalism, Sir Robert Hales, John Legge and John of Gaunt's personal physician had gathered with the Archbishop of Canterbury to receive the last rites. Not even allowing Sudbury to finish shriving the terrified men, the mob stormed the altar, knocked the communion cup from the archbishop's hand and dragged the four men and a monk named William Appelton down the stairs, through the Tower and out on to Tower Hill where a huge crowd was still milling around, howling for blood.

Archbishop Sudbury was thrown across a log as a man with a broadsword stepped forward. The first blow struck the archbishop's neck, slicing it open. When Sudbury cried out in pain and automatically raised his hand to the gushing wound, his executioner struck again, hacking off his fingers. Writhing in pain and bleeding profusely, the archbishop thrashed on the ground as his tormentor continued hacking at him. His skull was split open, as was his shoulder. After at least eight more strokes, the mangled corpse of Simon Sudbury, Archbishop of Canterbury and Chancellor of England, lay dead on Tower Hill. His bloody head was severed from his shoulders and his bishop's mitre nailed to the head, which was then stuck on a pike and paraded through the streets of London, along with those of his four companions, before being displayed on London Bridge.

While the Tower was being ransacked, his mother molested and his ministers murdered, King Richard was still earnestly trying to negotiate with the rebels at Mile End. To the boy's credit, more than forty thousand of the rebels, primarily those from Essex, agreed to the terms he had laid out and left Mile End carrying the letters of pardon he had offered to them earlier in the day. As the crowd began to disperse early in the evening, Richard and his party prepared to return to London. Before they had gone more than a mile, however, they met a herald who had slipped out of London with news of the assault on the Tower and the murders on Tower Hill. No one knew if the king's mother was alive or dead. Realising he could not return to London, the king's guards persuaded him to ride to Baynard's Castle. Once there, the fourteen-year-old king was reunited with his mother, cleaned up, fed and taken immediately to an emergency meeting of those few of the government who had made their way to Baynard's.

Despite all that had happened, Richard was still determined to stop the horrible, senseless violence and sent a page to war-torn London to find Wat Tyler and arrange for a meeting the next day at the Smithfield horse market, north of London. The scene that greeted the page on his return to the city had not improved. With few houses of the rich still standing, the mob had turned its vengeance on London's immigrant population. According to Geoffrey Chaucer, who witnessed the scene, 'there was a very great massacre of Flemings, and in one heap there were laying about forty headless bodies of persons who had been dragged forth from the churches and their houses; and hardly was there a street in the City in which there were not bodies laying of those who had been slain.'

At around five o'clock in the afternoon on Saturday 15 June, King Richard and a retinue of two hundred knights, soldiers, pages and the Lord Mayor arrived at Smithfield, where Wat Tyler and about twenty thousand rebels were waiting. This left nearly forty thousand of the mob still in London. Finally, to all intents and purposes, Wat Tyler now believed he had control of London, the government and the king. It was (according to Froissart) Tyler's plan to kill the king's men and the Lord Mayor and take Richard prisoner to parade around England as their mascot. With this grand plan in mind, all respect for the monarchy had vanished from Tyler's mind.

According to Froissart, and several other contemporary accounts, the meeting at Smithfield unfolded something like this: Tyler had commandeered a horse so he could approach the king at eye level and to make certain his followers could see him. Riding directly up to the king and brandishing a dagger in his left hand, Tyler reached out, took Richard's hand and shook it 'forcibly and roughly', saying, 'Brother, be of good comfort and joyful . . . and we shall be good companions'. Continuing in this well-rehearsed and intimidating manner, Tyler went on, 'Sir King, seest thou all yonder people? . . . they be at my commandment and have sworn to me faith and truth, to do all that I will have them.'

Trying to make the best of an obviously bad situation, Richard reiterated his promises of the day before, but believing himself now firmly in control this was no longer enough for Tyler. He insisted that all nobility, with the exception of the king, should be stripped of rank, title and possessions. All property belonging to the church, be it gold, land or buildings, would be confiscated and handed over to him and his followers. All bishops would be stripped of their titles and power. The list of wild, outrageous demands went on and on. When he finished, Tyler called for a mug of beer to wash out his mouth. Having done so, he spat the beer on the ground in front of the king.

Obviously frightened, King Richard remembered the words of the Earl of Salisbury at Friday's council meeting: 'Sir, if you appease the mob with fair words, that would be better; grant them all they ask . . .'. Calm negotiation was the only way he would save his own life and buy time to think of something. Consequently, Richard agreed to everything. It was all too easy. Tyler probably knew how outrageous his demands were and the king's easy compliance did not fool him. Of course, if Richard was telling the truth, he had literally surrendered his power to the mob and Tyler was king in all but name. To test the limits of his power, Tyler turned to the king's personal page and demanded that he hand over the Great Sword of State. '"I will not." The page shouted back, "It is the King's sword and you are not fit to hold it. You are only a villein.* If you and I were alone here, you durst not have spoken like that. . . ."' Swollen with his own sense of self-importance, Tyler was furious. Rising in his saddle and waving his dagger wildly, he shouted, 'By my faith, I shall never eat [again] till I have thy head!' The situation was on the verge of collapse.

Realising his king was in imminent danger, Lord Mayor Walworth spurred his horse forward, drove it between Tyler and the king and shouted that Tyler was a 'stinking wretch'. Furious, Tyler drove his dagger into the mayor's belly. Unknown to him, beneath his flowing gown of office Walworth had strapped on an armoured breastplate, and the knife glanced harmlessly to one side. The single moment of shock was all that Walworth needed. He drew his sword, striking the distracted Tyler across the forehead with the pommel and along the neck with the blade. When Tyler leaned back in the saddle, grabbing at his bleeding neck, he left himself open for the next blow. Walworth's blade drove deep into his stomach. Wheeling his horse around to pull himself free of the blade, Tyler rode only a few paces towards his men before tumbling to the ground, bleeding and writhing in agony.

This may have taken care of Wat Tyler, but the sight of their mortally wounded leader infuriated his thousands of followers. They drew their weapons; those who had bows cocked arrows into the string and drew. Seeing this shift in the mood of the crowd, the king's soldiers drew their swords, lowered their lances and prepared for an all-out fight. In the face of imminent death, it is to the young king's endless credit that he told his men to hold their positions and rode forward, alone, to face the angry rebels. 'Sirs', he said to them, 'would you shoot your king? I am your rightful captain. I will be your leader. Let him who loves me follow me.' With that, he turned his horse, exposing his back to the crowd, and rode slowly north, away from London. The now leaderless peasants lowered their weapons and, except for a few who remained behind to carry their fallen leader to nearby St Bartholomew's hospital, followed him.

---

* Villein was the medieval English word for anyone from a small village. It indicated a crude, ill-bred person and is the word from which the modern 'villain' is derived.

As soon as the king, and the mob, was out of sight, Sir Robert Knollys raced to London where he gathered his personal archers and soldiers and then returned to rescue the king. They found him, and the rebels, at Clerkenwell Fields, calmly talking, explaining their positions to each other. While Knollys had been gone, Walworth had despatched a group of men to retrieve the dying Wat Tyler from St Bartholomew's. By the time Knollys and his men had surrounded the rebels, Walworth had caught up with him. With the king rescued, Tyler was dragged on to the field and unceremoniously beheaded in full view of his former followers. Within hours, his head had replaced that of Archbishop Sudbury on London Bridge.

A week after the incident at Smithfield, a group of peasants returned to the burned-out shell of London, carrying the king's letters of pardon, and asking for the charters to end serfdom that he had promised them. Furious at the rebels' betrayal of his trust, Richard told them that because his promises had been extracted by force and deceit, they were not binding, ending with the terse condemnation, 'Serfs and villeins ye are and serfs and villeins ye shall remain'.

Many of the rebels, particularly those from Essex who disbanded after the first meeting at Mile End, did receive the pardons they had been promised, although they were made to pay 20 shillings apiece to have them ratified with the king's seal. Elsewhere, the uprisings continued for nearly two weeks, the last of them being put down on 25 June in Norwich. In retribution for the uprising, many of the rebels who could be identified were arrested and hanged. The exact number is unknown, but the figure of one hundred and fifty is generally accepted. Considering the extent of the uprising and the damage and murder it caused in London, by medieval standards the rebels got off remarkably easily.

The incident did, however, have long-lasting repercussions. There has never again been a poll tax successfully levied in England and within a century the institution of serfdom had been dismantled. Wat Tyler's rebellion was the first popular revolt in England and the only time in its thousand-year history that the Tower was taken by force. The murder of Archbishop Simon Sudbury and his three companions was the first time anyone had been taken from the Tower and publicly executed on Tower Hill. It set a precedent that would continue, under the auspices of the law, for the next three hundred and seventy years.

Three

A FAMILY AFFAIR

The Princes in the Tower
1483–4

ew figures in history are more controversial than England's King Richard III. To some he is a nasty little hunchback who allowed nothing to stand between him and the throne; to others, he is a tragically maligned man surrounded by enemies. Richard's most vicious detractor was none other than William Shakespeare, who transformed him from a tough yet attractive man into a club-footed hunchback with a withered arm whose mind was as bent and twisted as his body. In light of the popular concept of Richard, it is worth mentioning that contemporary records mention no physical deformities. Years later, the Countess of Desmond remembered him as 'the handsomest man in the room, except [for] his brother Edward, and [he] was very well made'. From surviving accounts, we know that Richard was shorter than average, slim, delicately featured, with a pale complexion and black hair. These descriptions, combined with his record as a capable soldier, make it highly unlikely that he was in any way handicapped. But the most gnawing question surrounding Richard is the fate of his nephews, who disappeared while being kept in the Tower under his protection.

England's Wars of the Roses (1455–85) were a brutal dynastic struggle for the crown carried out between two great families, the House of York and the House of Lancaster. Over several decades control of the kingdom shifted back and forth between the two. The struggle for the throne claimed the lives of more than two-thirds of the nobility in the kingdom.

In 1461, Henry VI, a Lancastrian, was forced to abdicate his throne by Edward IV, a Yorkist. For ten years Henry lived in exile while Edward tried to hold together a fractious, coalition government only marginally stabilised by his marriage to Elizabeth Woodville, a member of a powerful Lancastrian family. Edward set up his court in the Tower of London. The ancient fortress ensured his safety and its location in the centre of London kept him in close proximity to the citizens of the capital, whose support he desperately needed if he was to keep his tenuous hold on power. To nearly everyone's surprise Edward ruled wisely, if not comfortably. He set the monarchy on a stable financial footing for the first time, enacted protectionist taxes on imported goods and encouraged England's export trade.

Then, in 1471, Henry VI's queen, Margaret of Anjou, took up her husband's cause and again challenged the Yorkists. The two armies met at the Battle of Tewkesbury. King Henry's son, the Prince of Wales, led the Lancastrians while King Edward and his brother Richard, Duke of Gloucester, led the Yorkists. The result was a disaster for the Lancastrians. The heir to the throne was killed and days later, while Edward was celebrating his victory with a great feast, the imprisoned King Henry was murdered in the Tower.

Throughout these troubled years, Edward was unswervingly supported, both on the field of battle and in the council chamber, by his brother Richard. Created Duke of Gloucester in 1461 when his brother first seized the throne, Richard was also made Constable of England following his outstanding performance at Tewkesbury. In 1480 Edward granted him the additional title of Lieutenant in the North, and sent him to York to oversee the northern half of the kingdom. Although York had long been a Lancastrian stronghold, records show that Richard's cautious and scrupulously fair administration made him popular with nobles and commoners alike.

Despite the inauspicious start to Edward IV's reign, everything seemed to be going in his favour until early April 1483, when he contracted pneumonia and died a few days later. The crown now passed to the eldest of his two sons, twelve-year-old Edward, Prince of Wales. Edward and his ten-year-old brother, Prince Richard, were evidently both precociously bright boys who had spent most of their young lives in the care of their mother, Elizabeth (Woodville), who also had two daughters by King Edward and three older children by her first husband. Tragically, like so many children of the Middle Ages, young Edward was known to be sickly.

The suddenness of the king's death sent his allies, including his brother Richard, into a panic. With the king dead and his heirs under the control of their Lancastrian mother, it was likely that the tenuous coalition government would unravel and the House of Lancaster would again try to seize power – this time, through the child who now wore the crown. The only rallying point the Yorkists had left was Richard of Gloucester, who had been named in his late brother's will to serve as regent for the young king until he was old enough to wield power for himself.

Almost immediately, the rival factions began to square off. Queen Elizabeth quickly arranged for her son, now King Edward V, to be moved from the Welsh border town of Ludlow, where they were living, to London for his coronation. Travelling with him would be a small escort led by his half-brother Lord Richard Grey; his grandfather, the Earl Rivers; Sir Thomas Vaughan, who served as personal servant to both boys; and assorted soldiers loyal to the Woodville family. She also sent an urgent letter to her eldest son, half-brother to the young king, who was serving as the Constable of the Tower. Acting on the authority of his mother, the Constable smuggled a large part of the royal treasury out of London to be distributed among the Woodvilles and other staunch Lancastrians.

Moving almost as quickly, Richard of Gloucester travelled south from York with a band of heavily armed soldiers and an apparently new political ally, Henry Stafford, the Duke of Buckingham. Near the village of Stony Stratford, Richard and his men caught up with the new king's entourage. Dismounting, Richard knelt in front of his nephew, swore allegiance to him as his sovereign and proceeded to tell him there was a plot against the crown. Apparently no names were mentioned, but to anyone present it was obvious he was alluding to the Woodvilles. Before Rivers and his men realised what was happening, Richard drove them off, taking the new king under his own protection. Deserted by his family and friends and surrounded by a band of frightening soldiers and an uncle he hardly knew, the twelve-year-old king broke down in tears. In the tension of the moment, it is unlikely that Richard found time to offer the boy much comfort.

On 4 May Richard and King Edward arrived in London, where they were received with wild cheering and celebration. The new king, blond and fair, and his guardian, who was not much taller than his nephew, paraded through the streets on their way to the Tower. After receiving the keys to the Tower, Richard led the king to the palace of John Morton, Bishop of London, where he would be cared for until his coronation; now scheduled for Sunday 22 June.

By the time her son and brother-in-law arrived in London word of the incident at Stony Stratford had reached the queen mother. Terrified that the Yorkists were plotting to eliminate the Woodvilles and their allies, Elizabeth packed up her youngest son, Prince Richard, along with her three daughters, and headed to London, where she demanded sanctuary at Westminster Abbey.

As Richard set to work planning the coronation and dealing with the day-to-day workings of the government, word came to him that Bishop Morton was a Woodville man and not to be trusted. It was also possible that Morton was carrying messages between Queen Elizabeth at Westminster Abbey and King Edward. With the coronation still six weeks away, the bishop and the queen had ample time to poison the boy's mind against his uncle. On 19 May, using the pretext that the vast demands of a new government and preparing for the coronation required the king's constant attention, Richard ordered his nephew to be moved from the Bishop's Palace to the Tower. Once there he and his household were installed in the apartments formerly used by his father. That Edward was involved, at least nominally, in ruling the kingdom, is attested to by the fact that his signature appears on many surviving documents from this period.

To Richard's credit, he did not simply appoint political toadies to the new government. He selected men who were capable and experienced, regardless of their political leanings and social standing. He also kept many of the Lancastrians who had served under his late brother, probably hoping that if they were allowed to retain their offices they would be less likely to stir up trouble. But there was always the niggling fear that they would try to block every move Richard made. What Richard lacked was the force of personality – and marriage to a Woodville – that had allowed his brother to hold the warring factions in check. He had to find another way to keep his family in power. To this end he secretly set up a dual council. The official council still met in the Council Chamber at the Tower, but private meetings, limited to those loyal to the House of York, were held at his private residence, Crosby Palace.

Obviously, the Lancastrians had exactly the same fears about Richard as he had about them. Lord Hastings, the Lord Chamberlain, Lord Stanley and Bishop Morton were the leading Lancastrians on the council and they all felt Richard would do anything he could to marginalise their influence at court. The removal of the young king from Bishop Morton's palace was evidence enough of that.

What both sides did agree on was that having a minor as king would set England on a course to disaster. The same situation had occurred twice within the past century – under Richard II and Henry VI – and both times the kingdom had nearly fallen apart. Both Yorkists and Lancastrians were determined it would not happen again, and both were equally determined that stability would be maintained to their own best advantage.

30

The first overt move to consolidate power was made by Richard. Anxious to get the king's younger brother, Prince Richard, away from the influence of his mother and her faction, Richard asked the queen to send him to live with his brother at the Tower. Politically, she would have baulked at such a suggestion, so it was probably put to her that the young king was despondent and lonely in the Tower, and that his brother's presence would cheer him up. Whatever Richard said, it worked. By early June the boys were living together in the Royal Apartments in the White Tower.

Amid this slowly escalating war of wills, evidence came to light – probably through the Duke of Buckingham – that the marriage of the late King Edward IV to Elizabeth Woodville had been invalid. Records were produced showing that Edward had a previous marriage contract with another woman, Eleanor Talbot. Whether or not this marriage ever took place was irrelevant. According to medieval civil and canon law a marriage contract was as binding as a marriage itself. This meant that Edward IV had been a bigamist and his children by his marriage to Elizabeth Woodville were bastards. The new king, Edward V, had no right to the crown.

It was hardly unknown for a medieval court, or the church, to legitimise a bastard child so that they could claim their father's name, title and even his throne. Such legal manoeuvrings would certainly have suited the Woodvilles, but at the moment, Richard and the Yorkists held the upper hand. It was particularly convenient that if young Edward was successfully barred from the throne, the man best positioned to take his place was his uncle, Richard, Duke of Gloucester.

On Friday 20 June 1483, members of the Privy Council assembled for their regular meeting in the Council Chambers at the Tower of London. Everyone else had settled in long before Richard arrived. Apologising for having overslept, he immediately left the room again. Uneasy and irritated, the council members began mumbling to each other about the regent's reliability. Moments later Richard strode back into the room and began accusing one council member after another of plotting treason. William Hastings, the Lord Chamberlain; Lord Stanley, Archbishop Rotherham of York and Bishop Morton were all condemned by name. Loudly protesting their innocence, the men were interrupted when Richard's soldiers entered the room and arrested everyone who had been singled out. One by one they were marched off to the cells. All except Lord Hastings. He was dragged into the Tower yard, thrown across a beam that had been left lying there by workmen, and beheaded on the spot.

Later that day Richard summoned a meeting of the full council to explain his actions. The arrests and execution of Hastings had been a calculated act designed to undermine a Lancastrian plot to gain control of the government and King Edward. Unsaid was the fact that Richard had proved himself a man of action and not just his dead brother's puppet. Richard of Gloucester was not to be trifled with. By and large, the entire episode had been a *tour-de-force* exercise in sabre rattling. By executing Hastings, Richard had shown himself a force to be contended with and by arresting the others (who would later be released) he had demonstrated he was both wise and lenient; and he had done it all in a single morning. The lesson was not lost on the council, parliament, the church, or the populace. As a result of this impressive bit of theatrics Richard's popularity soared. And his message to those who opposed him was clear enough to cause the apparently miraculous reappearance of much of the Royal Treasury – which had disappeared weeks earlier on Queen Elizabeth's orders.

Within days there were make-Richard-king movements springing up everywhere. If Edward were crowned, between his youth and his questionable legitimacy there were sure to be years of instability. If Richard assumed the throne England would be led by a man of foresight and determination. Better still, his prowess on the battlefield had been proved many times and he would be capable of countering any threat the Lancastrians might pose. From pulpits across England, Richard's kingly qualities were praised. Parliament and the Council repeatedly asked him to accept the crown on behalf of the people. With little hesitation Richard accepted.

Of course, there was a cost. With Richard set to be the next king, the young princes lost nearly all their political importance. On 25 June, only five days after the council meeting, the boys were moved out of the Royal Apartments and into a large, single room in what was then called the Garden Tower (later known as the Bloody Tower). Their new accommodation was spartan and nearly all their servants were withdrawn. The boys were still seen playing in the Tower yards; shooting bows and arrows and tossing a ball with the wardens, but they no longer played any part in the future of the kingdom. On 6 July 1483 their uncle Richard, Duke of Gloucester, was crowned Richard III in Westminster Hall.

Among Richard's first acts as king were the customary bestowals of legal clemency. After cooling their heels in a cell for a few weeks – and hopefully rethinking their allegiance to Richard, who was now safely on the throne – Lord Stanley, Bishop Morton and Archbishop Rotherham were all released unharmed and restored to their titles and offices. There were, of course, less pleasant measures designed to ensure the Yorkists' hold on power. The Earl Rivers, his grandson Lord Richard Grey and Sir Thomas Vaughan (the Woodville party which had been with young King Edward when Richard intercepted them at Stony Stratford) were all arrested and summarily executed.

There is little doubt that Richard was so consumed with safeguarding the new government and consolidating his position that he neglected his nephews almost entirely. They were still the children of his beloved brother, but there were simply more important things to deal with than family visits. One of these 'important things' occurred only four months after his coronation.

In October, Henry Stafford, the Duke of Buckingham, who had been Richard's staunch supporter through the worst of the troubles, mounted a rebellion against the crown. By many accounts, Buckingham was acting on behalf of Henry Tudor, a Lancastrian who had been forced into exile at the age of fourteen following the Battle of Tewkesbury twelve years earlier. The uprising was suppressed and Buckingham was publicly executed at Salisbury shortly thereafter, but Richard's position was never again secure. At the heart of the king's problem was a growing concern about the princes in the Tower.

Ever since Edward had been barred from the throne and the boys moved out of the royal apartments, they had become less and less visible. Where were they now? Why weren't they seen any more? At least the guards at the Tower should know where they were. But there was simply no word. It had only been twelve years since Henry VI had died mysteriously in his cell after the Battle of Tewkesbury and, as always, people love to gossip about their leaders and their families.

The last known sightings of the boys were recorded both in the Great Chronicle of London and by the Italian spy and courtier, Dominic Mancini (to whom the story was told by the king's physician Dr Argentine). According to Mancini, Argentine said that 'all the attendants who had waited upon the King [Edward] were debarred access to him. He and his brother were withdrawn to the inner apartments of the Tower proper . . . [and they were] seen more rarely behind the bars of the windows . . . till at last they ceased to appear altogether.' According to the Great Chronicle, the boys were seen 'shooting and playing in the Garden of the Tower by sundry times' during the mayoralty of Sir Edmund Shay, which ran until 28 October 1483.

According to Mancini, the Croyland Chronicle and the writings of Philippe de Commines, before the end of the year rumours and accusations in connection with the boys' disappearance and supposed deaths were running wild. There were calls for the young princes to be brought before the public. Throughout the later months of the year massed demonstrations, sometimes bordering on riot, protested their disappearance all across the south of England. Strangely, Richard refused to make any comment as to the boys' whereabouts, their health or address any question concerning them.

But apparently everyone did not share the public's concern for the boys. Their mother, Elizabeth Woodville, seemed unperturbed about the disappearance of her sons. As rumours and accusations rose, Elizabeth sent her three daughters from Westminster to the Tower to live with their uncle Richard. Certainly Richard was no friend; he had already executed her father, Earl Rivers, and one of her sons, Lord Richard Grey. But these executions had been carried out according to the law as part of the big game of medieval power politics. Certainly if she had thought he was complicit in the death or disappearance of the princes she would never have handed her daughters over to him.

But Richard's life continued in a downward spiral. In April 1484, his son died at the age of ten. The following year his wife, Anne, followed their only child to the grave. With no heir and no wife to produce another, Richard again became politically vulnerable. In an attempt to bolster his position, he sent for another orphaned nephew, the Earl of Warwick – son of his late brother the Duke of Clarence – and appointed him heir to the Yorkist line. It was not enough. The combination of continuing rumours about the princes and the desperate Lancastrian longing to reclaim the kingdom brought Richard's enemies into the open. Chief among them was Henry Tudor, Duke of Richmond. Henry Tudor had been in exile in Brittany since the Battle of Tewkesbury. Then he was only fourteen, now he was twenty-eight.

Although officially barred from the throne because he was part of the Lancastrian line, Henry was determined to reclaim the crown for his family. And he had plenty of help inside England. His mother, Lady Margaret Beaufort, the Countess of Richmond and Derby, was ambitious for her son and had plenty of money and connections, both of which she devoted wholeheartedly to his cause. On 7 August 1485, Henry Tudor landed at Milford Haven in Wales with two thousand French mercenary troops and began marching eastward to meet Richard III.

Sixteen days later the two armies met in an open field near the town of Bosworth. Richard's army was more than twice the size of Henry's and it should have been an easy victory. The battle only lasted two hours and no more than a hundred men were lost on either side, but at a crucial point in the fighting Richard's allies, the Earl of Northumbria and Lord Stanley (the same Lord Stanley who Richard had briefly jailed after the council meeting of 20 June and whose army alone was larger than that of Henry Tudor) betrayed Richard, turning their men against the king and his forces.

When Richard's horse stumbled on marshy land, he was thrown to the ground. As Lord Stanley's men closed in around him, a loyal page fought his way through the crowd to bring Richard a horse – urging him to flee the field. Richard refused, shouting, 'I will not budge a foot, I will die King of England.' Now, nearly alone among his enemies, his sword broken and having only a war hammer with which to defend himself, Richard was hacked to death, crying 'Treason – treason', in Stanley's direction. His mangled body was stripped naked and flung across a horse to be paraded through the streets of nearby Leicester. Richard's crown, lost in the heat of battle, was picked up by Stanley who placed it on the head of Henry Tudor, whom he proclaimed King Henry VII.

Almost immediately, King Henry ordered the arrest and imprisonment of Richard's heir, the Earl of Warwick; and just as quickly rumours sprang up that Warwick had escaped. But Tower records show he was still there a year later when Margaret of Burgundy sent a cask of wine to him. Along with the new rumours about Warwick were the continuing rumours concerning the fate of the young King Edward and his brother Prince Richard.

Strangely, Henry Tudor did not seem concerned about the boys' fate, nor did he accuse Richard of having done away with them. Had he wanted to, in the absence of the boys themselves, he could have invented any number of stories about their disappearance that would have helped blacken Richard's name, but he assiduously avoided the subject. This alone is odd, considering the pains he took to accuse Richard of almost every other imaginable crime.

Four years after Henry VII took the throne there were a series of riots in North Yorkshire, which had been Richard's seat of government during his tenure as the Lieutenant of the North. To quell the riots, Henry selected the Earl of Northumberland; the same man who, along with Lord Stanley, had betrayed Richard at Bosworth. At Cocklodge, just outside the village of Thirsk, Northumberland was set upon by a mob that seized him, drove off his retainers, and meticulously murdered the earl. Obviously there were those who still believed Richard was not the ogre he was being portrayed as by King Henry and the rumourmongers in London.

The next, and possibly the strangest, development in the story came to light with the arrest of Sir James Tyrell, former 'knight of the body' to the late King Richard. Arrested on unrelated charges, Tyrell apparently confessed under torture to engineering the murder of the princes. Oddly, his confession was never made public during Henry VII's lifetime and was only brought to light by Sir Thomas More, during the reign of Henry VIII. According to More, Tyrell said he hired two men, Miles Forest, one of King Edward's keepers, and a groom named John Dighton, to carry out the murders. Tyrell supposedly obtained a warrant to receive the keys to the Garden Tower from the Tower Governor, Sir Robert Brackenbury, and passed them on to Forest and Dighton. Creeping into the boys' room late at night, Forest and Dighton smothered them with their pillows, hauled their naked bodies to the Wakefield Tower and buried them under a heap of stones. Supposedly, their bodies were later recovered by a priest and reburied as near to consecrated ground as possible; beneath a staircase leading into the Chapel of St John.

If this evidence was available to Henry VII, it would have provided the 'smoking gun' he needed to prove Richard III a child murderer and a usurper. Why did he not use this evidence? There are two possible explanations: (1) he knew it was not true – and we will come back to this possibility later – and (2) he did not know of Tyrell's confession. Why? Because More invented it years later to vilify Richard?

Sir Thomas More is unquestionably one of the most respected men of the Tudor period, but he was, at least at this time, doggedly devoted to Henry VIII and happy to go to any lengths to slander the Yorkists. Certainly, it was More who first transformed Richard from the physically attractive little man we met earlier into the deformed creature we meet in Shakespeare. More described Richard as 'little of stature, ill-featured of limbs, crook-backed, his left shoulder much higher than his right, hard favoured of visage. . . . He was malicious, wrathful and envious, from before his birth [and] ever forward.'

At this period, physical deformities were still believed to be a sign of spiritual corruption, and making Richard physically repugnant would have indicated that he was also morally bankrupt. It was almost certainly from More's malign description that Shakespeare created the psychotic monstrosity who appears in his 1593 play, *A Tragical History of Richard III*. And, as he was writing for another Tudor, Queen Elizabeth, there would have been good reason for the Bard to paint Richard as unpleasantly as possible.

Just as there were people during Richard's lifetime who never believed his complicity in the boys' murder, there were also those in the years after his death who defended him. The first accounts protesting his innocence appeared in 1603, immediately after the death of Queen Elizabeth, the last of the Tudor line. By 1684, the 'Rehabilitate Richard' movement moved into full swing when William Winstanley wrote of him, 'this worthy prince [hath] been blasted by malicious traducers, who like Shakespeare in his play of him, render him dreadfully black in his actions, a monster of nature rather than a man of admirable parts'.

But by Winstanley's time the case against Richard had already taken a turn for the worse. In 1674, nearly two centuries after the disappearance of the princes, workmen were making renovations to the old Royal Apartments near the White Tower. Buried beneath the foundation of a disused staircase they discovered the skeletons of two children. According to the observations made at the scene by John Knight, Principal Surgeon to Charles II, 'about Ten Feet in the ground were found the Bones of Two Striplings in (as it seem'd) a Wooden Chest, which upon the survey were found proportional to the Ages of those Two Brothers . . . about Thirteen and Eleven Years'.

These were not the first bones of children found buried in the Tower, but they were the only ones corresponding to the approximate ages of the two princes and, to make the case all the more compelling, they had been buried together. Convinced these were the remains of the princes, King Charles commissioned his Surveyor General of Works, Sir Christopher Wren, to design an urn of white marble in which the bones could be placed and moved to Westminster Abbey where, ironically, it was installed in the Chapel of Henry VII. On the urn is engraved an epitaph stating that within are the remains of the lost princes who were murdered in the Tower of London.

There the bones rested until 1933 when the Dean and Chapter of Westminster Abbey granted permission for the urn to be opened and the bones examined. The examination was only marginally more conclusive than the one made when the bones were discovered more than 250 years earlier. It was simply assumed they were male, and at the time there was no test to accurately determine how old the bones actually were. Consequently, they were replaced in the urn. Even if this is accepted as true, we are still left with the mystery of who, exactly, ordered the boys' death. There are four possible suspects:

Richard III. Let's assume for the moment that Richard ordered the murder of his nephews. Why did he never deny the rumours? It would have been easy enough, and far more politically advantageous, to say the boys had simply sickened and died. It was a common enough explanation for an untimely death during the Middle Ages. Having said this, he could have displayed the bodies in public and quashed the rumour mill that was slowly destroying his reputation. It had worked for his elder brother, King Edward IV, when he ordered the murder of his predecessor Henry VI – surely it would have worked for Richard. But the nagging question remains: did Richard have any reason to order their murders?

The Yorkist faction had already accepted that the boys were illegitimate and urged Richard to accept the throne, so neither of the boys presented any political threat to his claim to the throne. Richard was lovingly devoted to his brother, the boys' father, Edward IV. Would he have killed his nephews out of simple spite?

There were at least nine other legitimate, Yorkist claimants to the crown besides the boys, and three of these were male. One, the young Earl of Warwick (son of Richard's late brother the Duke of Clarence), was proclaimed heir to the throne by Richard himself. Beyond public rumour, there is no contemporary accusation that Richard was complicit in their death. The boys' mother, Queen Elizabeth, obviously did not believe Richard was guilty. If she had, would she have sent her daughters to live with him at court?

So, if Richard did not kill the boys, who did? There are three other likely candidates.

Henry Stafford, Duke of Buckingham. Buckingham's position in Richard's administration is unclear, at best. He apparently came very late as a supporter of Richard, not appearing in the records prior to the incident at Stony Stratford. By all accounts, Buckingham was excessively proud, ambitious and ruthless; the type of man who would do anything to advance himself. If supporting Richard was politically advantageous, fine; if betraying him was more advantageous, that was fine too.

What motive would Buckingham have for murdering the boys? He was a prince of the royal blood and a descendant of Edward III's youngest son. Could he have had designs on the crown himself? If so, what better way to topple Richard than murder his nephews and let the fall-out undermine

Richard's reputation. Could this have been the impetus for Buckingham's ill-fated attempt to overthrow Richard in the late summer of 1483?

There is also the possibility that Buckingham was working in league with Henry Tudor and his mother, Margaret Beaufort. Acting as their henchman, he might have ordered the boys' death in the hope it would make Richard so vulnerable that he could be dethroned. Again, Buckingham's revolt could have been an attempt to pave the way for Henry.

Having been forced into a dire marriage with a Woodville woman when little more than a child, Buckingham had no love for the Woodville clan. This animosity worsened when vast tracts of the land he owned in Wales were denied to him by the Woodville family's powerful influence in that area. If he did develop a loathing of the Woodvilles, who better to take it out on than Woodville children? Killing an enemy's child had already become a tragic part of the Wars of the Roses scenario and the boys were, after all, as much Woodvilles as they were Yorks.

Could it be that Buckingham's and Richard's shared hatred of the Woodvilles led the duke to do something dangerously stupid? Might he have murdered the boys on his own initiative in the belief that it would please Richard? If Richard was appalled by the news and threatened to strip Buckingham of his titles and possibly send him to trial, might this have been enough to trigger Buckingham's revolt? If these were his motives, did he have the means and opportunity? Yes. In his capacity as Constable of England, Buckingham would have had ready access to the Tower at any time.

If we assume that the last reported sighting of the boys took place shortly after Richard's coronation, that must mean that they disappeared from sight while Richard himself was on progress. Whether Buckingham was with Richard at this time is open to question. If he did not accompany the royal party, he was in London and therefore near the Tower. Even if he was with Richard during the week generally accepted as the time the boys disappeared, 7–14 August, the party was only in Reading and therefore well within a hard day's ride of London. Of course, all evidence against Buckingham is speculative. And if we assume the boys were not dead by 2 November 1483, Buckingham could not have been directly involved in their deaths. For 2 November was the day Buckingham himself was executed.

There is, however, one more intriguing scenario in which Buckingham stands large. Might he have discovered that Richard had ordered the death of the boys and this alone was enough to mount a revolt – with or without the support of the Lancastrians – designed to overthrow Richard?

Lady Margaret Beaufort, Countess of Richmond and Derby. Finding someone to accuse Margaret Beaufort of almost any crime against the House of York hardly requires the services of a Sherlock Holmes. Margaret was a Stanley. Her husband was the same Lord Stanley thrown into jail by Richard after the council meeting on 20 June, and the same Lord Stanley who betrayed his king at the Battle of Bosworth. How does this implicate her directly in a plot against Richard or his nephews? Lady Margaret Beaufort was not only a Stanley, she was also Henry Tudor's mother. It was Richard and his brother who had driven her son into exile in 1471 after the Battle of Tewkesbury and her only goal in life was to see her son back in England and on the throne.

Certainly, descriptions of Lady Beaufort meet the profile of a scheming, spiteful matriarch. In his 1646 five-volume *Life of Richard III*, Sir George Buck claimed to have found evidence against Margaret Beaufort in 'an old manuscript that I have seen'. According to Buck, 'Doctor Morton and a certain Countess, contriv[ed] the death of Edward V and others, resolv[ing] it by poison.' Dr Morton is the same Bishop Morton who was arrested at the same council meeting as Lord Stanley. There is no doubt that Morton and the Stanleys would have been in close contact, as they were among the leading Lancastrians in Richard's court. Buck also suggests that because he was a 'closet Lancastrian' Morton served as a go-between for the Stanleys and Buckingham himself – further strengthening the case against Buckingham.

If Margaret Beaufort was already neck-deep in a Lancastrian plot against Richard, and desperate to have her son on the throne, how great a step would it have been to arrange – possibly through Buckingham – to have the boys murdered?

Henry Tudor (Henry VII). If Richard III had no legitimate reason for killing his nephews, Henry Tudor had nothing *but* reasons for wanting them dead. Obviously, his primary goal was getting Richard out of the way, but any remaining Yorkist heirs were bound to impede his claim on the throne. Following the Battle of Bosworth he arrested, and later executed, Richard's hand-picked successor, the Earl of Warwick. Henry took measures to seek out and arrest every Yorkist claimant to the throne, keeping them in close confinement until he could do away with them with the least possible scandal.

He even moved against the boys' mother, Queen Elizabeth, by shipping her off to a convent barely two years after his ascension to the throne.

Why, in light of his endless accusations against Richard, did Henry never mention the death of the boys, even after Sir James Tyrell's supposed confession? Could it be that Henry knew the truth of the matter and took pains that it remained as quiet as possible? Assuming that Tyrell did confess to the murders as Sir Thomas More claimed, there is another intriguing possibility that bears examining. Could it be that the confession was intended as a smoke-screen to hide the boys' actual fate and prevent Henry from tracking them down?

There is circumstantial evidence dating from shortly after the boy's disappearance that they 'were not indeed murdered but conveyed secretly away, and were yet living'. Contemporary with this rumour is a story, which says, in part, 'that the princes and their mother Elizabeth Woodville lived in the hall by permission of their uncle'. The 'hall' in question is supposedly Gipping Hall near Stowmarket, Suffolk, which at the time was the home of James Tyrell. If this is true, it must have taken place after Elizabeth left the sanctuary of Westminster Abbey and placed her daughters in the custody of Richard. Certainly if she knew her sons were alive it would go a long way to explaining why she trusted Richard with her daughters.

Adding some credence to the claim that Tyrell was harbouring the boys is an interesting item found in the docket book of Richard's Privy Seal dated 1484. The entry refers to the fact that, acting on behalf of the king, Tyrell was sent 'over the sea into the parts of Flanders for diverse matters concerning greatly Ourselves . . .'. The 'ourselves' alluded to must certainly have meant Richard. Is it possible that Tyrell was escorting the boys to the safety of the continent or making arrangements for them to go later? If Richard was already in fear for his throne, he might have wanted the boys well out of the way for their own safety. If Henry Tudor, the Woodvilles and the Lancastrian party managed to unseat him, nowhere in England would be safe enough for the boys. Tyrell's trip might also explain why Elizabeth Woodville went to stay with them at Gipping Hall. If they were being spirited out of the country, it might have been her last chance to see them. Adding some weight to this strange tale are two bizarre uprisings that took place during Henry Tudor's reign. Even if Henry VII was never certain about the boys' fate, the uprisings frightened him enough to take them both very seriously.

Less than two years after Henry came to the throne a boy in his early teens appeared in Dublin claiming to be the Earl of Warwick. Clearly, since Warwick was imprisoned in the Tower, the boy was not who he claimed to be, but so many people believed the rumours that Warwick had escaped that it was an easy claim to make. The boy must have been relatively convincing, he even fooled Henry VI's widow, Margaret of Anjou. He fooled a lot of others too, because in May 1487, he was crowned King Edward VI by the Irish (who hated Henry VII and were anxious to find a way to unseat him).

Since Henry had the real Warwick behind bars he knew the boy in Ireland was an impostor. To prove this to the public he even had Warwick hauled out of the Tower and paraded through the streets of London all the way to St Paul's Cathedral. Why then did he simultaneously use this occasion to lock his mother-in-law Elizabeth Woodville (he had married one of the three daughters she had entrusted to Richard when she came out of sanctuary) in a convent and confiscate all her belongings?

In 1487, Margaret of Burgundy (the same Margaret of Burgundy who had sent a cask of wine to the real Warwick whom she knew to be locked in the Tower) backed the pretender, with an army of Irish and German mercenaries. With this support, the supposed Earl of Warwick promptly challenged the English. At the Battle of Stoke, in June of that year, the rebels were defeated and their young king taken prisoner. Now identified as 'Lambert Simnel' the boy was no longer the twelve- or thirteen-year-old described earlier, but only about ten years old. After deciding his enemies had used the boy as a dupe, Henry graciously took pity on him and put him to work in the royal kitchens where he is recorded to have died in about 1525.

Now here are the problems with the story. If Margaret of Burgundy, and presumably Margaret of Anjou, both knew the real Warwick was being held in the Tower, why did they identify the boy as Warwick? Why was Henry so quick to cloister Elizabeth Woodville when word of the pretender reached him, even though he had the real Warwick under lock and key? How did the twelve- or thirteen-year-old who was crowned king in Dublin turn out to be a ten-year-old boy named Lambert Simnel?

Could it be that the boy claiming to be the Earl of Warwick was actually Prince Richard, the younger of the two missing princes? If so, why would he pretend to be his own cousin (Warwick) rather than admit to his identity? Possibly because it provided him some protection and possibly because Warwick had been named Richard III's official heir while Prince Richard and his brother Edward V had been declared bastards and denied the right of accession. Did Henry Tudor lock up his mother-in-law to prevent her from recognising her own son? Did the Irish rebels make a last-minute substitution to keep the real Prince Richard from falling into Henry Tudor's hands? There is one last point worth considering. No one who threatened Henry VII, even from afar or in the minutest way, managed to escape the most severe punishment. Why then, did he allow Lambert Simnel to live out his life as a royal retainer?

In 1491, only four years after the curious incident of Lambert Simnel, an almost identical incident occurred in almost the same way. A boy named Perkin Warbeck appeared in Cork, Ireland, claiming to be none other than the Earl of Warwick. Then, inexplicably, he changed his story claiming to be Prince Richard of York, the younger of the two brothers. To prove his identity, the 'prince' travelled around Europe visiting his supposed relatives. He was fêted by Charles VIII of France and, as the other Prince Richard before him, identified by Margaret of Burgundy. Many others who had known the young princes also identified him.

By the time Warbeck returned to Ireland in 1493 he declared himself ready to claim his inheritance. He attempted to invade England through Scotland in 1495 with the help of James IV, who was also convinced of his identity. The invasion failed, so he tried again in 1496 and again in 1497. If the first two attempts failed to get off the ground, the third went disastrously wrong. In October 1497 the 'prince' was taken prisoner by the king's soldiers at the Battle of Taunton and brought before Henry VII to explain himself. The boy now admitted that he was not Prince Richard, but only Perkin 'Warbeque', the son of an illiterate boatman from Tournai, Flanders. How much of the story Henry believed we will never know, but where he had shown uncharacteristic leniency to Lambert Simnel, he had Warbeck thrown into the Tower. In the cell next to him was none other than the real Earl of Warwick.

The two remained locked in adjoining cells until late in 1499. The boys, both now about twenty-five, were accused of plotting to burn down the Tower of London in order to escape and make their way to Flanders where they planned to launch another bid to put Warwick on the throne. In retribution for this supposed plot, Henry ordered the execution of the boys, along with a Tower warder who was accused of being their accomplice. On 23 November 1499 the Earl of Warwick was beheaded on Tower Hill while Warbeck and the gaoler were hanged at Tyburn.

Henry VII could now rest easy, but the rest of us are left with an endless string of questions. How did the son of an illiterate Flemish boatman come to have the education, linguistic skills and social graces that allowed him to pass himself off as an English prince in front of half the crowned heads of Europe and still look so much like the missing prince that he could fool various members of his own family? Stranger still, of all the countries Perkin Warbeck might have hailed from, how is it that he just happened to be from the place Sir James Tyrell had travelled to on behalf of Richard III?

Whatever really happened to the princes following their mysterious disappearance, and the murder of Henry VI twelve years previously, the Tower had developed such a malign reputation that no future monarch of England would live in it. The venerable fortress now began the long descent from royal residence to state prison that would mark its future.

An interesting footnote to the centuries of accusations that have swirled around Richard III and the disappearance of his nephews took place in the United States in 1997. In an extraordinary mock trial, Richard III was brought up on charges of murdering his nephews. Presiding was a panel of three US Supreme Court judges. Cases for both prosecution and defence were duly presented. The judges returned a unanimous verdict of 'not guilty on all counts'.

PART II
State Prison of the Tudors

Four

THE WARDEN, THE WOLF AND THE WOMAN

John Wolfe and Alice Tankerville
1533–4

It is one of history's better-known facts that Henry VIII had marital problems. Less well known than his acrimonious relations with six successive wives, however, is the fact that in at least one instance, a clever and beautiful woman nearly got away with picking Henry's pocket without being married to him, or ever even having met him. Like two of Henry's wives her story, too, ended in the confines of the Tower of London.

In October 1531, agents of the king and parliament arrived at the London docks expecting to collect a shipment of 366 gold crowns that had been shipped from the continent to help replenish King Henry's perpetually depleted royal treasury. With a modern equivalent value of more than £700,000 it was, quite literally, a king's ransom. To the guards' surprise, despite having been transported in an iron bound chest, which was securely locked, chained to the floor of the ship and kept under constant guard while at sea and in port, the gold had vanished.

A massive investigation was launched to recover the gold and bring the perpetrators of the theft to justice, but it took nearly two years before the scanty trail of evidence pointed the finger at a ne'er-do-well sailor named John Wolfe. Wolfe had a reputation as a petty thief, sometime pirate and general thug, but there was little evidence to connect him with the theft beyond the fact that he had been part of the crew that was aboard while it lay at anchor in the London docks. Under the circumstances, however, that was enough for the crown to issue a warrant for Wolfe's arrest. By the early summer of 1533 he had been apprehended and dragged off to the Tower where he awaited arraignment on charges of conspiracy, theft and treason: not easy charges to face at any time, but especially not under the somewhat tyrannical reign of Henry VIII.

While Wolfe languished in his cell, his common-law wife Alice Tankerville, who, by all accounts, was a charmer, visited him almost daily. Over the course of her visits, the comely and seductive Alice made friends with two of her husband's jailers, William Denys and John Bawd. Denys and Bawd were both young and unmarried and more than a little taken with Alice's obvious charms. They allowed her to bring wine, decent food and treats to her husband, and Bawd and Denys probably received more than their fair share of the woman's attention in appreciation of their leniency.

Nearly six months after his arrest, the case against Wolfe collapsed for lack of evidence and he was released. Although free, he decided it would probably be a smart move to leave the country until things cooled off. Ireland seemed a good choice for an extended holiday, but before he left Wolfe met privately with John Bawd and asked him if he would look after Alice while he was gone. Already desperately smitten, Bawd readily agreed.

Only weeks after Wolfe's departure, new evidence turned up in the case of the king's missing gold and it would seem that it not only pointed directly at Wolfe himself, but also implicated Alice Tankerville as an accomplice. Wolfe, of course, was long gone; so to avoid losing any more time over the case both he and Alice Tankerville were tried *in absentia* by parliament. Even Alice, who was often seen around the Tower where she went to visit John Bawd, was not notified of the charges, or the trial, in which she had been named as a co-defendant. Within days the pair were found guilty of theft and treason and sentenced to death. Only then were formal arrest warrants issued.

In February 1534, Alice Tankerville was seized and thrown into a windowless cell in Coldharbour Tower, located near the west side of the original White Tower. The only light that filtered into her cell came through a tiny, barred window in the heavy oak cell door. Her hands and feet were shackled, and the shackles were attached to heavy chains looped through iron rings set into the wall. Here she would wait until John Wolfe was recaptured, the authorities decided to execute her alone, or she simply died. Even by the standards of the day Alice's treatment was so unusually harsh that the daughter of Sir Edmund Walsingham, the Lieutenant of the Tower, interceded with her father on Alice's behalf. Reluctantly, Walsingham agreed to remove the heavy irons so long as both her cell door and the outer door of Coldharbour Tower remained locked at all times. Food would have to be pushed through a gap beneath the cell door.

During Alice's confinement, one of the guards whose schedule placed him on guard duty in the Coldharbour Tower was her old friend, Will Denys. Distressed and concerned for this lovely woman who had been so nice to him while he had guarded her husband, Denys brought Alice small gifts and visited her even when he was not on duty. As his visits increased in regularity and length, gossip filtered back to his boss, Sir John Walsingham, and within a few short weeks Denys was out looking for a new job.

No matter, Alice Tankerville was a very resourceful young woman. Somehow, John Bawd had his schedule changed so he was Alice's guard on an almost daily basis. Through the tiny window in her cell door, Bawd's and Alice's relationship developed into a romance, at least on John Bawd's part, and together they conceived a daring escape plan. Alice told Bawd that Will Denys had once mentioned a possible escape route out of Coldharbour Tower, and urged him to verify its feasibility. Together they would work out the final details. At the risk of losing both his job and his head, Bawd agreed. He had already lost his heart to her, so no risk was thought too great to save his Alice from the sort of grisly death that inevitably awaited her.

Over the next few days, Bawd had a long conversation with a trusted friend named Jeffrey Harrison and a much shorter one with an hosteller who kept a stable not far from the Tower. He also purchased two lengths of rope from a dockside merchant named Sampson at a cost of 13 pence. Next he needed a copy of the key to the outside door of Coldharbour Tower, which had been constantly locked since Alice's shackles had been removed. There was no way his usual key could be used. When the last guard went off duty at ten o'clock at night, all keys had to be returned to the main guard office. Carefully, Bawd made a duplicate key, filing it away a bit at a time and hiding it in his uniform so he could test it in the lock until it worked perfectly. Finally, he found a smooth, round stick about 18 inches in length.

When this strange collection of tools was complete, John Bawd smuggled them in to work with him. Through the bars of Alice's cell door, he passed the key, the rope and the stick so she could hide them under the straw on her cell floor where they were far less likely to be noticed than if he put them in his trunk in the warder's dormitory. Now, the pair made their final plans and waited impatiently for a moonless night when the near-total darkness was most likely to cover their escape.

Two weeks later it was the new moon. That night, as his shift ended, Bawd told Alice to pass the rope back through the cell door. With the coil of rope over his shoulder, he hurried out of the tower before his replacement showed up for work. At ten o'clock that night, Alice's last guard of the day went off duty, dousing the torches on his way out as he always did. When she heard the 'clunk' of the lock in the outside door, Alice went to work. After tucking the duplicate key safely in her bodice, she took the stick Bawd had smuggled in to her, and reached through the gap under the cell door where food was passed to her. With the end of the stick she began fumbling blindly for the pin that secured the hasp on the door. After locating the pin she began tapping it upwards to drive it out of the hasp, jarring the door with her knee to help work it loose. After several nerve-racking minutes, the pin fell to the floor and the door swung open. Feeling her way along the darkened hall and down the steps to the outer door, Alice took the duplicate key from her bodice, unlocked the door and stepped into the darkness of the tower yard.

To make herself as invisible as possible, she pulled the hood of her long, dark cloak over her head. In the chill March night, Alice hurried away from Coldharbour Tower, feeling her way through the narrow alleyways and up the stone stairs leading to the flat roof of the tower straddling Traitors' Gate and the small wharf where the condemned were brought into the Tower from the Thames. Here, on the roof of St Thomas's Tower, John Bawd was waiting. He had tied one end of the rope to an old iron hook embedded in the stone parapet wall and now waited anxiously for Alice to arrive before dropping the rope down the outside of the tower so they could make good their escape. Peering over the parapet, they waited till the night watch passed on their regular rounds of the streets on the opposite side of the moat. Once passed, it would be at least half an hour before they returned. By then John and Alice would be long gone.

Sliding carefully down the rope, first John and then Alice landed silently on the tiny wharf next to Traitors' Gate. Untying the small boat used to ferry prisoners from the shore into the Tower, they glided silently across the moat and up to Iron Gate Steps on the far shore. As they stepped out, John pushed the boat back into the moat and towards the wharf; it might look strange if it were spotted tied to the shore and they had to do everything possible to buy time before their escape was discovered.

As the couple walked across the grassy verge towards a nearby road lined with cottages inhabited by Tower guards with families, Bawd told Alice that he had rented a pair of horses and tethered them nearby. These would carry them to the home of his friend Jeffrey Harrison who had agreed to let them hide out for a few days until the guard had stopped looking for them in the immediate vicinity of the Tower. This should give them enough time to escape London and find passage to the continent. Walking slowly towards the horses, the pair held each other close, talking in hushed tones. Undoubtedly they were excited to be so close to freedom and at the same time terrified they would be discovered. They clung to each other out of excitement, desperation and in the hope that a pair of young lovers would not attract any undue attention from anyone who might pass them on the road.

Just as they rounded the last corner on their way up Tower Hill to the waiting horses, they were confronted by a group of men carrying lanterns coming in the opposite direction down the narrow lane. The two huddled closer, trying to hide their faces from anyone who might recognise them. Glancing up, Bawd recognised the night watch. They were early. They shouldn't be at this point for at least another ten minutes. Had the escape taken longer than he thought? Too late. One of the guards, Charles Gore was an old friend and immediately recognised Bawd, calling out a greeting. Waving and mumbling a reply, Bawd and Alice hurried on, pressing themselves against the cottages to stay beyond the reach of the lantern light. But Gore was also an occasional guard of Alice Tankerville and when the pair squeezed past the guard he recognised her. In a few seconds of panic and confusion, the guard fell on John Bawd and Alice Tankerville, snatching away all hope of escape and freedom. There was now no doubt what the future held for either of them.

Alice was hauled back to her cell where a padlock was put on the door and a 24-hour guard posted outside. At the same time, John Bawd was taken temporarily to the Counter Gaol for questioning. Even without torture, he confessed everything, insisting that he was driven to betray his office and his king 'only by the love and affection he bore her'.

For Sir Edmund Walsingham, Lieutenant of the Tower and devoted servant of the crown, the next day must have been one of very mixed emotions. On the one hand, a member of his staff had nearly helped a condemned prisoner escape justice. If the breakout had been successful it would almost certainly have cost Sir Edmund his job, and considering the mercurial temperament of the king, it could also have cost him his head. On the other hand, the plotters had been recaptured and a messenger had brought word that John Wolfe had been apprehended attempting to slip back into England. Evidently, word of his trial and conviction had not reached him in Ireland. Now, everyone would pay for their crimes.

John Bawd was moved to the notorious cell known as 'Little Ease', a cramped hole so small a man could neither stand up nor lie down in it but was constantly forced to remain in a foetal position. Bawd's interment there is the first of a few scant references to Little Ease, and its exact location has never been determined. Some historians insist it was in the White Tower, but it is more likely that it was located in the cellars beneath the old Flint Tower which was rebuilt in the eighteenth century, obliterating any evidence of the cell. Wherever it was, Little Ease was undoubtedly a nasty place. Bawd was only allowed out for an occasional torturing; not to make him confess, he had already done that freely. The torture was simply a gruesome part of his punishment for treason, of which more was to come.

For Alice Tankerville and John Wolfe, the end came soon, but not quickly. On 31 March 1534 the pair were carted from the Tower to the stone retaining walls lining the Thames embankment. Here they were securely wrapped in chains and lowered into the water at low tide. Their guards and a crowd of ghoulish fun-seekers gathered to watch as the tide turned and began to creep back in. Inch by inch, the filthy water of the Thames crept up over their legs to their waist and on to their chest; finally drowning the helpless, terrified couple as they struggled frantically to hold their heads above the relentless rising tide. According to the official State Papers of Lord Lisle, an entry for Sunday, 28 March of that year states: 'Wolfe and his wife Alice Tankerville will be hanged in chains at low water mark upon the Thames on Tuesday. John Bawd is in Little Ease cell in the Tower and is to be racked and hanged.'

For his part in helping plot history's only attempted escape by a woman from the Tower of London, John Bawd was racked until his muscles tore and his arms and legs were pulled from their sockets, leaving him in excruciating pain and unable to move on his own. As a final humiliation he was wrapped in chains and suspended over the outer walls of the Tower complex where he slowly died of exposure and dehydration. His body was left to hang there for months, picked at by the crows and the Tower ravens, a festering public display intended to serve as an example to anyone foolish enough to think they could escape the king's justice.

For all this mayhem, tragedy and treason, and despite the legitimate efforts of the courts and official investigators, the historical record never mentions that Henry VIII's 366 gold crowns were ever recovered, leaving open the question of whether John Wolfe and Alice Tankerville were actually guilty of any involvement in the crime. If they were, their punishment, gruesome as it was, was no more than could be expected by a convicted traitor during the harsh reign of Henry VIII. If they were innocent, their deaths were not only horrible, but a gross miscarriage of justice.

Five

TREASON IN THE BEDROOM

Queen Katherine Howard
1540–2

Henry VIII came to the throne of England in 1509 as a rather awkward seventeen-year-old whose life had been sheltered from nearly all the world's realities. But within a few years he developed into the very model of a fairy-tale prince. Shortly before his twenty-fifth birthday the Venetian ambassador described him this way: 'His majesty is the handsomest potentate I ever set eyes on; above the usual height . . . his complexion [is] fair and bright, with auburn hair combed straight and short . . . his throat rather long and thick. . . . He speaks French, English and Latin and a little Italian, plays well on the lute and harpsichord, sings from books on sight, draws the bow with greater strength than any man in England, and jousts marvellously. Believe me he is in every respect a most accomplished Prince. . .'. But as is the case with so many people, time and the harsh realities of life turned Henry into something very different from what was promised in his youth.

By 1540 Henry had gone through three wives and was on the verge of taking a fourth. When his first Queen, Catherine of Aragon, grew fat and ugly and had only provided her husband with one child, a daughter, Henry divorced her in favour of the young, haughty Anne Boleyn. When she, too, could do no better than give him a single daughter, Henry trumped up sufficient evidence of adultery to send her to the block after less than three years of marriage. His third wife, Jane Seymour, was a gentle, pious woman who gave him the son he longed for but died less than a week after Prince Edward's birth.

Jane's death sent Henry, and by extension the entire English court, into a prolonged period of mourning. The once light-hearted monarch became morose and bitter. The masquerade parties, jousts and banquets gave way to sombre gatherings at which the king sought refuge in food and drink, gradually becoming a bloated caricature of his former self. The jousts and hunting parties, too, disappeared, partly as the result of a leg injury he had suffered during his marriage to Anne Boleyn. The wound never healed, leaving Henry with a weeping ulcer on one leg.

In an attempt to cheer up their king and endear themselves and their political goals to him, the reforming party at court – led by Henry's personal secretary Thomas Cromwell and the Archbishop of Canterbury Thomas Cranmer – connived a fourth marriage with Anne, the daughter of the Duke of Cleves. It was a disaster. The two hated each other at first sight. At the age of forty-eight Henry was grossly fat, gouty, prematurely aged and foul tempered. Anne was unschooled in the courtly graces of music, dancing and needlework; neither had she taken up the English habit of regular bathing. Worst of all, she could probably out-think Henry and insisted on arguing religion and politics with him. As a staunch Lutheran Protestant, Anne's views on church reform were just too liberal for Henry, even though he had long since broken with Roman Catholicism. Behind her back Henry took to calling her 'the great Flanders mare'. There was no doubt the marriage would not last.

With another divorce imminent, the conservative faction at court, led by Bishop Gardiner and Thomas Howard the Duke of Norfolk, who had been out of favour since Henry's ill-fated marriage to his niece Anne Boleyn, saw a way to get themselves, and their religious views, back in favour. If they could find a young woman more to the king's tastes, he might replace Anne with her. Better still, the fall of Anne might discredit the hated Thomas Cromwell. To this end, Norfolk inveigled a position in Anne's household for his niece Katherine Howard.

Only weeks after Anne officially came to court so did Katherine. At fifteen years of age, Katherine Howard was a silly, frivolous child with big brown eyes and auburn hair. Still plump with baby-fat, the 4 foot 11 inch Katherine was awestruck by the glitter of the court, and particularly by the monumental figure of King Henry, who presided over it. To keep her happy, and hopefully throw her directly in front of the king's wandering gaze, in the spring of 1540 her uncle secured her an invitation to a masked ball.

Katherine's upbringing had been nothing if not unconventional. Orphaned at the age of ten, she spent the next five years in the household of her step-grandmother, the Dowager Duchess of Norfolk. Although she was well advanced in years, the duchess kept a massive household peopled with youngsters collected from her extended family. Too old to oversee them properly, she generally left the children to their own devices. They were not abused, but neither were they educated, given the diversions necessary for young people, nor properly supervised. Housed in dormitories divided by sex, the youngsters were left with no more chaperoning than a locked door intended to keep the boys and girls apart at night. Obviously it did not work.

The gentlewomen's chamber was the site of almost nightly parties, which frequently included the young men of the household who simply crawled out of their own window and in through the window of the girls' chamber. Inevitably, along with the games, laughing and drinking came a lot of sexual experimentation. One of the first of the young men to catch Katherine Howard's thirteen-year-old eye was the duchess's music master, a man named Edward Manox. After a few romps in the bedroom, however, Katherine dumped him in favour of her distant cousin, the handsome and charming Francis Dereham. Dereham and Katherine became constant bed partners, excusing their illicit sex by insisting they were going to marry, even calling each other 'husband' and 'wife'. Outraged at being dumped, Manox wrote a letter to the dowager duchess detailing Katherine's latest affair. The duchess caught her granddaughter and Dereham in bed together and beat her; but it was only a momentary solution to a long-term problem. By any standards, Katherine Howard was a wild child.

Given the girl's own history, and the king's mercurial record with his past wives, Katherine was hardly the most appropriate marriage candidate to put before Henry VIII. But when Henry took notice of the tiny, vivacious girl, her uncle 'commended her pure and honest conditions'. That one recommendation was all it took. According to a contemporary account, 'The King's Highness did cast a fantasy to Katherine Howard the first time that ever his Grace saw her.' Undoubtedly, her uncle Norfolk encouraged the girl to return the king's attention; at the same time cautioning her to keep a discreet distance. If the king was allowed to take her for a mistress, he would not need her as a wife; and it was a royal marriage that Norfolk needed.

In no time Henry was doting on the girl. He lavished gifts of fine gowns and jewels on her. He threw feasts and entertainments to focus her childish, wandering attention. It could not have taken him long to realise that she was not only uneducated, but also none too bright, but the king didn't seem to care. She was young, pretty and fun-loving. She loved to dance and listen to the court musicians, just as he once had. In Henry's lonely mind, this was the woman who would reinvigorate him, bring back his youth and be the solace of his old age. With Katherine by his side, the deprivations of age and the approach of death would not be so terrible. He called her 'the very jewel of womanhood' and his 'rose without a thorn' – the perfect woman who would never give him the anxieties that had been so much a part of his previous marriages. One of Henry's courtiers wrote, 'He is so amorous of her he cannot treat her well enough. He [can] not, in public or in private, keep his hands off his acquisition.' She was, in short, the fantasy of every middle-aged man.

For her part, the teenager doted on the attention Henry showed her – especially when there were expensive gifts thrown in to the bargain. For a girl who had never had anything, Henry's extravagance only made her greedy for more, and she behaved like a spoilt child. Her petulance may have passed unnoticed by Henry, but it did not sit well with everyone. Henry's pious, eldest daughter Mary – who was nearly ten years older than Katherine – was scandalised by the affair and took every opportunity to voice her feelings to anyone who would listen. Thomas Cromwell, realising that Anne of Cleves was about to be cast off in favour of this silly child, manoeuvred frantically to save his position and his head. Even Katherine's former lover, the young Francis Dereham, heard the news of Henry's latest fancy and beat a hasty retreat to Ireland to take up piracy; it may have been dangerous, but not so much as having the king find out about his affair with Katherine.

For all the things that can be said against Henry and Katherine's pairing, there was also a positive side. The prematurely aged Henry was indeed reinvigorated. He went on a diet. He took regular exercise. He went riding every day, hunting and hawking as he had done in the past. With the new regimen the ulcers on his leg began to heal for the first time in years. He even seemed to be able to put the tragedy of Jane Seymour's death out of his mind. As his physical health improved, so did his attitude. Henry's physician, Dr Marillac, wrote: 'This King has taken a new rule of living. To rise between five and six, hear mass at seven, and then ride till dinner time which is at ten a.m.' The court again became a place of joy rather than mourning. There were feasts and dancing, music and celebrations. Even Henry's legislative judgement seemed more stable than it had been in recent years. Henry now had no doubts; he would marry Katherine Howard.

On 28 July 1540, just sixteen days after his divorce from Anne of Cleves, Bishop Edmund Bonner secretly married the 49-year-old Henry VIII to the seventeen-year-old Katherine Howard. In either an ironic twist of fate, or a cleverly arranged social *tour de force*, this was the exact day his old friend, right-hand man and engineer of the Cleves marriage, Thomas Cromwell, went to the block. Ten days later the marriage was publicly announced. To celebrate his new-found marital bliss Henry had coins struck in Katherine's honour. The legend on them read 'Truly a rose without a thorn.'

Somehow, Henry even managed to let the acrimony between him and Anne of Cleves dissipate. At Katherine's insistence Henry went to visit his ex-wife at Richmond and she was invited to dine with the royal couple at Hampton Court. When Anne began to curtsey to her successor, Katherine stopped her, insisting that it was not proper. For such a normally thoughtless girl, it was an impressive and touching gesture.

Despite Henry's best efforts, his health remained uncertain. At his best he could even dance with his new bride, but as often as not his bad leg and excessive weight kept him on the sidelines, often forcing him to sit and watch while Katherine danced with the younger men at court. By spring 1541, the king's health took a serious turn for the worse. The ulcer on his leg reappeared, and his weight soared. He became morose and depressed, sitting alone in his private chambers for days on end, unable to work and refusing to see anyone except his closest personal aide, Thomas Culpeper, who helped hoist his bulk out of bed and dress and wash him. He even refused to allow the court musicians to entertain him and often denied Katherine admittance to his rooms, probably because he did not want her to see him as an invalid. There was a moment of hopefulness in April 1541 when Katherine thought she was pregnant, but when it proved to be a false alarm Henry's spirits sank lower than ever.

To fill the long days and weeks without Henry, Katherine busied herself with putting together her own household. In the unthinking, generous way of children, everyone who approached her for favours and advancement was welcomed into Katherine's glittering little circle. She dressed herself and her ladies in the latest French clothes and everyone got an allowance. In an effort to curb the worst of her excesses, Lady Jane Rochford was appointed to serve as her chief lady-in-waiting. Jane Rochford was the sister-in-law of Katherine's cousin, the late Anne Boleyn. She had been married to Anne's brother George and had been instrumental in manufacturing the evidence that sent her husband and Anne to the block only five years earlier. Jane Rochford was an inveterate plotter and schemer and the worst possible candidate to be put in a position of authority over an impulsive, senseless girl like Katherine Howard.

Most of Katherine's household, however, consisted of lively young people near her own age, many of whom were friends and distant relations she had known during her five years at the Duchess of Norfolk's house. Unwisely, among those she took into her household was her former lover Edward Manox, whom she appointed her court musician. In her endless quest to find amusing companions, Katherine made friends with her husband's personal body servant, the handsome and charming Thomas Culpeper. As a trusted retainer of the king and not many years older than the queen, Culpeper seemed a perfectly acceptable companion – as long as he remained at a discreet distance.

With the innocence of a child, Katherine graced both those around her and those she hardly knew with random acts of kindness. The accumulating mountain of gifts sent by her doting husband were shared with her ladies-in-waiting, palace staff and Anne of Cleves, who commented on the new queen's 'utmost kindness'. When she heard of the plight of the ageing Countess of Salisbury – who had been kept prisoner in the cold, damp confines of the Tower for more than two years – Katherine begged Henry to allow her to send warm clothes to the old lady. With his permission she had her seamstress make a fur-lined nightgown, a fur-lined petticoat and a skirt of heavy wool. She even took up the cause of the poet Sir Thomas Wyatt whom Henry had condemned to the Tower on a frivolous charge. When Henry finally released Wyatt on Katherine's insistence, his popularity soared and he magnanimously gave the credit to Katherine.

Despite her ongoing arguments with Henry's older daughter, Mary, she befriended his younger daughter Elizabeth, the child of her cousin Anne Boleyn. She insisted that Elizabeth be returned to court, calling her 'kinswoman' and allowing her to attend official court functions. Although he had officially declared Elizabeth a bastard, Henry did not seem openly offended by this constant reminder of his time with Anne. As the summer of 1541 approached, Henry's health again improved and his spirits lightened so much that he proposed to undertake a 'progress' through his kingdom. With their combined households in tow, Henry and Katherine set off on an extended tour of the country in late July.

When the royal party reached Pontefract, Katherine was approached by another of her former lovers, Francis Dereham, who had recently returned from his adventures in Ireland. Either out of sheer excitement, or to keep Dereham from blurting out her past indiscretions, Katherine took him into her household as private secretary. Obviously Henry had been told nothing of his wife's past association with either Dereham or Manox. When the king and queen returned to Windsor at the end of October, Henry was in better spirits than he had been in years. Only days after their return, he ordered the Bishop of Lincoln to give a special service thanking God for his new happiness 'after sundry troubles of mind which had happened to him by [previous] marriages'.

What Henry could not know was that while he was away Archbishop Cranmer had been approached by a man named John Lascelles and his sister Mary Hall, who was a member of Katherine's household. Both Lascelles and Hall had worked for the Dowager Duchess of Norfolk while Katherine had lived there and Mary had slept in the same dormitory as Katherine where she witnessed the goings on with Manox and Dereham. When Katherine took these men into her new household it outraged Mary Hall's sense of propriety. Now, with the foolish young queen away from court, they babbled everything they knew to Cranmer. Mary Hall insisted that Manox had lain with the queen and 'felt the secret and other parts of her body' and went into lurid detail of her sex romps with Dereham and the thrashing she had received from the Duchess of Norfolk as punishment.

Although Cranmer had nothing against Katherine herself, he was a staunch Protestant and irritated to see the Catholic-leaning Howard clan amassing power and social influence. To him she was no more than an innocent child. This revelation, however, was deeply disturbing. If Katherine and Dereham had actually insisted that they were going to be married, by the law of the time this made Katherine a bigamist when she married Henry. It would not lead her to the same end as her cousin Anne Boleyn, but it would demand an immediate divorce and a lot of hushing-up. It would also discredit the Howards once and for all. It was a moral dilemma with which Cranmer wrestled for months before coming to a decision.

Finally, one morning around 1 November 1541, while Henry was attending mass in his private chapel, Cranmer crept up behind him and passed him a note outlining the allegations. Cranmer admitted that he had to do it in writing because he 'had not the heart to tell him by mouth'. Henry's initial reaction was exactly what might be expected. He dismissed the entire thing as malicious gossip spurred on by old acquaintances who were jealous of Katherine's good fortune. In conference with his council, he abused Cranmer and the rest, accusing them of trying to bring down this sweet girl for their own political ends 'under pretence of serving him [when they] were only temporising for their own profit, but . . . if God lent him health, he would take care that their projects should not succeed'.

Henry may have been furious, but he was no fool. He knew the allegations would have to be investigated. If any of them proved true it would certainly not amount to treason, but it would demand that his marriage be annulled. Of course, as head of the kingdom and the Church of England he could tidy up that little problem. There was no way some childish indiscretion, if it had actually happened, was going to ruin the rest of his life and that of his queen. Atypically, Henry even discussed the problem with Katherine, telling her that she had nothing to worry about and that if the worst came to the worst he would grant her a Royal Pardon.

As certain as he might have been of his wife's innocence, Henry also knew that legal procedure must be adhered to absolutely. The king could not be seen to flout the law. As he called those ministers he could trust into council, Henry told Katherine to stay in her private apartment. As he left her, he told her musicians to leave, saying 'it is no more the time to dance'. For three days Henry and his advisers wrangled over possible courses of action. Certainly there was nothing here that smacked of treason, but everyone even remotely associated with the accusations was to be rounded up and questioned. First, Dereham and Manox were to be taken to the Tower and questioned rigorously. Henry insisted that if they refused to cooperate, they were to be tortured, muttering '*Necessitas non legem habet*' – necessity knows no law. Also to be questioned were Katherine's friends who had come to court from the Dowager Duchess's household, including John Lascelles and Mary Hall, who had made the original accusation. The Dowager Duchess, too, along with Katherine's uncle Lord William Howard, his wife Margaret, her brother Henry and his wife along with her aunt Lady Bridgewater must all give depositions. With the exception of her uncle, the Duke of Norfolk, virtually the queen's entire family was brought in for questioning. Someone out there knew the truth and Henry was going to find out what it was.

Francis Dereham at first denied everything, but under torture admitted to having sex with the queen when she was thirteen years old. That he was telling the truth and not simply saying what his questioners wanted to hear was confirmed by his knowledge of a birthmark on Katherine's thigh. If that were not bad enough, an old friend of Dereham's insisted that he had overheard Dereham say that if 'the king were dead, I am sure I might marry her'. This alone was enough for a charge of treason against Dereham, but

Katherine still seemed relatively safe. It was not until one of the queen's ladies, Margaret Morton, made reference to the king's trusted body servant, Thomas Culpeper, that things began to turn nasty.

Under questioning, Morton said, 'I never mistrusted the Queen until at Hatfield I saw her look out of her chamber window on Master Culpeper after such sort that I thought there was love between them.' Pressing this point with Morton and others of the queen's ladies-in-waiting, tales of love letters and secret meetings between Katherine and Culpeper began to emerge. If the queen were carrying on with men after her marriage, it was no longer a matter of an awkward past that would have to be hushed up; it was high treason.

This new information was laid before Henry at a council meeting on the night of 5 November – a meeting that began at midnight and went on until nearly dawn. The Culpeper revelation hit Henry hard. His trusted servant, his friend who bandaged his bad leg and helped him dress was cuckolding him; lying with his young wife. Henry had even rewarded Culpeper with the gift of an entire abbey. How could he betray him like this? How could Katherine betray him? If the situation had been serious before, it was now verging on disastrous. Henry swore he would get to the bottom of the matter if it was the last thing he did. Even the queen's uncle Norfolk declared that he 'wished the Queen was burned'.

As the order went out for Culpeper's immediate arrest, Katherine was to be sent from the palace to Sion House, a converted convent a few miles east of Hampton Court, but she was not to be alarmed and given plenty of time to pack. Henry did not want to move too fast in case these new charges were no more than the malicious gossip he had believed the first rumours to have been.

Two days after the council meeting Henry was attending mass with most of the court when Katherine was given the news of her impending detainment. Frantic, she broke loose from her guards and ran screaming through the vast halls of Hampton Court towards the chapel – shouting her husband's name as she ran. The guards caught up with her as she started banging her fists against the thick oak door, shouting for Henry to save her. Undoubtedly everyone in the chapel heard her, but no one so much as turned their head. Henry VIII would never see his rose without a thorn again.

As Katherine was shipped off to Sion with only Lady Rochford, three other women and the guards to attend her, Thomas Culpeper was being 'put to the question' in the Tower. He was racked mercilessly. At first, he adamantly denied sleeping with Katherine, insisting that the most attention she had shown him was to call him her 'sweet little fool' and to give him a cap and a ring. To refresh his memory a knotted rope was placed around his head and tightened until the knots dug into his eyes until they exploded. Finally he confessed, admitting that Lady Rochford had encouraged his affair with the queen, made all the arrangements for their meetings, and carried letters back and forth between them. There was no doubt he was finally telling the truth, the king's agents had already discovered a letter in his apartment that corroborated his story and would provide all the evidence the court would need to convict him. Written in Katherine's own childish scrawl it read:

Master Culpeper,

I heartily recommend me unto you, praying you to send me word how that you do . . . for I never longed so much for a thing as I do to see you and speak to you . . . and when I think again that you shall depart from me again it makes my heart die to think what fortune I have that I cannot be always in your company. . . . I trust . . . that you will come when my Lady Rochford is here for then I shall be best at leisure to be at your command-ment . . . and I would you was with me now that you might see what pain I take in writing to you.

Yours as long as life endures,
Katheryn

The arrest of Lady Rochford was ordered to take place immediately. Then it would be Katherine's turn to answer some questions.

Isolated at Sion House, Katherine had no idea of Dereham, Manox or Culpeper's confessions nor the dire effect they were having on her future. She must, however, have had some idea of how desperate her situation was becoming when the king's deputation came to question her. Among those present were Archbishop Cranmer, Bishop Gardiner, the Earl of Sussex and her uncle the Duke of Norfolk.

At first Katherine denied everything, insisting, as her husband had done, that it was all gossip and lies concocted by jealous rivals and servants; but Katherine was no intellectual match for her inquisitors. Finally, she confessed to her pre-marital indiscretions with Manox and Dereham, saying that Dereham had used her 'in such a sort as a man doth his wife, many and sundry times'. Cranmer asked her if she had intended to marry Dereham, and that if she had, it would make her marriage to Henry invalid and it could be annulled, relieving her of any further guilt. Katherine steadfastly denied she had any ties to Dereham, insisting that she was married to Henry and was the rightful queen. What she obviously did not realise was that she was throwing away her one chance to save herself. If her marriage was invalid, any post-marital affairs could be swept under the carpet; if she were legally the queen, she had committed a crime that carried the status of treason.

But she consistently denied any affairs after her marriage. Cranmer was so moved by her terror that he did not press the point, nor did he mention her letter to Culpeper. They had the proof and there was obviously no point in bringing it up just to terrify her. In his report on the questioning, he said, 'Her state it would have pitied any man's heart to see . . . for fear she would enter into a frenzy.' Cranmer and the others repeated their questioning well into the evening, but it was obvious that the queen was near hysterics and would not tell them anything new.

Desperate to make all the bad things she had brought on herself go away, Katherine wrote the following letter to her husband:

I, Your Grace's most sorrowful subject and most vile wretch in the world . . . do only make my most humble submission and confession of my faults. . . . My sorrow I can by no writing express, nevertheless I trust your most benign nature will have some respect unto my youth, my ignorance, my frailness, my humble confession of my faults, and plain declaration of the same referring me wholly unto Your Grace's pity and mercy. . . . I most humbly beseech you to consider the subtle persuasions of young men and the ignorance and frailness of young women.

I was so desirous to be taken unto Your Grace's favour, and so blinded by the desire of worldly glory that I could not . . . consider how great a fault it was to conceal my former faults from Your Majesty, considering that I intended ever during my life to be faithful and true unto Your Majesty ever after.

Nevertheless, the sorrow of my offences was ever before my eyes, considering the infinite goodness of Your Majesty toward me, which was ever increasing and not diminishing.

Now, I refer the judgement of mine offences with my life and death wholly unto your most benign and merciful grace, to be considered by no justice of Your Majesty's laws but only by your infinite goodness, pity, compassion and mercy – without which I acknowledge myself worthy of the most extreme punishment.

Not realising that Henry already knew about her letter to Culpeper, Katherine conveniently neglected to mention her ongoing affairs in this plea for mercy. The absence of a full confession only worsened her cause.

By 13 November, everyone who had waited on the queen while she lived at Hampton Court had been questioned and re-questioned. Lady Rochford had been removed from Katherine's household at Sion and taken to the Tower. Although there is no evidence that Rochford was tortured she completely lost control of herself under cross-examination. On the verge of mental collapse and willing to do anything to save her own scheming life, she signed a confession accusing virtually everyone even remotely associated with either Katherine or Culpeper. More significantly, she revealed that Culpeper and the queen were having sexual relations even while the royal party was on progress. She also admitted that she had made arrangements for the two to meet at nearly every castle and great house visited during the course of the tour where she, or a servant acting on her orders, ferreted out back stairs, dark passageways and secret doors through which the teenage queen's lover could find his way to her without any chance of running into Henry or his court officials. She also confirmed Culpeper's story that she had carried love letters between the two. It was corroborative testimony, it was damning and it was all the evidence needed to convict the queen of treason.

Although there was no hard evidence that either Manox nor Dereham had had sex with Katherine after her marriage, their past record with her, combined with their presence in her royal household, was enough to make them more than marginally suspect. Hurt and enraged, Henry ordered that they be tried for high treason along with Culpeper. To suppress any gossip that he was simply trying to get rid of another unwanted wife, he also commanded that their trials be held in open court.

On 1 December 1541, Thomas Culpeper, Edward Manox and Francis Dereham were arraigned in London's Guild Hall on charges of 'presumptive treason'. Culpeper was additionally charged with criminal intercourse with the queen. Although all three initially entered pleas of 'not guilty', when faced with the mountain of evidence against them they finally admitted their guilt. Culpeper made a final statement to the court, saying, 'Gentlemen, do not seek to know more than that the King deprived me of the thing I love best in the world and, though you may hang me for it, she loves me as well as I love her, though up to this hour no wrong has ever passed between us.' In light of the evidence, it was a useless effort. All three were convicted as charged. The sentence was death. In an attempt to wring any last bit of information out of the men ten more days of senseless torture and questioning followed their sentencing.

Through the long weeks of investigation, arrests, questioning and trials, Henry had retained his composure. But in a council meeting shortly after Culpeper, Dereham and Manox's trial, his over-wrought state got the best of him during a meeting of the council. Suddenly demanding that someone bring him a sword, the king flew into such a rage that his ministers thought he had finally snapped. Shouting and screaming, Henry cried, 'That wicked woman! She never had such delight in her lovers as she shall have torture in death!' As his terrified advisers watched with ashen faces, the man who had single-handedly reshaped the English church, defied France and the Pope and discarded three previous wives shook, wept and finally vomited on the council table before his guards could restrain him and lead him from the room sobbing, 'Why must so sweet a thing die?' For all his past cruelty and callous behaviour, there is no doubt that Henry VIII was desperately in love with Katherine Howard; now she had betrayed him and he was too old to rebuild his life.

Ten days after their trial, Culpeper, Dereham and Manox were taken to Tyburn to die. As a concession to his rank, Culpeper, blinded by his torture, was led to the block for a swift end. The other two were hanged, drawn and quartered as common traitors. Their three heads were then placed on pikes and displayed on London Bridge.

In the hope of keeping Henry from further anxiety, the council assured him that he would not have to appear at Katherine's trial. An Act of Attainder – essentially a warrant stripping Katherine of her rights – would be issued in his name and the trial undertaken through regular legal channels. The Act, drawn up in late January 1542, only seventeen months after Katherine's marriage to the king, listed the charges and accusations against the queen in graphic terms, referring to her as 'abominable, base, carnal, voluptuous and vicious', and accusing her of deceiving the king when she 'led him by word and gesture to love her . . . [and] . . . arrogantly coupled herself with him in marriage.'

On Friday 12 February, Katherine was moved by barge from Sion House to the Tower, 10 miles down the Thames. In the flotilla was the barge of the

Lord Privy Seal, in which members of the council rode, the barge carrying the queen – who was dressed in black velvet – and the Duke of Suffolk's barge crowded with soldiers. As they floated silently into London, they passed beneath London Bridge where Katherine undoubtedly saw the heads of her former lovers staring blindly down at her.

Taken through Traitors' Gate, Katherine was led from the barge to an apartment in the building known as the Queen's House, where Lady Rochford was already waiting for her in complete hysteria. Only hours before, Rochford had been told that her confession had not saved her from condemnation. She would not stand trial, but whatever punishment was handed down to Katherine would be hers as well.

As the women waited to hear their fate, both of them teetered on the edge of mental breakdown. Katherine's uncle Norfolk commented that she 'refuses to drink or eat and weeps and cries like a madwoman, so that they must take away things by which she might hasten her death'. A cynical and battle-hardened old soldier, Norfolk may have had little sympathy for his promiscuous niece, but he openly wept for his grieving king. Although Katherine was given the opportunity to appear at her trial, she refused. Still, she thought that if she could get a letter to Henry, he would save her. He had always given her everything she had wanted. Now, surely, he would save her life. She was wrong.

On Sunday evening, the head warden came with the news that she was to be executed the following morning. Amazingly calm, Katherine asked only two things. First, that her execution be held in private, away from the stares of the public and, secondly, that someone bring the block to her so she could practise laying her head on it with dignity. Both requests were granted. In a bizarre spectacle, the queen spent all evening repeatedly approaching the grim block, kneeling, praying and leaning forward.

Stepping on to the scaffold the next morning, Katherine Howard, the nineteen-year-old Queen of England, addressed the small clutch of noblemen who surrounded her. In her final address, she said 'As to the act . . . for which I stand condemned, God and His holy angels take to witness my soul's salvation, that I die guiltless. What sins and follies of youth I have committed I will not excuse, but am assured that for them God hath brought this punishment upon me, and will, in His mercy, remit them; for which I pray you, pray with me unto His Son and my Saviour Christ. . . . [B]y the journey on which I am bound, I have not wronged the King . . . sin blinded me and greed of grandeur; and since mine is the fault, mine also is the suffering.' Finally, she asked that her family should not suffer for her crimes. Approaching the block, she died with the first stroke of the axe.

Next came Lady Jane Rochford who regained her sanity long enough not only to admit her part in Katherine's downfall, but in being complicit in wrongly condemning her husband and Anne Boleyn to the end she herself was about to suffer.

On hearing of Katherine's fate her predecessor, Anne of Cleves, said ironically, 'she was too much a child to deny herself any sweet thing she wanted'.

After her death, Henry granted Katherine's last request. Her family was freed from the Tower, but he confiscated large tracts of their vast estate holdings. After providing him with two such troublesome wives, the Howards would never find profit in Henry's court again. The king himself never recovered from the ordeal either mentally or physically. Throughout his few remaining years he intermittently insisted that he saw and heard Katherine's ghost running frantically through the hall leading towards the chapel of Hampton Court Palace where she had tried to reach him as he attended mass that morning in early November. He may have been right; hundreds of others have reported the same phenomenon in the centuries since.

Six

NINE DAYS A QUEEN

Lady Jane Grey
1553

Over the centuries hundreds of men and women have coveted the crown of England. Thousands more have died trying to seize or protect it for heirs and claimants, both rightful and otherwise. But in at least one instance a legitimate heir tried desperately to refuse the honour of becoming monarch but, much to her regret, allowed herself to be manipulated into accepting by a small clique of power-hungry men.

Henry VIII's complicated matrimonial experiments left behind a string of claimants to the throne. Clearly, the first in line was Edward, son of Henry's third wife, Jane Seymour. After Edward the claim became muddled as a result of Henry's half-dozen marriages and four ugly divorces. According to Henry's will the next in line was Mary, his eldest daughter by his first wife, Queen Catherine of Aragon, followed in line of succession by Elizabeth, offspring of the disgraced Anne Boleyn. While this might seem straightforward enough, King Henry had previously convinced his ministers to declare both Mary and Elizabeth bastards and, therefore, unable to succeed him. Thus the king had effectively reduced his own will to little more than a royal request.

When Henry died in 1547, Edward assumed the throne, but since he was only ten years old, he was given a 'Protector' to act as regent. The manipulative and ambitious John Dudley, Duke of Northumberland, filled this position. In addition to shepherding the young king, Dudley was also Head of the Royal Council, making him the most powerful man in England next to the king; a king whose decisions were heavily influenced by Dudley.

Even as a child Edward showed ample evidence of his strong-willed Tudor blood and eventually he should have been able to outgrow the influence of Northumberland. But Edward had always been a sickly child. He had probably contracted tuberculosis before he ascended the throne and early in 1553 an attack of measles weakened his already frail health. By April of that year the king was coughing up blood, and contemporary accounts of his condition indicate that may also have been receiving doses of a slow-acting poison. Royal surgeons held out little hope for the boy's recovery. Death was imminent.

Edward's councillors panicked. If Edward died childless, the throne could still revert to Princess Mary – a devout Catholic – who would undoubtedly outlaw the new Church of England and the entire council would lose their power and quite possibly their heads. Edward had to make a will of his own and set out a new line of succession that protected England's future. There is little question that the direction of the succession was engineered by Northumberland, but Edward was ultimately responsible for most of the wording of his will and the articles of succession, both of which were designed to protect the fledgling Church of England.

Edward knew that if his half-sister Mary were passed over in favour of the Protestant Elizabeth there would assuredly be legal, and possibly physical, challenges to the throne. It would be far better if both of them were denied the throne and another Protestant named to succeed him. Henry VIII's precaution of having declared both Mary and Elizabeth illegitimate gave Edward a perfectly legal means of accomplishing this end. From the minutes of Edward's Last Will and Testament comes the following: 'Item the Second: Our said executors shall not suffer any piece of religion to be altered. And they shall diligently travail to cause Godly ecclesiastical laws to be made and set forth . . .'. Following this was Edward's intent for the future of his sisters: 'Fifthly, my will is, that my sisters Mary and Elizabeth shall . . . be bound to live in quiet order . . . and . . . that they . . . shall have our gift of one thousand pounds yearly.' With that single sentence, King Edward VI pensioned off the two nearest claimants to the throne.

Now, a new monarch had to be selected. Outside Edward's immediate family there were no less than eight legitimate claimants to the crown and all except one of them were women. No matter who Edward named the next ruler of England would most likely be the kingdom's first female monarch. Immediately in line behind Henry VIII's three children was Frances Grey, Duchess of Suffolk. Following her was her eldest daughter Jane. Certainly, unlike Edward's sisters, the legitimacy of the wife and daughter of Henry Grey, Duke of Suffolk were beyond question. It was to these two women that Edward left his throne. In his Devise for the Succession, Edward stated: 'For lack of issue (male) of my body . . . to the Lady Frances's heirs male, for lack of such issue (before my death) to the Lady Jane and her heirs male.' In simple language, this meant that the throne would go first to Frances Grey and then, unless Frances gave birth to a son, to her daughter Jane. Twenty-four members of the council including the Protector, Northumberland and the Duke of Suffolk, Frances' husband and Jane's father witnessed this Devise.

It was at this point that the devious Northumberland implemented his master strategy. If he could arrange a marriage between Edward's cousin Jane Grey and one of his own sons, when Jane inherited the throne her husband would undoubtedly be crowned king – because there was no precedent for a female ruler – and Northumberland could then rule through him. Jane's parents zealously agreed to the proposed marriage, the Duchess of Suffolk even stepping aside from the line of succession in favour of her daughter. Whether Northumberland's only unmarried son, Guildford Dudley, or Lady Jane Grey, were consulted in the matter of their marriage remains a mystery. It is certain that neither of them was aware of the new Articles of Succession.

By all accounts Jane Grey was an extraordinary young woman. In 1546 she had been sent to court at the age of nine under the wardship of Queen Katherine Parr, last wife of Henry VIII. Katherine was a warm, pious, loving surrogate parent to Jane, but died in childbirth (by her third husband) less than two years after taking charge of Jane. Now Jane's wardship fell on the machiavellian John Dudley, Duke of Northumberland.

Despite the presence of Northumberland, Jane developed a mind of her own, probably out of self-defence. At the time her marriage was arranged in 1553, Jane was a tiny, delicate fifteen-year-old. Standing barely 5 feet tall, she had a startling mane of bright auburn hair and a pale, heavily freckled complexion. But it was her mind that really set Jane apart. She could read, write and speak Latin, Greek, French, Hebrew and Italian; she was also amazingly pious for a teenager and her most treasured possession was a copy of the New Testament in Greek.

While the years had taught Jane to fear and hate her guardian Northumberland, she was barely acquainted with the fourth of his five sons, Guildford. But bending to what she called 'the urgency of my mother and the violence of my father' she agreed to marry this twenty-year-old stranger. With Edward nearing death, the wedding had to be arranged as soon as possible. There was no time to have the elaborate wedding clothes made, so they were borrowed from the Master of the Royal Wardrobe. On 25 May 1553 Jane Grey and Guildford Dudley wed at the London home of the Duke and Duchess of Northumberland. On the same day Jane's younger sister Mary was married to Lord Herbert and Guildford Dudley's sister Catherine was married to the young Earl of Huntingdon. In one bold move, the Northumberlands had intermarried their family with nearly everyone of importance in the kingdom.

Almost six weeks to the day after the triple wedding, sixteen-year-old King Edward VI died at Greenwich, but no public announcement was made of his passing. There were too many preparations to be made and precautions to be taken. Immediately on Edward's death, Northumberland ordered the Tower brought to a full state of defence in the name of Queen Jane, and sent his son Lord Robert Dudley with a troop of cavalry to take Princess Mary prisoner. Mary had been kept more than 20 miles outside London and under heavy confinement throughout Edward's five-year reign but somehow, before Robert Dudley and his troops got to her, she had learned of her brother's death and escaped into the Suffolk countryside to begin rallying her own forces. It was not an auspicious beginning to the new reign.

On Sunday 9 July, Jane's sister Mary arrived by barge at Jane and Guildford Dudley's house. Here, Mary told Jane that she was ordered to come at once to their parents' home, Sion House, where there was important news from the king. Although Jane had been ill for several days and was running a fever, she agreed, and the two returned by barge to Sion. When they arrived at the Suffolks' home, the great hall was empty, but almost immediately members of the family and the council began filtering in. According to Jane's diary, they 'began to make me complimentary speeches, bending the[ir] knee . . . all of which made me blush. . . . My distress was still further increased when . . . my mother-in-law entered and paid me homage.' Jane's embarrassment and confusion were heightened when Lords Pembroke and Huntington entered the room, knelt and kissed her hand; 'with unwonted caresses they did me reverence as was not at all suitable to my state'. Obviously, Jane knew something was very wrong, but she was not kept guessing for long.

Within minutes, Jane's father-in-law, Northumberland, entered the hall and announced to Jane what everyone else in the room already knew. The king was dead and Jane Grey was to succeed him. When the announcement was over, the assembled company knelt before Jane, stating, according to Jane's diary, 'that they . . . swore to shed their blood and give their lives to maintain the same'. Already weak from fever, Jane collapsed and fainted. In her own words, 'On hearing this I remained stunned and out of myself and I call on those present to bear witness who saw me fall to the ground weeping piteously and dolefully lamenting the death of the king, I swooned and lay as dead.'

When she was roused, Jane insisted, 'The crown is not my right and pleaseth me not.' But once again, out of loyalty to her parents, she allowed herself to be persuaded that it was her duty to her family and the kingdom to take the throne. Finally, she agreed and addressed herself not to those in the room, but to God, 'if what hath been given me is lawfully mine, may I . . . govern to Thy glory and service, and to the advantage of the realm.' Later, Jane would write, 'It did not become me to accept . . . [it showed] a lack of prudence'.

The following day, Monday 10 July, at around three in the afternoon, Jane, her husband, family and in-laws, travelled by barge from Sion House to London where the new queen could be kept safely behind the ancient walls of the Tower. For the official procession into the Tower, Jane was dressed in the splendour befitting her new station in life. Her brocaded gown was heavily decorated with seed pearls and the bodice beneath it was bright green, embroidered with gold. Behind her, the train of her gown was borne by her mother and at her side was Guildford who, reportedly, was 'showing her much attention'. To make Jane's diminutive figure visible to the crowds that had gathered, over her shoes she wore a pair of wooden clogs with soles 3 inches thick. A merchant from Genoa who witnessed the scene described her as 'graceful and well made, and when she smiles she shows her teeth. . . . In all she is a charming person *graziosa e animata*' (graceful and lively).

At the gates of the Tower Jane was greeted by the Marquis of Winchester, the Lord Chancellor, and Sir John Bridges, the Lieutenant of the Tower, who knelt to present her with the keys to the ancient fortress. But before Jane could step forward to accept, her father-in-law intervened, taking the keys and handing them to Jane. It was clear that from now on, all power, even the symbolic power of the Tower keys, would pass through Northumberland's hands before being transferred to the new monarch.

As Queen Jane stepped into the Tower a herald proclaimed her, 'Jane, by the Grace of God, Queen of England, France and Ireland, Defender of the Faith and Church of England and Ireland, under Christ on Earth, the Supreme Head'. It was far too heavy a burden to lay on an unprepared fifteen-year-old, and far too delicate a responsibility to slip into the hands of Northumberland.

The following day, Tuesday, the Lord High Treasurer brought the crown to Jane to check its fit and make arrangements for any necessary adjustments. At first, Jane refused, insisting that she had not asked to see the regalia. She was told, 'You must take it . . . and soon I will have another made to crown your husband with.' To the Lord Treasurer the phrase had been completely innocent, but to Jane it revealed the extent of Northumberland's entire ugly plot. This wasn't about her and never had been. The plan was to make Guildford Dudley king; she was nothing but a pawn in a massive game of power politics. Was Guildford a part of the plot? Were her parents? Understandably, Jane was furious. She called her council and confronted them with what she knew and what she suspected. Then she informed them that under no circumstances would she allow Guildford Dudley to become king. Her parents were beside themselves and her in-laws were fuming, but Jane stood her ground.

That same evening, word came to the tower that Princess Mary still eluded capture and was now asserting her right to the crown, demanding that Jane relinquish the throne immediately. The council responded by formally rejecting Mary's claims and asserting the rights of 'our Sovereign lady Queen Jane'. But if the councillors feared Mary and her religion, they also hated the scheming, power-hungry Northumberland, and their support for Jane was largely a matter of political expediency. For their own protection as much as Jane's, the council demanded that Jane's father, the Duke of Suffolk, lead an army to capture Mary and defeat whatever forces she might have assembled. Jane refused. Her father would remain at the Tower to protect her; Northumberland would lead the hunt for Mary. Little could Jane have known that the populace of England hated her father-in-law as much as she did. Four days later, on Saturday the 15th, Northumberland and his army set out to suppress the Marian rebellion, heading north towards Cambridge, Mary's last known location.

With the coercive influence of Northumberland now absent from court, the ministerial will to oppose Mary began to falter, a matter not helped when word arrived on Sunday that Mary was openly being proclaimed queen in towns and cities throughout the south and common people everywhere were refusing to take up arms against her. In truth, popular support for Mary was not as strong as it was made to seem. Most people were aware of the possibility of religious upheaval if she took the throne, but she was Henry VIII's rightful heir and that alone brought her a lot of support.

Both sides in the growing confrontation were now actively campaigning for their chosen candidate and doing their best to raise an army large enough to defeat the opposition. While there is no doubt that Mary was firmly in charge of her party, we have no way of knowing if Jane even understood the terrible implications of all this. As a teenage girl who had led a sheltered and privileged life, she can hardly have been expected to grasp the real gravity of her situation. What we do know is that the stress of the situation was already taking a horrible physical toll on the girl. Her hair had begun to fall out and her skin was peeling. Sleep became impossible.

When some of the ships of the Royal Navy stationed at Yarmouth mutinied and defected to Mary's side, the already timorous ministers went into a panic and began looking for the quickest way out of the Tower and as far as possible from the teenage girl they had put on the throne. At around seven o'clock in the evening of the 16th, the tower warders, loyal to Jane, locked the Tower gates, preventing the ministers from leaving. The keys to the Tower were then handed to Jane.

Despite these precautions, by Tuesday the 18th virtually the entire council had abandoned Jane and the Tower, slipping away one at a time to meet at Baynard's Castle where they unanimously declared the hated Northumberland a traitor and asserted Mary's right to the crown. To give weight to their action they drafted a letter to the Duke of Suffolk demanding that his daughter relinquish the throne which only nine days earlier she had tried so hard to refuse.

When a copy of the letter was delivered to Suffolk, who had remained in the Tower with his daughter, he rode immediately to Baynard's Castle where he added his name to the proclamation acknowledging Mary as rightful queen. This done, he returned to the Tower to confront Jane whom he found sitting alone in her chair of state in the empty audience chamber. 'Come down off there, child. That is no place for you', he told her sadly, and proceeded to tear the canopy bearing Jane's device from its place above the throne. Then he told her to remove her crown and royal robes.

Not surprisingly, Jane's reaction was one of immeasurable relief. Exhausted beyond words, she is reported to have replied to her father, 'I much more willingly put them off than I put them on. Out of obedience to you and my mother, I have grievously sinned. Now I willingly relinquish the crown.' Finally, she asked him 'May I go home now?' Guilt-ridden, Henry Grey could not bring himself to answer his daughter. He and his wife had already decided they would leave the Tower, abandoning their daughter as a hostage to Mary, as a guarantee of their own future good behaviour.

Among those in the council who had actively plotted Jane's downfall was the Earl of Arundel. When Northumberland left the Tower on his way to confront Mary's army, Arundel had made a great show of support for the enterprise, insisting that he would gladly have gone along, but his age and duties at the Tower prevented it. In truth, only hours after Northumberland left London, Arundel had slipped away and was on his way to Cambridge to join Mary's followers. There he would meet up with Northumberland on the afternoon of 20 July.

Even before Northumberland reached Cambridge he realised that his cause had virtually no popular backing. At best, the towns and villages the army passed through were indifferent; at worst, they were openly hostile to the duke and his men. By the time they arrived in Cambridge, Northumberland knew his cause was lost and he made a public announcement supporting Mary, saying, 'Queen Mary is a merciful woman who will pardon me.' Standing in the crowd that had gathered to hear him was none other than the Earl of Arundel. Stepping forward at the end of the speech, Arundel shouted, 'Do not flatter yourself. [Even] if the Queen were inclined to pardon, those who rule her will destroy thee, whomsoever else be spared.'

Realising there was no escape, Northumberland and his army disarmed, most of them slipping away into the countryside, while Northumberland, the would-be kingmaker, and his closest followers were taken into custody and marched off to London.

Even as Northumberland was laying down his arms, Queen Mary was marching on London with an army more than ten thousand strong.

At thirty-seven years of age Mary Tudor was already a sour-tempered old woman who had grown to mistrust and dislike almost everyone, mostly as a result of the abuse she and her mother had received at the hands of her father. Mary's only consolation, and the guiding force in her life, was her fanatically strong Catholic faith – which she clung to with an almost morbid devotion. When Mary entered the Tower, many of her old supporters, pillars of the Roman Catholic church, were brought out of the cells where they had been kept in confinement since her father reformed the church nearly fifteen years earlier. Casting her cold eyes over the sorry lot of bent and malnourished old men, Mary said 'You are my prisoners!' Then she kissed each one of them on the cheek, set them free and began plotting her revenge on everyone who had kept her off the throne and those who had supported her father's new Church of England.

Jane Dudley was removed from the state apartments to the Gentleman Gaoler's lodgings on Tower Green where she would be kept in relative comfort, but under close guard. Guildford Dudley was taken to the Beauchamp Tower to be joined there three days later, on 24 July, by Northumberland, his father and his three brothers, Robert, Ambrose and Henry. Three weeks later, on 18 August, the Duke of Northumberland was taken to trial at Westminster where he was immediately found guilty of treason, with the execution set for five days later. In an attempt to save his head, Northumberland converted to the Catholic faith and made a public statement enumerating all the troubles Protestantism had brought to England. It was a good ploy, but Mary was not fooled. Even on the morning of his execution, the wily duke played for every possible minute of time. The execution had to be delayed for nearly an hour when he demanded to hear mass. On the scaffold, the duke begged for his life, pleading that 'even the life of a dog' was better than death. Finally realising that there would be no reprieve, he wrung his hands crying 'This must be!' and lowered his head on to the block.

With Northumberland's death, Mary relaxed the conditions of Jane's confinement. She was allowed 93 shillings a week to spend, allowed to walk in the Tower gardens, occasionally going outside the Tower and as far as Tower Hill, but always under heavy guard. Occasionally she was allowed to share dinner with the Gentleman Gaoler, Mr Partridge, and his wife. It was at one such dinner eleven days after her father-in-law's execution that she fell into conversation with another dinner guest, Rowland Lea. During their discussion, talk came around to her father-in-law, his plots and his humiliating end. According to Lea's diary, Jane said, 'He hath brought me and our stock in most miserable calamity and misery by his exceeding ambition.' Of Northumberland's eleventh-hour religious conversion, she said, 'Perchance he thereby hoped to have his pardon . . . what man is there living, I pray you, although he had been innocent, that would hope of life in that case, being in the field against the Queen in person as General, and after being so hated and evil spoken of by the common [people]? Who was [to] judge that he should hope for pardon, whose life was so odious to all men? But . . . like as his life was wicked and full of dissimulation, so was his end . . . I pray God, I nor no friend of mine die so.' Here was obviously a great personal statement of faith, because Jane knew that she, too, was about to go on trial for her life on charges of treason.

But even the hardened Mary could not believe that Jane Grey was a traitor; she had simply been a pawn in a massive game of power politics. To that end, the day before Jane's trial, Mary called her to court and told her privately that although a verdict of guilty was certain, she and her husband would be pardoned and, as soon as possible, set free.

On 13 November, Jane and Guildford, along with two of his brothers, Ambrose and Henry, were sent to trial at the Guildhall surrounded by a guard of four hundred soldiers. They all pleaded guilty to the charge of treason, and the sentence of death was only a matter of form. True to her word, on the following day Queen Mary arranged their pardon.

Everything might have gone according to plan had Mary not made a proclamation in early December, announcing her intention to marry Prince (soon to be King) Philip of Spain. Hostility against her Catholic religion now overshadowed the public's belief in her inherited right to the throne. Visions of Spanish rule and the Spanish Inquisition being imported into England sent waves of panic through the church and lay community alike.

Among the tens of thousands of incensed Englishmen was Sir Thomas Wyatt. Wyatt had never been particularly political, nor especially religious. Even his background was not notably auspicious; his father had been executed for committing adultery with Anne Boleyn. But the thought of England becoming a Spanish satellite was too much for Wyatt to bear and he began raising an army to oppose the queen and, if necessary, to drive her from the throne. One of those who flocked to Wyatt's cause was the Duke of Suffolk, father of the captive Lady Jane. Undoubtedly, some of Suffolk's patriotic fervour was spurred on by guilt for having manipulated, and then abandoned, his daughter. Whatever the case, by mid-January Wyatt and Suffolk had an army of more than four thousand men, which they led to Rochester, seizing the city and sending out a call for support from Londoners. Initially Wyatt's chances looked good. When the Duke of Norfolk led an army into the field to subdue the rebellion, hundreds of his men deserted to join Wyatt's cause.

On 3 February 1554, Wyatt's army entered the outskirts of London, through the Southwark district and moved towards the Tower where they took up position across the river, demanding custody of both Queen Mary and Lady Jane Grey. It probably came as no surprise that their demand was rejected out of hand. Without hesitation, Wyatt and Suffolk began bombarding the Tower walls, irrespective of the danger their artillery might present to Jane Grey. But Wyatt's guns were no match for the massive cannon and mortars mounted on the walls of the Tower. Within an hour, Wyatt

Richard II, aged fourteen, leaves the Tower to meet Wat Tyler and his rebels during the Peasants' Revolt of 1381. (*Authors' collection*)

Murder of the two young princes – Edward V and his brother Richard (original painted by James Northcote in 1790). (*Authors' collection*)

This fifteenth-century image from Froissart's *Chronicles* incorrectly shows the murders of Archbishop Simon Sudbury and his companions taking place in St John's Chapel, when, in fact, they took place on Tower Hill. (*Authors' collection*)

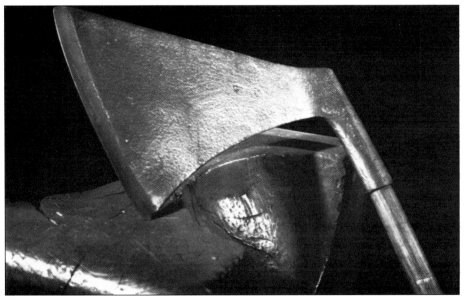

The headsman's block and axe displayed at the Tower of London. (*Authors' collection*)

Woodcut dated 1497 depicting the Tower of London. (*Authors' collection*)

The doorway to Little Ease from an 1883 painted postcard. (*Authors' collection*)

Queen Katherine Howard. (*Authors' collection*)

'IANE' carved into the walls in one of the rooms in the Beauchamp Tower, believed to be by the hand of Guildford Dudley. (*Courtesy The Royal Armouries, HM Tower of London*)

Woodcut from a pamphlet of 1662 showing traitors being hanged, drawn and quartered. (*Authors' collection*)

Perspective view of Tower Hill and the place of execution of the Lords Kilmarnock and Balmerino on 18 August 1776 – note the ring of guards encircling the scaffold at the time of execution. (*The Guildhall Library*)

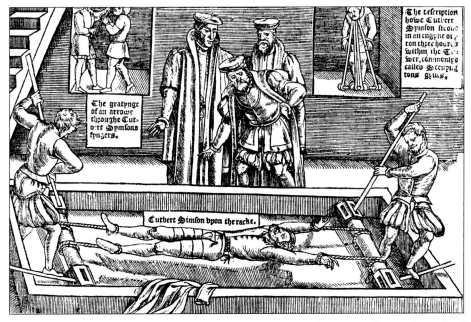

Cuthbert Symson being tortured and broken upon the rack. (*From John Foxe's* Book of Martyrs, *1563*)

Seventeenth-century regicides are hanged, drawn and quartered on Tower Hill shortly after the Restoration of the Monarchy. (*Authors' collection*)

A late eighteenth-century print showing the execution, hanging, drawing and quartering of the Gunpowder Plot conspirators. (*Hulton Getty Collection, London*)

Nineteenth-century representation of heads displayed on Bridge Gate, Tower Bridge. (*Authors' collection*)

Near contemporary portrayal of the trial of the Babington conspirators. (*Authors' collection*)

The Tower of London at night as viewed from the Thames, and engraved by H. Winkler in 1834. (*Author's collection*)

began abandoning his position, slowly retreating through the streets of London. Suffolk stood his ground longer but, eventually, he too had to give up the fight. It wasn't long before, Wyatt and nearly three hundred of his supporters, including Jane's father, were captured by the queen's forces near Temple Bar and hauled unceremoniously back to a Tower already overcrowded by the arrests made when Mary took the throne. Never in its long history had the Tower held so many prisoners at one time.

More than one hundred of Wyatt's rebels would eventually be hanged or beheaded, forty-five of them on one day alone. Wyatt himself would be among the last to go. When his turn came, Wyatt was subjected to all the public humiliation and pain of the worst of medieval tortures: being hanged, drawn and quartered. But even with the deaths of Northumberland and Wyatt, Mary's fears were not put to rest. So long as Jane Grey remained a focus of public sympathy, Mary would not rest easy. Jane Grey would have to die. Two days after Wyatt's execution, Jane and Guildford were told that their pardon had been rescinded and they would go to the block in a matter of days.

On hearing the news, Jane's ladies-in-waiting broke down in tears, but Jane tried to comfort them, saying 'O faithful companions of my sorrows . . . are we not born into life to suffer adversity and even disgrace? When has the time been that the innocent were not exposed to violence and oppression? The quarrel is God's, but undoubtedly the victory is ours.'

It would seem that even the hard-hearted Mary had no taste for killing her sixteen-year-old cousin and sent her personal confessor, Dr John Feckenham, to Jane with a message of hope. If she would convert to Catholicism, the execution might still be called off. On 8 February, Feckenham took the message to Jane and urged her to convert, but Jane told him that she did not have time for a religious controversy. Feckenham took her statement literally and reported to the queen that Jane needed more time to search her soul. Mary agreed to a three-day stay of execution. Excitedly, Feckenham rushed back to Jane with the news. Realising that he had completely misunderstood her intent, Jane said, 'You are much deceived, sir, if you think I have any desire for longer life; for I assure you . . . my life has been so tedious to me that I long for nothing so much as death; and since it is the Queen's pleasure, I am most willing to undergo it.'

Desperate to save the girl, Feckenham even proposed that he and Jane debate their respective beliefs publicly. Exhausted and frustrated, Jane answered, 'This disputation may be fit for the living, but not for the dying.

Leave me to make peace with God.' When Feckenham replied that he was afraid that he would not see Jane again, she told him, 'that is true, unless God . . . opens the eyes of your heart'. Implicit in this answer was Jane's belief that Feckenham, as a Catholic, would not be accepted into heaven. It was a sentiment that was undoubtedly not lost on Feckenham.

Although he had failed to convert Jane to the Roman Catholic Church and thereby save her life, Feckenham had been deeply moved by the girl's piety and strength of character. As a final gesture to Jane, he asked Queen Mary if he might accompany her young cousin to the scaffold. Probably hoping for a last-minute conversion, Mary gave her consent.

Even with the certainty of death hanging over her, Jane seems to have spent her last few days relatively composed, if not calm. She occupied her time writing in her diary, recalling the facts of her short, turbulent reign and sending letters to friends and family. Among those to whom she wrote was her cousin, the queen. Here, she admitted her guilt and explained the circumstances that led her to the end of her young life. 'Although my fault be such that but for the goodness and clemency of the Queen, I can have no hope of finding pardon . . . [my own] lack of prudence . . . deserve[s] heavy punishment. . . . It being known that the error imputed to me had not been altogether caused by myself.'

She also wrote to her father who was being confined in the nearby Martin tower. 'Father', she began, 'although it hath pleased God to hasten my death by you, by whom my life should have rather been lengthened, yet can I so patiently take it, that I yield to God more hearty thanks. . . . I count myself blessed that . . . my guiltless blood may cry before the Lord, "Mercy to the innocent".' She closed the letter 'I am your obedient daughter till death, Jane Dudley.'

On the very eve of her execution, she wrote in her diary the following words, 'If justice be done with my body, my soul will find mercy with God. If my faults deserve punishment, my youth, at least, and my imprudence, were worthy of excuse; God and posterity will show me favour.' While Jane occupied her mind with writing, in the nearby Beauchamp tower her twenty-year-old husband spent his time thinking about Jane and the life they might have had together. On the wall of his cell he carved a single word in Latin script – IANE. It remains there to this day.

On the morning of 12 February, just six days after Wyatt's rebellion had been put down, Jane and Guildford Dudley were scheduled to go to the block.

In a last-minute request to the queen, Guildford asked that he might spend a few minutes with his wife before going to his execution. Obviously moved, Mary consented. Jane, however, did not. Instead, she sent a note to her husband, insisting that to meet under their present circumstances would be too painful and could only drain whatever emotional strength they still had. The letter said, in part, that they should 'omit these moments of grief' and that they would 'shortly meet in a better world where friendships were happy and unions indissoluble'. Jane did agree to watch from the window of her cell as Guildford was led through from the Tower and to wave to him as he passed.

Once on Tower Hill, Guildford's courage failed him. Terrified and shaking, he could not bring himself to make the customary final speech for fear he would break down in tears. Sinking to his knees before the ugly oak block, he muttered, 'Pray for me, pray for me, pray for me.' Transfixed with emotion, Jane had remained at the window of her cell long after Guildford and the guards passed out of sight and through the gates of the Tower. She was still standing there nearly twenty minutes later when the handcart bearing her husband's body trundled back in through the gates. By his side, wrapped in a blood-soaked cloth, was a large round object. It was his head. Slumping to the floor, Jane sobbed 'Oh! Guildford! Guildford!'

Less than an hour later it was Jane's turn on the block. To spare her the public humiliation of an execution on Tower Hill, a special scaffold had been erected on Tower Green inside the walls of the Tower compound.

As Lady Jane Grey mounted the steps of the scaffold, wearing the same black dress she had worn at her trial, she commented to those around her, 'Good people, I am come hither to die, and by law I am condemned to do the same. . . . I pray you all . . . to hear my witness, that I die a good Christian woman, and that I do look to be saved by no other means but only by the mercy of God in the blood of His only Son Jesus Christ. . . . And now, good people, while I am alive, I pray you assist me with my prayers.'

Having knelt and prayed, Jane turned to Dr Feckenham, who had been waiting on the scaffold when she arrived, and asked if she might be allowed to recite the 51st Psalm. Choked with emotion, Feckenham could not answer, but nodded his assent. Then, only minutes before her death, in a loud, clear voice, Jane repeated the psalm, from memory and without flaw. By the time she rose, Feckenham was in tears. Jane stepped over to him and said, 'God will abundantly requite you, good sir, for your humanity to me' – and then added wryly, 'though your discourses gave me more uneasiness than all the terrors of my approaching death.' With that she kissed him on the cheek and squeezed his hand, as though she had enough strength for both of them.

Now, Jane calmly stepped towards the block and removed her outer gown. But as she prepared to kneel, she was told that there would be a five-minute wait in case of a last-minute reprieve. For five long minutes the entire company stood there in dead silence. Jane stared at the ugly black oak block in front of her while everyone else stared at her. The reprieve never came.

Finally, the executioner stepped forward and knelt down beside Jane, asking her forgiveness for what he was about to do. He then instructed her to approach the block. For a moment Jane looked confused. 'Stand upon the straw, madame' he said quietly. Turning one last time, Jane said to him: 'I pray you dispatch me quickly', then added, 'You will not take it off before I lay me down?' 'No, Madame', he assured her.

Kneeling in front of the block, Jane tied a white handkerchief around her eyes and then felt for the block. But she had kneeled too soon. The block was out of reach. Now panicking, she waved her hands in the air first one way and then another, muttering, 'Where is it? What shall I do? Where is it?' Frozen in horror, no one on the scaffold seemed able to move. Finally, one of the small crowd surrounding the scaffold mounted the steps and guided her hands to the block. As she crawled forward on her knees and laid her head into the hollow, Lady Jane Grey, Queen of England for nine days, said in a firm voice, 'Lord, into thy hands I commend my spirit.'

When the executioner had finished his work, according to law he picked up the bleeding head of the sixteen-year-old girl, held it high in the air, and proclaimed, 'So perish all the Queen's enemies. Behold – the head of a traitor!'

In the seven months since Jane Grey had first entered the Tower to be declared Queen of England, she had never left. England's most unwilling monarch, who had reigned for only nine days, was laid to rest in front of the altar of St Peter ad Vincula Church in the Tower compound next to her husband, Guildford Dudley. Jane's father, Henry Grey, Duke of Suffolk, followed his daughter to the block eleven days later on 23 February 1554. Guildford Dudley's brother John died in his cell, but his brothers Ambrose and Robert escaped death; Robert went on to be elevated to the title of Earl of Leicester and is best remembered as 'Robin', Queen Elizabeth I's friend, confidant and lover.

But in the months and years before Elizabeth came to the throne, many of Queen Mary's supporters would come to regret their choice of sides in the war between Jane and Mary. Her vicious persecution of Protestants would send hundreds to the block or the stake, there to be burned as heretics. Nor would posterity remember her kindly, referring to her not as Queen Mary Tudor but simply as Bloody Mary.

Seven

THE DEVIL'S DANCING BEAR

Bishop Edmund Bonner and Cuthbert Symson
1553–9

W hen Mary Tudor came to the throne of England in August 1553 crowds of supporters swarmed through the streets of London to welcome her. Across the city and throughout southern England church bells rang in celebration. The short, violent term of Jane Grey's reign was over and the uncertainty of the sickly young Edward VI's five-year reign was past. Stability had finally returned to England. Or so it seemed for the moment.

In truth, Mary Tudor was a woman bent on vengeance. Her father, Henry VIII, had divorced her mother, Queen Catherine of Aragon, and declared Mary illegitimate in an effort to bar her from the throne. He had also outlawed the Roman Catholic Church to which Mary was so devoutly attached that throughout her life she reportedly wore a nun's habit beneath her gown. Now, at last, Mary was in a position to wreak a very personal revenge on everyone who had supported the religious upheavals that had so nearly deprived her of the crown.

On the very day Mary entered London those hard-line Catholics who had survived her father's purges were released from the Tower and brought before the queen. Kissing each of them on the cheek, she released them from their years of imprisonment and reinstated them in their old positions. The Protestant-leaning Church of England was outlawed and Protestants in the church and government were stripped of office and instructed to convert back to Catholicism. If they resisted, they were clapped in the Tower.

The main points of contention between Protestants and Catholics – beyond recognising the Pope as supreme head of the church – were purely dogmatic details. The most obvious difference was that the Roman Church insisted the mass be said in Latin rather than the common tongue. More subtle, but even more central to the faith, was the act of communion. According to Catholic doctrine the wine and bread used in the celebration of communion literally became the body and blood of Christ after having been blessed and ingested, through a miracle called Transubstantiation. Protestants believed that the communion was a purely symbolic representation of Jesus' death and resurrection. This seemingly tiny article of faith would lead to more confusion, death and destruction of religious property on both sides of the argument than we, today, can possibly imagine.

In her drive to bring England back to the Catholic faith, Mary needed the support of law. To that end she reinstituted the medieval heresy statutes of 1401 which allowed ecclesiastical courts to deal with all cases of religious impropriety, many of which were considered capital crimes punishable first by excommunication by church authorities and then being burnt at the stake on order of the civil courts. But such a massive legal change was going to take time. So, as an interim step, Mary passed a law allowing local constables and churchwardens to arrest anyone they suspected of heresy and keep them confined until they repented their sins. This convenient intermediary step removed the necessity of a trial; the accused was simply held without bail as long as necessary. To establish these first steps on the long road to reform, and later to enforce the revived heresy laws, Mary needed administrators as merciless as she was.

Among those released from the Tower on Mary's triumphal entry into London had been Bishop Edmund Bonner. Just two days after his release Bonner was restored to his old position as Bishop of London and charged by Mary with ensuring the populace quickly readopted the Catholic faith; willingly if possible, forcibly if necessary. It was a job for which Edmund Bonner would prove ideally suited.

Born about 1500, Bonner had grown to be an outstanding student during his years at Pembroke College, Oxford. In 1519 he graduated with degrees in both civic and canon law and later that same year took the vows of a priest. But Bonner's main concern was neither with theology nor matters of the spirit. He was a lawyer through and through. Taking the vows of the church simply gained him access to the halls of power where he could manipulate people, and the law, to suit his own best interests. A huge bear of a man with cold, steel-blue eyes and massive hairy hands, Bonner cut an imposing figure in the robes of a judicial cleric. Between his outstanding record at Oxford and his dominating physical presence it was only a matter of time before somebody of importance noticed Bonner. That somebody was Thomas Cromwell, Henry VIII's right-hand man and holder of the Privy Seal.

With degrees in both secular and church law, Bonner was Cromwell's ideal choice to serve as ambassador to the Vatican. And when Henry's religious upheavals brought down an order of excommunication from the Pope in 1533, it was Bonner who tried to have the order reversed. His attempt failed, but his efforts did not go unrequited. Between 1532 and 1543 Edmund Bonner served in various ambassadorial capacities throughout Europe, but in almost every post his crude, overbearing, dictatorial manner alienated him from foreign counterparts and English associates alike. Consistently, Cromwell protected his protégé from all criticism. This man would eventually have his use.

In 1539 Bonner was made Bishop of London, where his first assignment was as head of the London Ecclesiastical Court. Here he would bring to trial anyone who refused to acknowledge Henry VIII as the supreme head of the new Church of England or who spoke out against the 'Six Articles of Faith', which established Henry's church as England's official religion. Almost immediately he was accused of excessive cruelty and both religious and political bias. Ultimately, Bonner proved no more popular at home than he had in foreign courts. But when Henry VIII died in 1547, Bonner refused to support the religious policies of the new king, Edward VI. As a result, he was imprisoned in the Tower in 1549 where he remained until Mary came to the throne four years later.

Where Bonner had once willingly persecuted Catholics who rejected Henry VIII's new Church of England, he was now just as happy to ferret out anyone unwilling to reject Henry's reforms and convert back to Roman Catholicism. Edmund Bonner had no beliefs of his own; whichever way the political wind blew was the direction Bonner's ship would sail. Bonner was now saying 'Hail Mary' in more ways than one.

By 1553 England was undergoing the third imposed reversal of religion in a quarter of a century. The upheaval had already cost the lives of hundreds of devout Christians on both sides of the argument and now it was starting all over again. Religious paranoia swept across England as tolerance was replaced by suspicion and fanaticism. The only thing people now had in common with their neighbours was a shared sense of hysteria. As Mary's religious reforms split the kingdom, both Protestants and Catholics turned militant in a desperate effort to retain their religious freedom. Then, four months after Mary took the throne, things worsened.

In December 1553 Queen Mary announced that she would marry Prince Philip of Spain – a devout and hard-line Roman Catholic. Those who were initially frightened of Mary and her reforms now feared that the spectre of the Spanish Inquisition was about to spread across England. Religious panic swept the kingdom. Knives were thrown at preachers and priests while they delivered sermons and churches were ransacked and desecrated by mobs bent on destroying everyone who did not believe as they did. Street brawls and riots in favour of, or in opposition to, both the Church of England and Roman Catholicism became almost daily occurrences.

Mary, of course, could not understand that she was the root of the problem. Even at this point she could have diffused the situation by allowing the civil courts to deal with the problem. But to Mary this was a religious matter; anyone opposed to her reforms was at best a heretic and, at worst, probably in league with the devil. Even pleas from the staunchly Catholic Spanish Ambassador to slow the pace of her reforms were rejected. As civil order deteriorated, Mary hardened her position. Those who supported her were protecting the 'true' church and therefore innocent of wrongdoing. But all those who refused to renounce the Church of England would be arrested and tried by ecclesiastical courts; and in London the ecclesiastical and civil courts were both firmly in the hands of Bishop Edmund Bonner.

Once re-established in his former office of bishop, Bonner had quickly been appointed a Royal Commissioner and charged with carrying out the civil side of the religious reforms. In this dual capacity it became almost impossible to tell when he was acting as a civil authority and when as an ecclesiastic, and Mary's government provided the legal framework within which charges of heresy would be judged.

To add legal weight to the inquisition, Bishop Bonner compiled a list of 'Articles' – an exhaustive series of questions, which the accused were required to answer satisfactorily if they hoped to escape the creative horrors of the Tower's torture chamber. In all there were 133 questions, 37 specifically for the clergy, 11 for deacons and 16 concerning church ornaments and religious objects. There were also 41 general questions for laymen along with questions specifically designed for those in a variety of professions, including 8 for schoolmasters, 6 for midwives and 5 for old people. The list went on and on. For everyone there were questions on the nature of Holy Communion and the Eucharist (mostly dealing with the mystery of Transubstantiation) and queries on how often people made confession, attended church services and whether they took part in religious processions during Lent. How well an individual scored on the test determined whether they would go free, be offered a chance to reform their wayward life, or be sent to trial as a heretic.

Bishop Bonner dutifully involved himself in every aspect of each case that came before his bench. From the first examination on the Articles through any necessary torture, the trial itself, the order of excommunication and final sentencing by the civil court to death at the stake. In simpler cases, to avoid lengthy and costly trials, Bonner personally acted as judge, jury and prosecution. The nicety of an advocate was dispensed with entirely.

Sometimes it took relatively little persuasion to get people to reveal whether a person was simply misled or was an actual heretic. When a man named James Tomkins appeared before Bonner he at first refused to accept reintegration into the Catholic faith. To demonstrate what awaited him if he remained obstinate the burly Bonner seized Tomkins' wrist and pulled his hand over a lighted candle, holding it there until the flesh on his palm blistered and burnt. The strong-willed Tomkins refused to recant, but Bonner had all the confession he needed. Tomkins was a heretic and would be dealt with accordingly.

On one occasion a teenager named Thomas Hindshaw was brought to Bonner's court for some minor religious offence. Not wanting to seem too harsh on the first examination of a young offender, Bonner simply had Hindshaw hauled to the cells and locked in the stocks for a day and a night. Stocks were leg immobilisers made of two boards with cut-outs large enough to receive a person's ankles. These, in turn, were mounted on a frame fixed into the ground. A person locked in the stocks was forced to sit on a bench with their legs extended and knees straight, making it nearly impossible to change position. Even over short periods they could cause excruciating pain, but they did no permanent damage.

The day after Hindshaw was sent to the stocks, Bonner's archdeacon, Dr Harpsfield, went to question the boy. When Harpsfield asked him if his experience had persuaded him of anything, Hindshaw replied, 'I am persuaded that you labour to promote the dark kingdom of the devil, not for the love of truth.' Angry and frustrated, Harpsfield reported the boy's insolence to Bonner who, in a fury, took personal charge of the questioning. In what was described by a witness as 'a passion almost preventing articulation', Bonner screamed at the boy, 'Dost thou answer my archdeacon thus, thou naughty boy? . . . I'll soon handle thee well enough for it, be assured.' Taking up two stout willow branches, he then forced the boy to kneel against a bench and proceeded to whip him until sheer exhaustion forced him to stop.

Sometimes, more persuasive methods were required to extract confessions. For these occasions there were red-hot irons and thumbscrews, which could shatter the knuckle in a victim's thumb. There were bilboes, which compressed the ankle joint until the bone shattered. There were iron collars and the 'breaks', which snapped off a victim's teeth one at a time. But the most popular was always the rack.

Eventually almost anyone subjected to torture would confess to anything so long as it made the pain stop. Once a confession was forthcoming, the accused was returned to court and tried based on their confession. The severity of the sentence was determined by the offence. If it were a minor offence, like failure to attend church regularly, the penance might be no more than a public admitting of their 'crime', the promise never to sin again and a reaffirmation of their belief in the supremacy of the Catholic Church. For more serious charges, such as ministering to a Protestant congregation or reading the Bible in English, the sentence was likely to be far more severe. For anyone who refused to recant, or for those charged with a second offence, there was only one sentence: death by burning.

To Edmund Bonner, it all made little difference who was on trial or the accusations levelled against them. All were hounded with merciless vindictiveness. In at least one instance a witness so infuriated Bonner with a less than forthcoming answer that he hit him over the head with a heavy stick. Like all diligent workers, Bonner burned large quantities of midnight oil in pursuit of his job, and frequently this meant taking his work home with him. When witnesses proved reluctant to confess their sins, but their offences were not great enough to have them condemned to full-scale torture, Bonner would have them transferred from public prisons to the coal shed behind his home. There, locked in the stocks and chained to the wall, they could be visited at all hours of the night where their questioning could continue at the bishop's pleasure. In one instance, he recorded in his diary 'six obstinate heretics that do remain in my house'.

In the first two years, Bonner held the dual office of Royal Commissioner and Bishop of London, around four hundred and fifty people in the Archdiocese of London passed through his court, more than one hundred of them simply for having failed to attend church. Of those accused of more serious offences, eighty-nine were burned alive for their religious beliefs. Bonner obviously enjoyed the torments he inflicted on his victims and before long everyone in London knew his name and spoke it with fear. Since it was Queen Mary's decision that only Protestants would be charged as heretics, Bonner, as her enforcer, became a particular target for the hatred of Protestants. Political and religious tracts referred to him as 'the bloody sheep bite [i.e. sheep dog] of London' and 'Bloody Bonner'. The Protestant writer Foxe referred to him as a cannibal and to his victims as 'his food'. But the nickname that stuck was 'the Devil's Dancing Bear', undoubtedly a reference to his massive size and huge, hairy, paw-like hands.

If Bonner brought on the hatred of the rapidly shrinking Protestant community he did nothing to endear himself to right-thinking Catholics, either. One Catholic who appeared in his court on purely civil charges told the judge,'You have lost the hearts of twenty-thousand that were rank papists within these [last] twelve months.'

Despite the growing furore over his unbridled cruelty, Bonner insisted he was actually a gentle man who only desired to show people the error of their ways. He once said, 'God knoweth I never sought any man's blood in all my life', even insisting that his sadism was actually an act of Christian charity. 'Charity', he wrote, 'commands that all governors should correct offenders within their jurisdiction . . . those that be evil, [out] of love, we ought to procure them into correction.' How and why this correction would be accomplished, he explained as 'he who is in authority must be as a good surgeon [who] cutteth away a putrefied and festered member, for the love he hath to the whole body, least it infect other members adjoining it'. To prove his good intentions, Bishop Bonner even wrote and published a tract on the nature of Christian love. Thanks to Bonner's peculiar brand of Christian love, by the beginning of 1555 there were fewer than two hundred practising Protestants left in London. The rest had converted, fled, been imprisoned or burned.

But even Bonner's brutal tactics were not enough to satisfy the bloodthirsty queen. When Mary discovered that only eight heretics were burnt between 20 January and 24 May 1555, she was incensed that more progress was not being made to root out the heretics she firmly believed were overrunning her kingdom. At the end of May she and her council sent a remonstrative letter to Bonner ordering him to proceed 'with greater diligence'. As a result of these urgings, in June and July a backlog of sixteen condemned heretics were sent to the stake and thirteen more men and women had been condemned to death and awaited execution.

By the middle of summer 1556, a Bonner spy named Roger Sergeant infiltrated one of the last active Protestant congregations in London. In the parish of St Edmonds in the Limehouse district, a small group of Protestants continued to meet, usually at the Swan Tavern or the King's Head Inn. The minister of this small group was John Rough, a Scotsman who had fled to the continent at the beginning of Mary's persecutions, but returned to take up the ministry despite the ever-present threat of arrest and almost certain death. When Roger Sergeant discovered the group, John Rough had been back in England less than a month. After attending only two services, and collecting as many names and descriptions as he could, Sergeant reported his findings to Bonner. Immediately a warrant was issued for the arrest of John Rough. Seized from his bed in the middle of the night while his terrified wife pleaded with the soldiers to release her husband, Rough simply disappeared until he turned up several months later tied to a stake, surrounded by wood and kindling.

Left without a pastor, the terrified congregation was in imminent danger of falling apart. The job of calming their fears, keeping them together and finding safe places to worship fell on the congregation's only deacon, Cuthbert Symson. For more than a year Symson did his best to keep his friends true to their faith and his own frayed nerves from shattering. A respected member of society, Symson was a relatively wealthy man with a high-profile job. He was paymaster to all the London prisons, including the Tower. If he thought his social position would help deflect any possible charges of heresy, he was wrong. On 12 December 1557, Cuthbert Symson (along with two other members of the congregation, Hugh Foxe and John Devinish) was arrested on charges of attending church services in English and denying the doctrine of Transubstantiation. The following day the three were committed to the Tower for pre-trial questioning.

Somehow, Symson managed to chronicle his ordeal and later his wife smuggled the manuscript out of prison. The following paragraphs are predominantly in Symson's own words:

On the thirteenth of December I was committed by the Council to the Tower of London. On the Thursday after, I was called to the wardroom, before the Constable of the Tower and the Recorder of the Tower, master

Cholmley; who commanded me to tell whom I did will to come to the English service. I answered [that] I would declare nothing. Whereupon I was set in a rack of iron, [for] the space of three hours as I judged.

As the ropes on Symson's hands and feet pulled tight, his arm and leg muscles were stretched and pulled nearly to the breaking point. When he fainted from the pain, he was revived. Then the process began again: 'Then they asked me [again] if I would tell them. I answered as before.' After three hours of this torture, Symson was no longer able to stand, let alone walk.

Then I was unbound and carried to my lodging again. On the Sunday after, I was brought into the same place again, before the lieutenant and the Recorder of London and they did examine me. As before I had said, so I answered [again]. Then the lieutenant did swear by God I should tell. They did bind my two forefingers together and put a small arrow betwixt them and drew it through so fast that the blood flowed and that the arrow brake. Then they racked me twice. Then I was carried to my lodgings again and ten days after [that] the lieutenant asked me if I would confess that which before they had asked me. I said I had said as much as I would.

Over the next few weeks Cuthbert Symson was taken to the rack twice more. Still he refused to divulge the names of his congregation: 'Three weeks after [my last time on the rack] I was sent to the priest, where I was greatly assaulted, and at whose hand I received the pope's curse for bearing witness to the resurrection of Christ. I forgive all the world, and thus I leave the world in the hope of a joyful resurrection.'

The priest mentioned here was undoubtedly Bishop Bonner and, based on the reference to 'the pope's curse', the occasion was probably the ecclesiastical court where sentence of excommunication was pronounced. Frustrated at Symson's continued refusal to divulge the names of his fellow Protestants, Bonner ordered him to be transferred from the Tower to the makeshift prison in his coal shed.

Here, locked in the stocks for more than three weeks and kept on a diet of bread and water, Symson was continually questioned along with several other 'guests'. It was probably while he was here that Symson's wife managed to smuggle the account of his ordeal to the outside world. Attached to the short diary was a note to his wife telling her to be brave and remain strong in her faith. Finally, on 19 March 1558, Cuthbert Symson and his fellow parishioners Hugh Foxe and John Devinish were taken for their civil trial where final sentence would be handed down.

Over the months even Edmund Bonner had gained a grudging admiration for the man who had withstood so much pain and still refused to surrender the names of his friends. In a statement to the court Bonner said, 'Ye see this man, what a personable man he is. And furthermore, concerning his patience, I affirm that if he were not a heretic, he is a man of the greatest patience that yet ever came before me: for I tell you, he hath been thrice racked upon one day in the Tower. Also in my house he hath felt some sorrow, and yet I never saw his patience broken.' Of course, Symson's patience was not enough to save him from a horrible death. Nine days after their trial, Symson, Foxe and Devinish were committed to the flames at Smithfield.

While no account of Symson's martyrdom survives, there is a contemporary account of another burning that took place on the order of Edmund Bonner. The following is a portion of that account:

> his nether parts did burn first . . . but the flame only singed his upper parts. . . . In this fire he said with a loud voice, 'Lord Jesus, have mercy upon me! Lord Jesus, receive my spirit.' And these were the last words he was heard to utter. But when he was [burnt] black in the mouth, and his tongue so swollen that he could not speak, yet his lips [moved] until they were shrunk to the gums: and he knocked his breast with his hands until one of his arms fell off, and then knocked still with the other, while the fat, water and blood dropped out at his fingers' ends, until his strength was gone and his hand clave fast upon his breast. Then . . . bowing forwards, he yielded up his spirit. Thus was he there three quarters of an hour or more in the fire.

On 17 November 1558, less than eight months after Cuthbert Symson's execution, Queen Mary Tudor, now commonly known as 'Bloody Mary', died of uterine cancer. Following Mary to the throne was her younger sister, Elizabeth. The new monarch immediately set about righting the injustices of her sister's reign. Hard-line Catholics were replaced by moderate Protestants and, unlike her sister, Elizabeth was not willing to execute people for either their faith or even their actions under the previous reign – not even the

Bishop of London, Edmund Bonner. But when Elizabeth received Bonner in court, as a sign of her contempt she refused to allow him to kiss her hand.

On 25 June 1559 Elizabeth outlawed the saying of the Catholic mass, but Bonner would not comply. Twice the Royal Council sent him letters to cease, finally ordering him to resign his bishopric. Still Bonner refused. On 20 April 1560, Elizabeth's patience came to an end; the Devil's Dancing Bear was arrested and sent to the Tower to await trial.

The case against Bonner was irrefutable. However many 'heretics' had been sent to the stake during Mary's reign, the number of victims sentenced from Bonner's court was disproportionately large. More than one-third of all Protestants that had died during Mary's five-year reign were from the diocese of London. In all, one hundred and thirteen Londoners had been burned at the stake. Of these, Bonner sentenced eighty-nine personally and the execution of the other twenty-four had been signed by him. Bonner was stripped of his power and sent to Marshalsea prison in perpetuity.

Strangely, over the ten years of his incarceration, Bonner remained cheerful, never complaining about his captivity. A visitor referred to him as being 'a most courteous man and gentlemanly both in manners and appearance'. But there, in the cold, damp cell, Bonner had nearly a decade to contemplate the crimes he had committed in the name of God and his sovereign. On 5 September 1569, Edmund Bonner died, taking his case to a court far higher and more just than those he had held.

Eight

THE SPYMASTER

Francis Walsingham and Anthony Babington
1585–6

The Elizabethan age is remembered today as an almost magical, glittering time filled with music, magnificent clothes and great works of literature. There is little doubt that it seemed less idyllic at the time, particularly to Queen Elizabeth. Over a reign of thirty-eight years, her father, Henry VIII, had transformed himself from a handsome, enlightened young king into a grotesquely fat butcher who sent two wives, dozens of friends and hundreds of enemies to the scaffold. He ripped his kingdom apart by making war on the Catholic Church, viciously persecuting Catholics and extremist Protestants alike, and some of the persecution spilled over on to the young Elizabeth.

At the tender age of three, Elizabeth became trapped in her father's maelstrom when he declared her illegitimate as a part of his plan to rid himself of her mother, Anne Boleyn. Anne herself had been beheaded on Tower Green in May 1536, six months before Elizabeth's third birthday. From that day on, the Tower would be a place of nightmares for Elizabeth.

When her elder half-sister, the fanatically Catholic Mary Tudor, came to the throne in 1553, Elizabeth found that being a Protestant princess in a Catholic kingdom made her a dangerous liability. Protestant plotters bent on overthrowing Mary did so in her name. In the religious pogroms that dominated Mary's reign, Elizabeth was arrested and sent to the Tower. She was transported in the dead of night to prevent crowds of supporters from gathering along the banks of the Thames. By the time Elizabeth's barge reached Traitors' Gate, the 21-year-old princess was too terrified to step out of the boat. The charge was treason. The penalty was death. Before Elizabeth could be brought to trial, Mary came to believe she was pregnant. With the lineage apparently secure, Elizabeth no longer seemed such a threat and was released to house arrest at Hatfield House. But Mary was not pregnant. The swelling was a massive, malignant tumour. When the queen died in November 1558 the crown passed to her younger sister, Princess Elizabeth.

According to long-standing tradition, Elizabeth was transported to the Tower of London to await her coronation. This time, her journey to the Tower was a joyous occasion. Bloody Mary was dead and a new monarch was taking the throne. In celebration, the Tower cannons were fired continuously for more than half an hour. But the grim old Tower was still a place of terror for the new queen. When she left its confines for Westminster Abbey and her coronation, Elizabeth swore never to set foot in the Tower again. Her enemies would not be so lucky.

The new reign did not have an auspicious start. At twenty-five, Elizabeth was nervous and highly strung; she had inherited a kingdom exhausted by religious factionalism, turmoil and state-sanctioned cruelty, and her ministers urged immediate action to heal the nation. Overwhelmed, Elizabeth became a master of procrastination and reconciliation. Adhering to what she called her 'golden mean', the queen walked a treacherous political middle ground in an effort to keep her kingdom from sliding into the same turmoil that had marked the reigns of her father and sister. Religiously, Elizabeth was liberal and tolerant. In her own words, 'There is one God and one Christ Jesus, and all the rest is a dispute over petty trifles.' Unfortunately, many of her subjects were not so open-minded.

Elizabeth knew she was treading through a minefield of enemies anxious to bring her down. She commented, 'I must deal with nobles of diverse humours . . . and people who, although they make great demonstrations of love towards me, are nevertheless fickle and inconstant and I must fear everything.' Out of sheer necessity she became an astute politician who, according to her contemporary Sir John Hayward, kept 'her eyes set upon one, [while] her ear listened to another, her judgment on a third, and to a fourth she addressed her speech'.

No matter how terrified she was, Elizabeth never let her fear show. When the Spanish Ambassador informed her that because she was a heretic, the King of Spain was considering declaring war on England, she calmly said, 'I am more afraid of making a fault in my Latin than of all the Kings of Spain, France and Scotland . . . and all their confederates. I have the heart of a man, not of a woman, and I am not afraid of anything.' Cautiously, courageously, Elizabeth set about protecting her kingdom, insisting that those who administered the law in her name be strong, but fair; harsh measures were only to be used when the life of the kingdom, or of the queen herself were in peril.

In spite of her tolerant attitude, or perhaps because of it, Elizabeth's court became a hotbed of intrigue. Spies and plotters swarmed around her like flies drawn to over-ripe fruit, each jockeying for position in an effort to influence the queen, the government and the nation. Because the line between religion and secular politics had been virtually obliterated during the reigns of her father, her brother Edward and her sister Mary, most of the spies were Catholics bent on returning England to the Catholic Church by whatever means necessary. Many of the spies were funded and instructed in espionage by Jesuit priests who had been specially trained by England's staunchly Catholic enemies France, Spain and Rome. If there were more Catholic plots against Elizabeth than there had been Protestant plots against her sister Mary, it was because the Catholics were better organised and far better funded than the Protestants could ever hope to be. In the face of all the plotting and manoeuvring, Elizabeth and her council were forced into constant vigilance as the kingdom teetered on the narrow edge of religious turmoil.

To keep the rival factions in check, Elizabeth and her Secretary of State, Lord Burghley, relied on Sir Francis Walsingham. Walsingham's job was to spy on the spies and it was a position for which he was eminently suited. A staunch Protestant, Walsingham had fled to continental Europe when Mary Tudor came to the throne and reinstituted the Catholic religion. During Mary's five-year reign, Walsingham wandered the courts of Europe studying law, language and, significantly, the different methods employed by various governments to gather intelligence. Cultured, well-educated, and a cousin of the playwright Sir Francis Bacon, Walsingham used his good name and engaging manner to ferret out information and secrets in one country after another. Everything he learned was passed on to other English exiles and Protestant activists back home. By the time Elizabeth came to the throne Walsingham had become a brilliant, if slightly machiavellian, politician. Once called to court, he would devote the next thirty years and his entire personal fortune to keeping his queen well informed and out of danger.

Of all the threats to Elizabeth's position and the stability of the realm, the greatest came in the form of her cousin, Mary Stuart, Queen of Scots. Born the daughter of James V of Scotland and Marie de Guise of France, at sixteen Mary was wed to Francis II of France. Two years later her husband died and the childless Mary no longer had any place at the French court. Consequently, in 1560, the eighteen-year-old widow returned home to claim her throne. But Scotland was a far cry from France. Poor, backward and fanatically Protestant, Scotland was not at all what the cultured, spoiled and staunchly Catholic Mary had in mind.

The lairds of Scotland, led by her brother James, had no more use for Mary than she had for them. After eight disastrous years of intrigue, factionalism, mismanagement, clan warfare and murder, Mary fled across the border to England in the hope of finding sanctuary and raising an army to crush her brother and his allies. It is more than likely that she also had her eye on Elizabeth's throne. Certainly her strong claim to the throne, her religion and continental connections, combined with the vastly greater appeal of ruling England than being stuck in Scotland, would have made this an enticing possibility. What Mary did not know was that Elizabeth and Walsingham knew as much about her plans as she did. When she crossed the border into England she was promptly arrested and would remain an unhappy guest of her cousin for the next eighteen years.

If Elizabeth knew how politically dangerous Mary was, Walsingham was even more concerned than his sovereign. Year after year he urged Elizabeth to do away with Mary on the grounds that she was a rallying point for both English and continental Catholics bent on toppling Elizabeth. But the queen would not hear of it. She would not be a party to murdering her cousin and her own position was not so secure that she could risk setting the precedent of murdering another monarch, particularly one with connections to the entire Catholic community in Europe.

Once it became clear that most of Mary's support came not from Scotland or Europe, but from English Catholics, Walsingham urged Elizabeth to send Mary back to Scotland where her own brother and his supporters would surely kill her. Again, Elizabeth refused. It was still no better than murder; Mary would simply remain in England where her every move could be kept under close watch. In 1585, seventeen years after Mary's arrest, parliament passed a bill known as the Bond of Association, obviously aimed directly at Mary and her continuing manipulations to free herself and take control of England. The bond stated that if anyone plotted against the crown on behalf of any claimant to the throne, then the pretender in whose name they were acting, whether they were aware of the plot or not, was as guilty as the plotters and subject to execution as a traitor. Now all Walsingham had to do was wait until the next Catholic plot bubbled to the surface, and Elizabeth would have to defy the law if she wanted to protect her cousin.

Only months after the Bond of Association was enacted, a Walsingham spy named Gilbert Gifford came to his master with word of a new plot to put Mary Stuart on the throne of England. According to Gifford, the chief conspirators were a Jesuit priest named Father John Ballard and Anthony Babington. Handsome and well-bred, the 26-year-old Babington came from a family so well connected that he had served as a page to Mary Tudor during her years on the throne. Obviously the Babingtons, or at least Anthony, had not welcomed Elizabeth's return to liberalised religion.

Babington had already gathered more than a dozen like-minded young men, and together they were plotting to free Mary Stuart. Foolishly, in his zeal Babington had told far too many people of his plans. Among his thirteen followers were Gifford who, though a Catholic, was loyal to his queen, and at least one other member of Walsingham's nexus of informants. To Walsingham's absolute joy, once the group was organised enough to make contact with the Scottish queen, they elected Gifford as their courier. As he began moving encoded letters back and forth between Babington and the imprisoned queen, Gifford took them to Walsingham first so they could be copied. The originals remained with the spymaster and forged copies were delivered in their place. Meanwhile, Walsingham's code-breaker, Thomas Phelippse, began unravelling the ciphers. Amazingly, the key fell right into Walsingham's hands. It seems that Mary could no more interpret the code than Phelippse, and when the time came to deliver the key to her, it was passed through Gifford's hands. Babington and his friends may have been zealous, but when it came to conspiracy they were rank amateurs.

As letter followed letter, the extent of the plot, and the names of the plotters, all came into Walsingham's possession. Once there was enough information to convince Queen Elizabeth of Babington's intentions, he presented his case to the crown. Elizabeth agreed that Babington had to be stopped. 'In such cases', she said, 'there is no middle course, we must lay aside clemency and adopt extreme measures . . . when the welfare of my state is concerned, I dare not indulge my own inclinations. . . . If they shall not seem to you to confess plainly their knowledge, then we warrant that you cause them . . . to be brought to the rack and first to move them with fear thereof to deal plainly with their answers. Then, should the sight of the instrument not induce them to confess, you shall cause them to be put to the rack and to find the taste thereof till they shall deal more plainly or until you shall see fit.' All Walsingham had to do now was wait for the conspirators to provide enough evidence to issue a warrant – and the next letter was a blockbuster.

In his own handwriting, Babington now outlined a plan to rescue Mary. He opened with 'Most mighty, most excellent, my dread sovereign Lady and Queen . . .'. Shortly thereafter he referred to Queen Elizabeth as 'a mortal enemy both by faith and faction to your Majesty', and insisted that he and his men were devoted to 'The deliverance of your Majesty [and] the dispatch of the usurping Competitor. . . . For the dispatch of the usurper, from the obedience of whom we are by the excommunication of her [by the Pope] made free, there are six noble gentlemen, all my private friends, who . . . will undertake that tragical execution.' Babington was planning to assassinate Queen Elizabeth.

As if to sweeten the pot, he asked for Mary's advice and blessing in carrying out the plan 'by your wisdom to direct us and by your princely authority to enable such as may advance the affair. Upon the XIIth of this month I will be at Lichfield, expecting your Majesty's answer. Your Majesty's most faithful subject and sworn servant, Anthony Babington.' Now Walsingham even knew where and when to find Babington.

Obviously Babington was reticent about committing regicide. He justified his course by stating the obvious; Elizabeth had been excommunicated by Rome. Still he asked for Mary's blessing to keep the blood off his hands. Babington's hesitancy was Walsingham's blessing, for not only had he put a noose around his own neck, but by asking for Mary's help he had made her a party to the plot. All Walsingham needed to do was wait for Mary's answer to have an airtight case he could take to Elizabeth. As he waited, Walsingham closed the snare around Babington and his men. When the group met at Lichfield, a battalion of soldiers was there to greet them. Swooping down on the unsuspecting rebels, they arrested Babington and fifteen others, hauling them away to London and the Tower. Two of their number, Gilbert Gifford and Thomas Harrison, were quickly released because they were in the employ of the spymaster; the rest were sent for trial on charges of treason. While Walsingham waited for the trial to begin, Mary obligingly answered Babington's letter.

It would have been politically astute for Mary to have told her cousin, the queen, all about Babington and his plot. It might have persuaded Elizabeth to trust her and it might even have bought her freedom, but Mary rarely exercised good sense. On the off-chance that the plot would succeed, Mary gushed with enthusiasm. It was a decision she would live to regret: 'For diverse and important considerations . . . I can but greatly praise and commend your common desire', she began. Almost immediately she quizzed Babington as to how much and what kind of support he had – 'for to ground substantially this enterprise and to bring it to good success, you must first examine deeply: What forces, as well on foot as on horse, you might raise amongst you. . . . Of what towns, ports and havens you may assure yourselves. . . . What place you esteem fittest and of greatest advantage to assemble the principal company of your forces.' If all this were not enough to show Mary's complicity, she now offered to arrange for foreign troops to invade England to ensure the success of the plan: 'What foreign forces, as well on horse as foot, you require . . .'. Obviously she was in contact with France and Spain and was willing to arrange a full-scale invasion on behalf of her cause.

As to her rescue, Mary suggested 'fifty, or three score men, well horsed and armed, come to take me as they may easily [do], my keeper having with him ordinarily but eighteen or twenty horsemen only.' For her part in the ensuing uprising, Mary said, 'take me forth from this place . . . to set me in the midst of a good army . . . where I may safely stay [until] the . . . arrival of said foreign succours . . .'. After pages of details, offers and suggestions, Walsingham must have been desperate to know Mary's view on the queen's assassination. Finally, it came: 'The affairs being thus prepared and forces in readiness both within and without the realm, then shall it be time to set the six gentlemen to work.'

When code-breaker Thomas Phelippse translated these lines, he could not resist drawing a little gallows in the margin of the letter. The implication was clear. Mary Stuart had just hanged herself. As damning as all this was, Walsingham was still not happy. The Scottish queen had not specifically endorsed Elizabeth's murder. She was clearly involved in the plot, and was obviously guilty of breaking the Bond of Association, but would it be enough to make Queen Elizabeth change her approach after nearly two decades of protecting Mary? While Walsingham pondered his next move, the courts had decided the fate of Babington and his fellow conspirators.

Of the sixteen arrested, fourteen (excluding Gifford and Harrison) had been convicted of treason and sentenced to death. According to the law, the Queen had to sign the traitors' death warrants. The warrant not only stated the time and place of their death, but also the manner in which they were to be executed. Had they been noblemen, they might have got away with the block, but they were not and faced the worst execution imaginable – being hanged, drawn and quartered. Their sentence read as follows: 'You shall be led hence to remain [at the Tower] until the day of execution. And from there you shall be drawn on a hurdle through the open streets to the place of execution, there to be hanged and cut down alive, and your body shall be opened, your heart and bowels plucked out, and your privy members cut off and thrown into the fire before your eyes. Then your head to be stricken off from your body and your body shall be divided into four quarters, to be disposed of at the [Queen's] pleasure. And may God have mercy on your soul.'

Surprising though it may seem, medieval executioners were adept enough at their craft to keep the hapless victim not only alive, but also conscious throughout the grisly procedures. The almost unspeakable act of castration was to demonstrate to the public that traitors would not be allowed to breed more traitors.

On 20 September 1586 Babington and six of his companions were taken from the Tower to Lincoln's Inn Field. The remaining eight were to follow the next day. Almost as bad as the executions themselves was the fact that the remaining victims were forced to watch their companions go through the horrifying ordeal before their turn came. The first to go was Father Ballard. As he was hanged, revived, stripped naked, tied to a ladder and raised so that the crowd of spectators had a clear view of the proceedings to come, Babington shouted that the plot to murder Queen Elizabeth had been 'a deed lawful and meritorious'. An eyewitness recalled Babington's reaction to Ballard's torture. 'Babington looked on with an undaunted countenance, steadily gazing on that variety of tortures which he himself, in a moment [was] to pass through. . . . When the executioner began his tremendous work on Babington, the spirit of this haughty and heroic man cried out amidst the agony, "*Parce mihi, Domine Jesu*"' (Spare me Lord Jesus).

Although hanging, drawing and quartering had been in use for centuries, because this was the first time in Elizabeth's long reign that it had been used, it is unlikely that the Queen actually understood how barbaric it was. On hearing the details of the executions and the public's horrified reaction, she ordered that the remaining eight conspirators should simply be hanged. There would never be another public dismemberment in the realm of England.

Even with Babington and his men out of the way, Walsingham was uneasy. They had only been a symptom of a much larger disease; one that could only be cured by removing Mary Stuart's head. Mary had obviously been complicit in the plot, but he needed enough proof to convince Elizabeth that she was too dangerous to remain alive. He found the solution in her letter to Babington. Beneath her signature, Walsingham had his forger insert a brief paragraph that made it look as though, at the last minute, Mary had decided to approve of Babington's plan to murder Elizabeth. The forged postscript read 'I would be glad to know the names of the six gentlemen which are to accomplish the designment, for it may be I shall be able, upon knowledge of the parties, to give you some further advice necessary to be followed therein, as also from time to time particularly how to proceed . . .'. The paragraph closed with, 'Let the great plot proceed.' Now, with Mary apparently complicit in the conspiracy to commit regicide, Walsingham went to the queen.

Elizabeth was furious. For eighteen years she had done everything she could to keep her scheming, plotting cousin from the block, but the woman simply would not let go. Elizabeth could no longer avoid the problem. Mary Queen of Scots, cousin to the English throne, would be tried for high treason. When told that Mary would be moved from Dudley Castle to Fotheringay Castle to await trial, Elizabeth knew the end was near. Under her breath she muttered, 'Jesu, that dreadful place'. Even now, however, Elizabeth tried to give Mary a way out. In a last letter to her cousin, she wrote 'You have in various ways and manners attempted to take my life and bring my kingdom to destruction by bloodshed. These treasons will be proved to you and all made manifest. It is my will that you answer the nobles and peers of the kingdom as if I were myself present. Act plainly without reserve and you will sooner be able to obtain favour of me.'

Mary's trial was an unprecedented affair. Never in history had any court tried the legitimate and reigning monarch of another country. Mary tried to use this fact in her favour, insisting that as a foreigner she was not subject to the laws of England and the court had no jurisdiction over her. Next, she insisted that since the judges were not monarchs themselves, they were not her 'peers' and therefore not qualified to sit in judgement on her. It was a clever tactic, but it didn't work. On 14–15 October 1586, Mary was tried as a common traitor.

Eventually, she did admit of her complicity in the plot to free herself, but repeatedly denied that she approved of the murder of Elizabeth – a fact that she stated three times in the two-day trial. Significantly, Mary's letter with the forged postscript was never produced at the trial. In truth, none of it mattered now. Mary had plotted and schemed too long and too often to walk away. When Elizabeth signed the death warrant, she muttered '*ne feriare feri*' (strike lest thou be stricken). On 8 February 1587 Mary Queen of Scots was beheaded in the great hall of Fotheringay Castle. She was forty-four years old and had spent nearly half her life in captivity.

But when Elizabeth herself died in 1603, it would be Mary's son, James VI of Scotland, who would take the English crown. As James VI of Scotland and James I of England, he united the two kingdoms under a single crown. A feat that dozens of monarchs had tried to accomplish by force finally happened by an accident of birth.

PART III
Turmoil and Treason

Nine

GUNPOWDER, TREASON AND PLOT

Guy 'Guido' Fawkes
1604–5

Following the Catholic conspiracies centred on Mary Queen of Scots, religious bigotry and hatred bubbled to the surface all over England. All Catholics were viewed with suspicion and assumed to be agents of a foreign power (the Pope) bent on the destruction of England and its monarchy. Queen Elizabeth's strength of character generally kept the hatred in check, but following her death in 1603 the violence crept into the open. Gangs of Protestant thugs destroyed Catholic homes searching for rosaries, holy relics and 'priest holes' where the dreaded Jesuits might be hiding. Any of these fanatical Protestants who were caught were prosecuted and imprisoned, but the law was half-hearted in its efforts to track them down, and this laxity only encouraged them. Sooner or later the situation was bound to come to a head, and when it did the results were nearly catastrophic.

Scotland's King James VI was beset with problems from the moment he accepted the crown left vacant by the death of Queen Elizabeth. Scottish Presbyterians, Roman Catholics and the Church of England alike hounded him to designate an 'official' religion. Although he had little time for the straight-laced, puritanical Presbyterians, he was far more afraid of the Catholics, even though theirs was the church of his mother, Mary Queen of Scots. Too many plots had been hatched by her and her followers against the English crown for James to trust any of them, particularly now that he was king.

Owing to his family's violent history, James had a virtual paranoia of assassination and political upheaval. His mother had been beheaded, his grandfather had been shot dead and the Scottish lairds had blown up his father, Lord Darnley. Desperate to keep all of his subjects happy, James began negotiating a peace with staunchly Catholic Spain and commissioned an English translation of the Bible that would accommodate all the various Christian sects.

Judging by James's private correspondence with his Secretary of State, Robert Cecil, it is obvious that he genuinely wanted to remain on good terms with all his subjects, no matter what their religious beliefs may have been. The only exception to this ecumenical view was the Jesuits. Both James and Cecil saw them as fanatics bent on stirring up anti-government and anti-Protestant sentiments on every possible occasion. In a memorandum, Cecil referred to them as 'absolute seducers of the people from temporal obedience and consequent persuaders to rebellion'. In reaction to the Jesuit 'problem' King James initiated the Hampton Court Conference designed to impose harsher penalties on any Jesuit priest caught in England as well as anyone remotely associated with them. These apparently conflicting attitudes towards the Church of Rome led King James to be referred to as the 'wisest fool in Christendom'. It was not the most positive judgement a new reign could hope for.

In March 1604, only weeks after the Hampton Court Conference got under way, three English gentlemen met at the home of John Wright in the London suburb of Lambeth. The three were Wright himself, Robert Catesby and Thomas Wintour. The only things they had in common were high social position, the fact that they were all in their early thirties, and the firm belief that they were being persecuted because of their devotion to and practice of Catholicism.

Catesby was Wintour's cousin and a close friend of Wright; he was also an inveterate plotter who had been involved in the Duke of Essex's abortive rebellion against Queen Elizabeth some years earlier. Now he had come to the conclusion that despite King James's assurances that honest Catholics were in no danger, the situation was sure to get worse unless devoted Catholics took matters into their own hands. Later, one of the group recalled that Catesby 'bethought him of a way at one instant to deliver us from all our bonds and without any foreign help to replant the Catholic religion [in England]'. As the three men talked on into the night, Catesby insisted that the only solution to the spiralling crisis was to eliminate the royal family, all the ministers of state and the entire parliament – and do it all at a single blow. With the government dead, they could seize the king's young daughter, Princess

Elizabeth, declare her queen and raise a general revolt against all the Protestant sects.

Obviously, such an audacious, brutal and seemingly impractical plot did not sit well with Wintour and Wright. But Catesby convinced them that their cause would be justified in the eyes of God and therefore worth any risk and any cost. The others were finally persuaded to agree. But three men could not possibly carry out such a plan alone. They would need help and the assistance of people with the right technical expertise. Catesby had a friend named Thomas Percy, who was both brave and a good Catholic and would make a fine addition to the group, but he did not have the specific skills they would need. After much thought, Thom Wintour said he might know just the man they needed, but he was on the continent. First they would have to locate him and then persuade him to join them. His name was Guy Fawkes.

Fawkes had been born near York into a Protestant family in April 1570. His father was a notary to the York ecclesiastical court and the consistory court of the local archbishop. It was a respectable, conservative background. So too, apparently, was the rest of Fawkes' early life. At the age of twenty he married Maria Pulleyn and a year later she gave them a son. Fawkes' inheritance of 4 acres of farmland and a barn was respectable, though modest. But somewhere along the line something had changed. Shortly after the birth of his son, Guy Fawkes sold his land, left his wife and infant son and went to the Low Countries to join a group of exiled English Catholic mercenaries fighting there in the pay of the Spanish king.

At twenty-two Fawkes was already a tall, powerfully built man with thick reddish-brown hair and beard. By all accounts, he was also a natural soldier, being described as a man 'of excellent good natural parts, very resolute and universally learned'. Apparently well liked both personally and for his fighting abilities, Guy Fawkes – who now called himself Guido – was 'thought by all the most distinguished in the Archduke's camp for nobility and exemplary temperance, of mild cheerful demeanour, an enemy of broils and disputes, a faithful friend, and remarkable for his punctual attendance upon religious observance'. As a result, he gained 'considerable fame among soldiers'; he also gained advancement from common foot soldier to a 'miner', where he received extensive training in tunnelling, munitions and explosives.

After serving in the Low Countries for a decade, Fawkes resigned his commission to go to Spain with the intention of 'enlighten[ing] King Philip II concerning the true position of the Romanists in England'. What he actually wanted was to persuade King Philip to finance a Catholic uprising to depose King James. Philip may or may not have met Fawkes personally, but after more than a year in Spain, Fawkes realised his mission was going nowhere. He had, however, run into an old school friend from York, Christopher Wright, who happened to be the brother of another boyhood friend (and Catesby's co-conspirator) John Wright. Together they discussed politics and religion, the sad state of affairs in England and what could be done about it. Undoubtedly, Fawkes told Wright about his abortive plan to get the Spanish to back a Catholic uprising in England, but whether or not Wright divulged any of his brother's plans is unclear. What is certain is that soon after Fawkes returned to England he received word – probably through one of the Wright brothers – that a man named Thomas Wintour wanted to see him.

In May 1604, roughly two months after Catesby, Wintour and Wright had first met, they met again in a private room at the Duck and Drake Inn in the fashionable Strand district of London. Catesby had brought along Thomas Percy and Wintour had brought Fawkes. Before divulging the exact nature of the plot to overthrow the government, Catesby swore the men to secrecy. To solemnise their vow of silence, they heard mass and were given communion by a Jesuit priest named Father John Gerard. This done, Catesby began laying out the details of one of the most bizarre and improbable plots in English history.

There was only one day in the year when the royal family, the chief government ministers and both houses of parliament were assembled in the same place at the same time – the State Opening of Parliament, traditionally held on 5 November. But King James was still putting together his government and would not convene his first parliament until November 1605; still more than twenty months away. Because this would be the king's first official public speech, the House of Lords would be packed with government officials of every rank. The only people not in attendance would be the king's two youngest children, Duke Charles and Princess Elizabeth.

According to Catesby's plan, if enough barrels of gunpowder could be stashed in the cellars directly below the House of Lords, they could blow the entire government sky-high at a single sweep. Before anyone knew what had happened, the plotters would be well on their way to kidnapping Duke Charles and Princess Elizabeth. Charles would probably be killed and Elizabeth placed on the throne by Catesby and his men. Obviously, there would be no mention that the princess's rescuers had been responsible for murdering the entire government. It was the perfect coup d'état.

As the men listened, open-mouthed, to the audacious plan, Catesby explained that he knew there was a nearly unused cellar directly beneath the House of Lords. All the men had to do was rent a house in the neighbourhood and dig a tunnel beneath the houses separating their location from the room beneath parliament. Fawkes' experience as a miner and explosives expert would ensure that the tunnel was dug properly and the gunpowder placed so as to do as much damage as possible.

Since the area around parliament was a warren of twisting alleyways and narrow streets filled with churches, public meeting rooms, taverns, wine merchants and brothels, their movements should go completely unnoticed.

Amazingly, no one backed out of the conspiracy and the group proceeded to the next step; renting a house near the parliament building in the name of Thomas Percy. Under the fictitious name of John Johnson, Fawkes pretended to be Percy's servant and assumed the responsibility of watching the premises, guarding it against unwanted visitors. According to Fawkes' later confession, 'we lay in the house and had shot and powder, being resolved to die in that place before we should yield or be taken'.

Around the end of September, Fawkes was told to begin preparations for work on the mine, but their activity was delayed for more than two months because the Commissioners for the Union between England and Scotland were meeting next door and any strange noises might alert the authorities. Finally, in early December, the men began tunnelling. But even at the best of times it was slow going, particularly for those in the group who were not used to hard physical labour. Things only got worse at the end of the second week when, according to Fawkes, 'we came to the very foundation of the Wall of the House, which was about three yards thick and [we] found it a matter of great difficulty'. Obviously more hands were needed if the work was going to be completed in less than a year.

Into the plot were brought Catesby's servant, Thomas Bates, John Wright's brother Christopher (who had initially contacted Fawkes in Spain) and Thom Wintour's brother Robert. Catesby also brought in his cousin Francis Tresham, and the Wintour brothers conscripted their brother-in-law John Grant. To their number they also added Sir Everard Digby, Robert Keys, Hugh Owen and Ambrose Rookwood. With the exception of Fawkes and Bates, all the new members were related to the original five either by blood or marriage.

With more hands, the work moved apace, but it was a long way from the rented house to the cellars of parliament. In March 1605, work came to a screeching halt when, according to Fawkes, 'As they were working on the wall, they heard a rushing in the cellar as of the removing of coals, where upon we feared we had been discovered: and they sent me off to the [nearby] cellar, [where I found] the coal [was] selling and that the cellar was to be let.' Amazingly, the cellar now up for rent had been their target all along.

Thomas Percy was immediately sent to take a one-year lease on the storeroom and the men began shuttling in barrels of gunpowder from their warehouse across the Thames. At this point, they had already acquired twenty barrels and were in the process of buying more. To hide this growing mountain of explosives, they brought in cartloads of firewood, which were piled on top of the barrels. Mixed in with the wood and gunpowder were hundreds of iron bars, which would act like shrapnel when the gunpowder was eventually detonated.

The hard work being almost over, the men could only wait till the opening of parliament in November. According to Fawkes, 'About Easter, the Parliament being [in recess] till October next, we dispersed ourselves and I retired to the Low Countries by advice and direction of the rest . . . lest . . . by my longer stay I might have [aroused] suspicions . . .'. Presumably, one of Fawkes' duties on the continent would be to alert English Catholics in exile to the coming unexpected change of government back home.

In Fawkes' absence, Percy and the others continued to ferry more powder, iron bars and wood from across the river and haul them into the cellar. Again, according to Fawkes' account, 'I returned about the beginning of September . . . and then receiving the keys again [from] Percy, we brought in more powder and billets to cover the same again, and so I went for a time into the country till the 30 of October'. As Fawkes nervously waited to be called back to London only days before the final, awful move some of the others began to have moral misgivings about what they planned to do.

To cleanse their guilty consciences, Robert Catesby and Thomas Wintour confessed the entire affair to their priest, the Jesuit Father Greenway, and at least Catesby discussed it further with Father John Gerard who had given communion to the five original members of the plot more than a year earlier. At the same time as Catesby and Wintour were seeking absolution, Sir Everard Digby was unburdening his soul to Jesuit Superior Father Garnet. He needed to know if the Pope would approve of the death of so many innocent people in the name of the church; particularly considering that there were Catholics among the king's ministers and in both houses of parliament.

Francis Tresham went to his own priest with the same concerns, but in his case they were even more personal; William Parker who held the title of Lord Monteagle was a member of the House of Lords, a Catholic and Tresham's cousin by marriage.

On 18 October, Catesby, Wintour and Tresham met to discuss the possibility of warning a few, key Catholic members of the government not to attend the opening of parliament. The specific results of their meeting are not known, but they probably decided it would be too dangerous even to hint that something was amiss. Everyone agreed they would keep their peace and live with the consequences, but one of them was growing increasingly uncomfortable.

Almost two weeks later, and only ten days before King James was scheduled to open parliament, Lord Monteagle had just sat down to dinner at his home in Hoxton when a letter arrived by special messenger. It read as follows: 'My lord, out of the love I bear to some of your friends, I have a care for your preservation. Therefore I would advise you, as you tender your life, to devise some excuse to shift of your attendance of this Parliament, for God and man hath concurred to punish the wickedness of this time . . . and I hope God will give you the grace to make good use of it, to whose protection I commend you.' Not surprisingly the letter was unsigned.

Monteagle was certainly no friend of the new king. He believed, and had said, that 'the King is odious to all sorts', but whatever the letter hinted at, it was obviously a lot bigger than political loyalties. Leaving his supper to go cold, Monteagle hurried to find Secretary of State Robert Cecil.

Somehow, it only took hours for news of the letter to find its way to the ears of Catesby and Wintour. Immediately they accused Tresham of trying to warn his cousin, but he vehemently denied it. A week later the five leading conspirators agreed that since nothing seemed to have been done to heighten security around the houses of parliament, the whole thing must have been laughed off as a bad joke or had been lost in the government bureaucracy. But just to be on the safe side, all of them except Fawkes made plans to get out of London immediately, though Francis Tresham decided to remain in London at the last minute. Guy Fawkes had no choice but to stay behind and light the fuse at the appointed time. Once the government was dead, he was to make a break for the Low Countries and spread the word that Catholicism was about to be restored in England.

Whether it actually took nine days for Robert Cecil to act, or whether he was simply biding his time to avoid scaring off the plotters remains uncertain, but on Monday afternoon, 4 November, his men went into action. Accompanied by the Lord Chamberlain, Lord Monteagle and John Whyniard, Thomas Howard the Earl of Suffolk led a thorough search of the parliament buildings. When they reached an exterior door leading to a rented-out cellar, they encountered a tall, powerfully built man with bristling beard and hair who identified himself as John Johnson, a porter in the employ of a Mr Thomas Percy. Dutifully and calmly he unlocked the cellar door while the ministers carried out a perfunctory search of the cellars. Their search uncovered no more than a pile of timbers and brushwood. Later that afternoon the delegation met with Cecil and the king, describing their search and admitting they had found nothing. They did, however, say that the man Johnson had appeared to be 'a very bad and desperate fellow' who 'seemed to be a man shrewd enough, but up to no good'. Everyone decided the cellar would have to be searched again and this time they should take a magistrate and soldiers with them.

A few minutes before midnight, the men returned to the cellar, accompanied by Sir Thomas Knyvett, the magistrate of Westminster and a band of armed men. When they arrived, the man 'Johnson' was still there guarding the door. Knyvett ordered him to hand over the keys and ordered several of the guards to keep Johnson under close guard while they searched the rooms. Ploughing through the pile of logs and wood, it was only minutes before they found thirty-five barrels of gunpowder and hundreds of iron bars. Rushing back to where the guards were holding Johnson under restraint, Knyvett ordered a body search. In Johnson's clothes they discovered a watch, a length of slow-burning match and the 'touchwood' he would need to light it. The man calling himself Johnson was placed under arrest and escorted to Whitehall Palace for a personal meeting with King James.

By one o'clock in the morning on 5 November, a large group of government officials and soldiers had crowded into the king's bedroom. With them was Guy Fawkes. Fawkes still insisted his name was Johnson, but now calmly admitted he had intended to blow up the House of Lords when the government assembled there to hear the king's speech. His only regret, he said, was that he had obviously failed, because his intent was 'To blow the Scottish beggars back to their native mountains . . .', and if he had been given the opportunity he would have gladly blown up the men who had arrested him, the Houses of Parliament and himself with them. For all his bravado, he adamantly refused to name any of his fellow conspirators. Realising they weren't going to get any more out of the man that night, Cecil ordered him to be taken to the Tower where he could think things over before being questioned in much greater depth in the morning.

After spending the night in the miserably cramped cell known as 'Little Ease' – where a man could neither stand up straight nor lie down and stretch out – Fawkes was taken to the Council Chamber in the Lieutenant's Lodgings. He again insisted that his name was Johnson; he was a Catholic and had intended to blow up the king and parliament and only regretted that he had not succeeded. Everything else he said was a lie, and everyone in the room knew it. It would now be up to the king to decide how rigorous the next round of questioning would be.

Back in Whitehall, King James I was a very shaken, but determined, man. This was all too reminiscent of the death of his father, Lord Darnley, who had been blown apart when James was still an infant. But no matter how personally frightening the plot was, the investigation had to be slow, thorough and carried out strictly according to the law. To oversee the investigation into what was already being called 'the Gunpowder Plot', James appointed Robert Cecil, the Earl of Nottingham, the Lord High Admiral, the Earl of Devon, Lord Lieutenant of Ireland and the Earl of Northampton, the Lord Privy Seal. Cecil was obviously just as concerned as the king, but he already had suspicions that somewhere, somehow, the Jesuits were behind the whole thing. Cecil is quoted as having said 'we cannot hope to have good government while large numbers of people go around obeying foreign rulers'. Implicit, but unsaid, was the fact that the 'people' indicated were Jesuit-leaning Catholics and the foreign ruler in question was the Pope.

While the commission was organising itself, the king spent all of 6 November writing up a list of sixteen questions that he personally wanted answers to. The King's questions were:

(1) As [to who] he is, for I can never yet hear of any man that knows him.
(2) Where he was born?
(3) What were his parents' names?
(4) What age he is?
(5) Where he hath lived?
(6) How he hath lived and by what trade of life?
(7) How he received the wounds (i.e. scars) on his breast?
(8) If he was ever in service, with any other . . . person, and what they were, and [for] how long?

(9) How came he in [that] person's service, by what means and at what time?

(10) What time did his master hire this house?

(11) How soon after the possessing of it did he begin his devilish preparations?

(12) When and where did he learn to speak French?

(13) What gentlewoman's letter it was that was found upon him?

(14) Wherefore doth she give him another name in it than he gives to himself?

(15) If he was ever a papist, and if so, who brought him up to it?

(16) How was he converted, where, when and by whom [to] this course of his life . . . because I have diverse motives leading me to suspect that he hath remained long beyond the seas and, either is a priest, or hath long served some priest . . .

Amended to the bottom of the list was a note expressly ordering that the prisoner be 'put to the question'; a euphemism for torture. While English common law now expressly forbade the use of torture, it was permissible if specifically ordered by the monarch or the Privy Council. Considering the magnitude of the crime in question, James had no qualms about ordering its use to ferret out every bit of information and the names of everyone involved. The amendment read, in part, 'if he will not other ways confess, the gentler tortures are to be first used unto him et sic per gradus ad mia tenditur (and so on by degrees proceeding to the worst), and so God speed your good work. James R'

The man in charge of the Tower and any prisoners kept there was Sir William Waad, one of the most active, and least sympathetic, men to hold the job for many years. When he was appointed Lieutenant of the Tower in 1605, Waad was already sixty years old and had a long and distinguished career as diplomat, spy and investigator of Catholic plots dating from the days of Sir Francis Walsingham's investigation into the Babington plot. Hard, efficient, crafty and unemotional, Waad was an expert at the game of alternately consoling and threatening his prisoners; and he never hesitated to back up the threats with action.

When Waad assumed his post only months before the Gunpowder Plot was uncovered, he brought with him a small group of hand-picked interrogators under the assumption that his own men would be far more efficient at extracting information than the Yeoman Warders whose main job was protecting the Tower compound. With Waad by his side, Guy Fawkes was taken to face his first, official interrogation on the morning of 7 November. Not surprisingly, the Lord Chief Justice could get nothing new out of Fawkes, so Waad was given the list of questions from the king and told to put the prisoner to 'the question'.

Before the torture began, Fawkes was shown the terrifying array of implements which might be used on him should the need arise. The rack, iron gauntlets and the scavenger's daughter, an iron neckband connected by a bar to knee shackles: when the device was tightened the victim's head was pulled towards their knees, slowly dislocating their spine. Each one was held in front of his face to start breaking down his psychological resolve. It only took half an hour on the rack – his muscles and joints pulled and stretched till the ropes bit into his wrists and ankles, chafing them till blisters were raised and broke open – that a few truths began to emerge. First was his name – Guy, or Guido, Fawkes. Then, in an attempt to justify anything he might say, he confessed that God must have not approved of the plot or it would have succeeded, so it was only proper that he felt ashamed for his own part in it. But he swore he would never divulge the names of the others involved. Waad told him they already knew the names of some of his friends, and that tomorrow the two of them would visit the rack again, and together they would find out everything else there was to know.

As he was returned to the cramped confines of Little Ease, Fawkes not only realised he would not be able to move enough to relieve the pain of the racking, but was informed of an aspect of 'the question' that took place outside the torture chamber. According to the rules of torture the prisoner 'shall have three morsels of barley bread a day, and that he shall have the water next [to] the prison, so that it shall not be current (meaning stagnant water taken from the moat), and that he shall not eat the same day upon which he drinks, nor drink the same day upon which he eats; and he shall so continue till he die'. And so Guy Fawkes completed his first day of questioning.

The next morning the racking lasted for two full hours. Before he finally broke down and confessed, Fawkes' muscles and ligaments had been torn, his shoulders had been dislocated and both wrists and ankles were so torn that the ropes holding them were soaked with blood. Finally, he delivered the names of the four other men who were at the centre of the plot and, according to Waad's notes, 'He told us that since he undertook this action he did every day pray to God he might perform that which might be for the advancement of the Catholic Faith and the saving of his own soul.' A written transcript of the confession was drawn up.

The following day, 9 November, after being informed that some of his comrades had already been arrested, he told everything else he knew without further torture. A full, extended version of the confession was now prepared and read in part:

> I confesse, that a practice in general was first broken unto me, against his Majesty for relief of the Catholic cause, and not invented or propounded by myself. And this was first propounded unto me about Easter Last [when I had been] twelve months beyond the seas in the Low Countrys . . . by Thomas Wintour, who came there upon with me into England and there we imparted our purpose to three other Gentlemen more, namely, Robert Catesby, Thomas Percy and John Wright, who all five consulting together to the means how to execute the same . . .

Nearly insensible with pain, Fawkes could hardly hold the quill to sign his name. After scratching out 'Guido' the pen fell from his hand. It was enough. The commission had the names of all the chief conspirators and all the information they needed to condemn them. Fawkes would spend the next forty-five days in Little Ease awaiting trial and the inevitable verdict.

By the time Guy Fawkes was arrested in the small hours of 5 November the remaining plotters, with the exception of Tresham, had already left London. Still, it was only a matter of days before word of Fawkes' arrest reached them. Even if they had not heard of Fawkes' arrest, the lack of news concerning the fate of parliament would have alerted them that something had gone terribly wrong. Nevertheless, Catesby was determined the plot would move forward in one form or another and pressed on to their appointed meeting place at Holbech House on the Worcestershire/Staffordshire border.

When Catesby and several of the others arrived at Holbech with a fresh cartload of gunpowder, they found Everard Digby waiting to tell them he had enlisted nearly four dozen new recruits. In spite of the foiled plot against parliament, this was hopeful news. After delivering the message, Digby set off to round up the new forces. Unfortunately, Catesby's load of gunpowder had become damp in the drizzling rain that had dogged their journey. Foolishly, the seven men now lodged at Holbech House decided the best way to dry the powder was to spread it out in front of a roaring fire. Once spread across the floor of the great hall the powder could not explode, but a flying spark from the fire ignited it, badly burning some of the men and nearly engulfing the house. It was taken as a very bad sign.

By the next morning, 8 November, three of the company, Robert Wintour, Stephen Littleton and Hugh Owen had fled in panic, leaving only Robert Catesby, the Wright brothers, John and Christopher, and Thomas Percy to clean up the mess and decide what to do next. They did not have long to wait. Shortly before midday, the Sheriff of Worcester arrived with a large posse, surrounded the house and ordered the men to surrender. In the ensuing battle, Catesby, the Wrights and Percy were all fatally shot. With the core group now dead and Fawkes in the Tower, the remaining men, along with scores of other suspected Jesuit rabble-rousers, were rounded up and shipped off to the Tower.

It took time to collect them all. Wintour and Littleton were on the loose for nearly two months, but eventually everyone with the exception of Hugh Owen was taken into custody. Those captured included Fathers Garnet, Gerard and Oldcorne and others with only titular involvement in the plot, but no Jesuit was going to escape Cecil's dragnet.

Their crime was so horrible, their absolute conviction in their cause so unshakeable, that Waad, his inquisitors and the regular Tower Warders were unable to exercise any restraint in dealing with the prisoners. One after another the prisoners were racked, hung in manacles and deprived of food and drink. The indictment presented at their trial, claimed that 'There [were] twenty and three several days spent in Examinations'.

In the face of such gruesome treatment, some of the men held up amazingly well. Thomas Wintour, the only surviving member of the original group, was astoundingly blasé, saying, 'I have often hazarded my life upon far lighter terms, and now would not refuse any good occasion wherein I might do service to the Catholic cause.' Sir Everard Digby was more zealous about his part in the affair: 'Oh! How full of joy I should die, if I could do anything for the Cause which I love more than my life', adding that, had the assembled parliament actually been blown to kingdom come, 'I do not think there were three worth saving that [w]ould have been lost.' Eventually, strong or weak, zealous or stalwart, one by one the accused added their signatures to the confession based on Fawkes' testimony. Of course, the Jesuit priests were another matter entirely. They had not actually been a part of the conspiracy but had only abetted it. They would require special handling.

Cecil had decided to rid England once and for all of the malign, manipulative influence of the Jesuits. In order to extract the greatest possible amount of information from the priests, he cautioned Waad to take special care of them. These men were accustomed to devious methods and thought nothing of laying down their lives for their cause. Simple torture might fail completely on men who considered martyrdom the most desirable death they could hope for.

Exhibiting remarkable finesse, William Waad put Father Henry Garnet into a dry, relatively airy cell and provided him with decent food and wine. He even made a sincere effort to chat civilly with Garnet. According to Garnet's diary, he found his gaoler 'very kindly in his usage and familiarity'. The cordial rapport between the two increased dramatically when Waad admitted that he wanted to be taken into the Catholic faith. In an apparently sympathetic gesture, Father Garnet was even allowed to visit some of the other prisoners, particularly fellow priest Father Oldcorne, with whom he was allowed to spend hours at a time, on a fairly regular basis. What Garnet did not know was that a hole in the stone wall of his cell allowed Waad and his secretary to overhear the two men's conversations. Every word was copied down. When presented with the record of his conversations, Henry Garnet confessed to knowing virtually every detail of the plot, but insisted 'it was not my part (as I thought) to disclose it'.

On Monday 27 January 1606, the day Fathers Garnet and Oldcorne were arrested, the eight surviving core members of the Gunpowder Plot went to trial. Robert Wintour, Thomas Wintour, Guy Fawkes, John Grant, Ambrose Rookwood, Robert Keyes, Thomas Bates and Sir Everard Digby were tried together in what, for its time, must have been a media circus. Francis Tresham escaped his fate, having died in the Tower of natural causes on 23 December.

To avoid any hint of religious persecution or bigotry, the king and Privy Council made sure that seated among the nine commissioners presiding at the trial were two Roman Catholics. The commissioners included: Sir John Popham, the Lord Chief Justice of England; Justice of the Common-Pleas Court, Sir Peter Warburton; the Earl of Nottingham; the Earl of Salisbury; the Earl of Suffolk; the Earl of Worcester; Thomas Fleming, the Lord Chief Baron of the Exchequer; the Earl of Devonshire and the Earl of Northampton.

Once the court was assembled, the indictment against the eight prisoners was read aloud. Page after page of legal jargon, enumerating the crimes and intended crimes of the men were presented. No attempt was made to spare the court, nor the defendants, the full horror of what they had intended to do. Below is a brief excerpt from the opening passage of the indictment:

That whereas our Sovereign Lord the King had, by the Advice and Assent of his Council, for divers weighty and urgent Occasions concerning, his Majesty, the State, and Defence of the Church and Kingdom of England, appointed a Parliament to be holden at his City of Westminster; That Henry Garnet, Superior of the Jesuits within the Realm of England, (called also by the several names of Wally, Darcy, Roberts, Farmer, and Henry Philips) Oswald Tesmond Jesuit, otherwise called Oswald Greenwell, John Gerrard Jesuit, (called also by the several names of Lee and Brooke) Robert Winter, Thomas Winter, Gentlemen, Guy Fawkes Gent. otherwise called Guy Johnson, Robert Keyes Gent. and Thomas Bates Yeoman, late Servant to Robert Catesby Esquire; together with the said Robert Catesby and Thomas Percy Esquires, John Wright and Christopher Wright Gentlemen, in open Rebellion and Insurrection against his Majesty, lately slain, and Francis Tresham Esq; lately dead; as false Traitors against our said Sovereign Lord the King . . . that it was lawful and meritorious to kill our said Sovereign Lord the King, and all other Hereticks [i.e. non-Catholics] within this Realm of England, for the Advancing and Enlargement of the pretended and usurped Authority and Jurisdiction of the Bishop of Rome, and for the restoring of the superstitious Romish Religion within this Realm of England . . .

The indictment went on to recount the details of the affair as it had been explained in the confessions of Fawkes and Wintour, and claimed that the plot, and by implication all those involved in it, were the most monstrous, horrible conspiracy: 'The Tongue of Man never deliver'd, The Ear of Man never heard, The Heart of Man never conceived, Nor the Malice of hellish or earthly Devil ever practised. . . . And surely of these things we may truly say . . . the Offences themselves . . . are so exorbitant and transcendent, and aggregated of so many bloody and fearful Crimes, as they cannot be aggravated by any Inference. . . .' The government had, to say the least, a strong case against the accused.

The evidence was duly presented and weighed but neither the verdict, nor the sentence, was ever in doubt. Guilty of treason: death by being hanged, drawn and quartered. Sentence to be carried out immediately.

There were so many men to be despatched, and the work of hacking a man to pieces while he was still alive so time-consuming and exhausting, that two days were allowed for the executions, and still the executioner had to bring in two assistants.

The first to go would be Digby, Wintour, Grant and Bates. On Thursday 30 January 1606, these four were dragged on hurdles to St Paul's Churchyard and slowly, horrifically, put to death. The following day came the turn of Wintour, Rookwood, Keys and Fawkes, but theirs was to be a different place of execution. They were taken to the Old Palace Yard at Westminster, only a few yards from the cellars where they had planted their cache of gunpowder beneath the Houses of Parliament.

After watching his three comrades torn to pieces before him, the last to go was Guido Fawkes. By then, the floor of the scaffold was awash with the blood and gore of the other three. Too crippled by his racking to walk, Fawkes was helped to the foot of the scaffold by his guards; but he insisted on mounting the steps himself. A contemporary account recorded the scene: 'Last of all came the great[est] devil of all, Guy Fawkes, alias Johnson, who should have put fire to the powder. His body being weak with the torture and sickness he was scarce able to go up the ladder. . . . He made no speech, but with his crosses and idle ceremonies made his end . . .'.

But Guy Fawkes had one last trick up his sleeve. After the hangman placed the noose around his neck, Fawkes flung himself from the edge of the scaffolding, breaking his neck instantly. The castration, disembowelling, beheading and quartering would continue, but Fawkes would feel none of it. He died, according to the above account, 'to the great joy of all the beholders that the land was ended of so wicked a villainy'.

Following his execution it was suggested that Fawkes' body parts be hung in chains outside parliament as a warning to other would-be traitors, but the idea was rejected. To be certain the point was not lost, the bodies of the four conspirators who had died at Holbech House were exhumed and beheaded. Within three months, most of the tertiary associates, including John Wintour, Ralph Ashley, Steven Littleton, Humphrey Littleton, Father Oldcorne and Father Garnet had also gone to the scaffold. Father Nicholas Owen officially committed suicide in the Tower in March 1606, but there is substantial evidence that he died under torture.

Father John Gerard spent some months in the Tower, but managed to escape to the continent, and after deserting his companions at Holbech

House, Hugh Owen somehow eluded the search for the plotters and made his way to Rome.

The Gunpowder Plot was the most extensive and celebrated plot ever devised against the Crown of England. To commemorate its collapse, Sir William Waad erected a plaque in the Council Chamber of the Lieutenant's Lodgings. With appropriately flowery language, the plaque reads: 'To Almighty God, guardian arrester and avenger, who has punished this great and incredible conspiracy against our most merciful lord, the King . . . [which was] . . . moved by the treasonable hope of overthrowing the Kingdom . . . [by] the Jesuits of perfidious and serpentlike ungodliness, with others equally insane, were suddenly, wonderfully and divinely detected, at the very moment when ruin was impending, on the fifth day of November in the year of grace 1605 . . .'. Following is a list of the conspirators' names. But in the public mind it is the little poem, still occasionally recited on 5 November, Guy Fawkes' Night, that best commemorates the plot to blow up parliament:

> Remember, Remember, the fifth of November:
> Gunpowder, Treason and Plot.
> We know of no reason why Gunpowder Treason
> Should ever be forgot . . .

Ten

A RIGHT ROYAL HEIST

Colonel Thomas Blood
1670–1

W hen Thomas Blood was born in Ireland around 1618 he seemed to have a bright future. His father was a man of means, having made his fortune in iron manufacturing, and so well connected that by the time his son had turned twenty-one he had secured him a post as Justice of the Peace. By the time Thomas had grown to manhood he was a tall, dark, handsome man with a hawkish nose, a full mouth, blue eyes and enough Irish charm to make him a natural leader.

When the English parliament went to war against the forces of King Charles I in 1642, Thomas Blood rushed to England to join Oliver Cromwell's army in its fight against the Crown. There, he was commissioned as a lieutenant and assigned to the Commission of Peace, a body of spies responsible for subverting Royalist activities. Blood's natural talent for duplicity and deceit soon made itself apparent as he played both sides against the middle, waylaying Royalist shipments of arms, supplies and gold, skimming off a hefty profit for himself before turning the rest over to his superiors. Profiteers have always been a part of war, but Thomas Blood was a master of the art.

When King Charles was captured and sentenced to death by Cromwell's parliament in 1649, England was destined to spend the next ten years suffering under the strict, puritanical rule of the Parliamentarian Common-wealth. But despite legal restrictions on even the simplest pleasures, the Commonwealth was a lawless time; and Thomas Blood made the most of it. Having received grants of land and property in his native Ireland as a reward for his services to parliament, Blood continued to amass cash with the help of the extensive network of spies and smugglers he had developed during the war. By 1650 he had affected the title of Colonel, although there is no evidence that he had ever earned such an exalted rank, and married the attractive young daughter of a well-to-do Lancashire landowner known to us only as Miss Holcroft. Life looked sweet for Colonel Blood, but the good life was already winding its way to an unhappy end.

After a four-year dictatorial reign as Lord Protector of England, Oliver Cromwell died in 1658 and within a year young Charles II was called from exile in France to assume his father's throne. Recognising the importance of putting on a good show, Charles set out to re-establish the monarchy with a display of pomp and grandeur that would have astounded even Elizabeth I. Affectionately called 'the Merry Monarch', Charles II was determined to wow his subjects with one grand ceremony after another. But missing from the necessary list of accoutrements were those imperial symbols of royal power, the crown, sceptre and orb. It seems that when the royal sceptre was presented to Oliver Cromwell six years earlier, he had snapped, 'Take away that bauble'. And taken away they were, but no one has ever determined exactly where they went. What we do know is that these hallmarks of royal authority were sold at bargain-basement prices. According to Sir Edward Walker's 1660 account: 'through the Rapine of the late unhappy times, all the Royal Ornaments and Regalia heretofore preserved from age to age . . . were taken away, sold and destroyed . . .'. Now, if Charles was going to look like a proper king, he needed new regalia.

Vast amounts of money, which Charles could not afford, were spent to make a new set of royal accoutrements, produced by the royal jeweller, who happened to be Charles's cousin. To keep the new 'baubles' safe, the old Martin Tower in the inner ward of the Tower of London was converted into a royal jewel room. Built directly into the walls of the Tower complex, the Martin Tower seemed an ideally safe location for the new Crown Jewels.

While Charles busied himself with his new look, his government was charged with securing the peace, fending off plots by disgruntled parliamentarians, and finding cash to finance the new king and government. Integral to the plan was stripping former supporters of Cromwell's government of their money and land. Deprived of their wealth, the rebels should be in no position to make trouble for the Crown. One of the men charged with carrying out these orders was James Butler, 1st Duke of Ormond and Lord Lieutenant of Ireland.

Former parliamentarian operatives were thrown out of their homes and forced to forfeit their land and money. One of those who felt the sting of this retribution was Colonel Thomas Blood. Not accustomed to being either homeless or penniless, Blood's wife quickly abandoned her husband and returned to England. Angry and hurt, Blood vowed to take revenge on the English and their new king.

Only months after his eviction in 1662, Blood joined a group of former parliamentarians and Irish republicans who were plotting to drive the English out of Ireland. Blood's skill in manipulating people quickly made him one of the group's primary movers as they planned their nationwide uprising. Gathering together some of his old friends from the war, and probably still his confederates in his continuing illegal activities, among Blood's closest allies in the plot were James Desborough, Edward Perrot and John Kelfy. Together, they and the other leaders of the revolution laid their plans. Central to the plot was the seizure of Dublin Castle where the Duke of Ormond would be taken hostage and used as a bargaining chip in their dealings with the Crown. Not only was Ormond the king's representative in Ireland, he had cost Blood everything he owned and it was his turn to suffer.

Tragically for Blood, the plan unravelled only days before it went into motion. The revolutionaries had been unmasked. Dozens of them, including Blood's brother-in-law, were arrested, tried and hanged. Blood and his small band of followers were luckier, for they escaped and scattered, but there was now a £1,000 reward on Blood's head and considering that the average yearly wage of a craftsman was scarcely more than £10, it was a huge inducement for anyone to turn him in. But the clever Blood managed to flee to Holland before making his way back to England under an assumed name, passing himself off as a doctor and apothecary dealing in herbal medicines and quack cures.

In London, Blood was seen hanging around Petty Wales, a seedy neighbourhood with a bad reputation that ran from the River Thames to Tower Hill. It is likely that he was rounding up his old gang while he hatched his next plot, and it didn't take the resourceful Blood long to put his new plan into action. On 6 December 1670, James Butler, Duke of Ormond and Blood's old nemesis, was snatched from his carriage while on official business in London. The kidnapping took place on a busy London street, in the middle of the day. It had all the earmarks of bad, bold Thomas Blood.

Whether Blood planned to hold Ormond for ransom, or simply kill him, has never been determined, but within days of the kidnapping Blood could sense the law closing in on him, and Ormond was released unharmed. Once again,

Blood and his comrades slipped through the government's fingers, but another £1,000 was added to the price on his head.

Deciding it was time to leave England for a while, Blood went to Scotland, where he involved himself in a rebel uprising and was sighted at the Battle of Pentland Hills on 27 November 1666. Like all Blood's previous plans, Pentland Hills went awry. Vastly superior English forces gunned down more than 500 rebels and the rest, including Blood, ran for their lives, scrambling across the rugged Scottish landscape.

With three failed plots behind him, Blood was broke and desperate. He had to make one final play that would net him enough money to escape England forever. In a plot as bizarre as it was bold, Blood decided he would steal the new Crown Jewels of England. Gathering together his old comrades Desborough, Perrot and Kelfy, Blood now added two more members to his gang. One of them was a young woman whose name remains a mystery and the other was Thomas Hunt, a pleasant-looking, well-spoken young man who would play a central role in Blood's latest far-fetched scheme.

It had been easy for Blood to find out where the Crown Jewels were kept, for then, like now, they were on public display; King Charles wanted his subjects to be able to see the grandeur of the restored monarchy. The warden in charge of the jewels was Mr Talbot Edwards, a retired military officer who lived in apartments on the upper floors of the Martin Tower, by now called the Jewel Tower. In a room immediately below Edward's apartment the royal regalia was stored in a cage made of heavy iron bars. Although the cage was large enough to walk around in, no one was allowed access except Edwards and official representatives of the king. Visitors were allowed to enter the room and peer at the crown, orb and sceptre through the bars, paying Talbot Edwards a few pennies for his time and trouble in showing them around.

In April 1670, one of Edward's visitors was a country preacher accompanied by his wife. Paying Edwards his modest fee, the couple followed the old man into the jewel room. As they stood admiring their king's ceremonial gear, the parson's wife slumped against the wall, insisting she was completely overcome at the sight of such magnificence, complained of a 'qualm upon her stomach' and asked for a glass of wine to calm her. Concerned and compassionate by nature, Edwards invited the parson and his wife upstairs to his quarters where the lady could lie down until she felt better.

Leading the pair up the winding stone stairs, Edwards handed the woman over to his wife and provided wine for her and her husband. After a short rest, the lady insisted she was fully restored and again apologised for being a nuisance. Her husband, too, expressed his thanks and the pair left. The kindly country preacher and his wife were, of course, none other than Blood and his female accomplice, and Blood now knew all he needed about the layout of the jewel room, the access route through the tower and the location of Edwards' apartments. He also knew that on a table near the iron jewel cage there was a brace of unpleasant-looking pistols in a heavy wooden box.

Several days later, 'Parson' Blood returned to the Martin Tower. This time he had several pairs of finely embroidered gloves, which he gave to Mrs Edwards in gratitude for her kindness to his wife. Thrilled at such a thoughtful gesture, Mrs Edwards invited the Reverend and his wife to dinner. It was the beginning of a friendship that Colonel Blood would milk for all it was worth. The two couples became close friends, dining together often and sharing confidences. Sometimes the Edwards' daughter, Elizabeth, who lived with her parents in the tower rooms, joined them. The parson and his wife quickly became familiar faces around the Tower of London. All the guards knew them by sight and their comings and goings became accepted in the heavily guarded fortress. One evening after dinner, Blood and Edwards strolled the grounds of the Tower's inner ward. As they did so, Edwards confessed that he was worried about his daughter's future. He was over seventy and could not expect to live much longer. When he died, his wife would get a small widow's pension that would see her through, but what would become of his daughter? Already near thirty and not yet married, how would she survive?

With the concern expected of a man of faith and a close friend, the 'Reverend' Blood said he might be able to help. He had a nephew, who was also his ward, and the boy was both single and had a yearly income of nearly £200 a year. It was not a lordly sum, but certainly provided the life of a gentleman. Blood went on to explain that he had been thinking the pair would make a fine match but had been reticent to mention the matter for fear of overstepping his bounds. Accustomed to living on a soldier's pay, Edwards must have been dumbfounded. Immediately he agreed. The next time the good parson and his wife came to dinner, they should bring their nephew with them and if he and Edwards' daughter liked each other, the matter would be settled. Blood agreed. Edwards later recalled Blood's words: 'If your daughter be free, and you approve of it, I will bring him hither to see her and we will endeavour to make it a match.'

Only days later Blood, his 'wife' and their 'nephew', in reality the newest member of the gang, Tom Hunt, gathered at the Martin Tower for dinner with the Edwards family. Handsome and charming, Hunt quickly won the attention of Elizabeth Edwards. After a pleasant dinner filled with laughter, wine and good conversation, Blood asked Edwards if his nephew could be allowed to see the Crown Jewels. Talbot Edwards was delighted to show off the jewels and while the women cleared the table, the men descended to the jewel room.

While Hunt peered dutifully at the hoard of gold and gems, Blood mentioned that he had noticed a fine brace of pistols next to the jewel cage and said they would make a fine gift for his neighbour, a nobleman who collected guns. Would he consider selling them? Edwards hesitated, but Blood's offer of considerably more than the pistols' actual value was enough to convince him to part with the weapons. By the time Blood, Hunt and their female accomplice left the Tower, Hunt was fully familiar with the layout of the Martin Tower and Talbot Edwards had surrendered his only means of defence.

Blood and company again dined with the Edwards on 8 May 1671. Over the course of the meal, Blood mentioned that he had two friends staying with him and they would love to see the Crown Jewels. The problem was, they had to leave London early the next morning and would be gone by the time the Tower was open to the public. Ever ready to help a friend, Talbot Edwards said he would be glad to let Blood and his companions in earlier than usual if they would meet him at the main gate at seven o'clock the next morning. Obviously, Blood agreed.

In the grey hours before dawn, Blood and his accomplices made their final preparations. Each man armed himself with a short dagger, Blood had the newly purchased brace of pistols hidden beneath his long travelling cloak and Desborough, Perrot, Hunt and Kelfy had one pistol each. John Kelfy also had a leather travelling bag in which Blood had placed a wooden mallet, a file and a gag to silence Talbot Edwards. Shortly before six on the morning of 9 May, the group set off through the London mist towards the great Tower complex and the Crown Jewels of England.

Just before seven o'clock they reached the main gate of the Tower where Talbot Edwards was already waiting for them. Greeting everyone warmly, Edwards led Blood and three of the men towards the centre of the Tower maze. Desborough remained behind with the horses safely outside the Tower walls. As the group reached the inner ward, Tom Hunt excused himself, saying he would like to stay in the courtyard. He had already seen the crown, and he would rather wait outside in the hopes of catching a glimpse of Elizabeth. Smiling at the thought of young love, Edwards said it would be perfectly all right and led the rest of the group into the Martin Tower and down the narrow stairs to the jewel room. Hunt could now serve as a lookout without arousing any suspicion.

Leading the way to the jewel room, Edwards approached the massive lock on the jewel cage door. As he bent down to put the key in the lock, Colonel Blood threw his long cape over the old man's head and held his arms tight at his sides. Kelfy opened his travelling bag and Perrot pulled out a nasty-looking wooden plug with a leather thong attached to it. Shoving the plug roughly in Talbot Edwards' mouth, he tied the thongs behind his neck to hold the gag tightly in place. Before releasing his struggling captive, Blood told Edwards that if he didn't cause any trouble, he wouldn't be hurt. Perrot then smashed the old man across the back of the head with the wooden mallet and Blood let him slide to the ground.

Entering the cage, the three men went to work. Blood grabbed the wooden mallet from Perrot and began hammering away at the crown until it was flat enough to fit, unseen, beneath his loose-fitting cassock while Perrot shoved the orb of state into his balloon-bottomed knee breeches which made him walk as though he was holding a cantaloupe melon between his knees. In order to fit the massive sceptre into his travelling bag, Kelfy began sawing it in half with the file. While the men were busily stowing away the king's treasure, Talbot Edwards roused himself enough to begin moaning and puffing against the wooden gag. In a fury, one of the men, probably Perrot, waddled out of the cage as fast as his orb-filled trousers would let him, drew his dagger and stabbed the keeper of the jewel house in the belly.

Outside in the courtyard, things were not going any better. As Tom Hunt stood guard, a young man who introduced himself as Wythe Edwards, son of Talbot Edwards, approached him. He said he had just come home on leave from the Royal Navy and wanted to see his parents and sister, and did the young man know if they were at home? Panic-stricken, Hunt began saying anything he could think of to detain Wythe from entering the tower. He was Elizabeth's fiancé, and he was very glad to meet his future brother-in-law and no, he had not seen the Edwards all morning. Of course there was a limit to how long he could detain the man and eventually he had to step aside and let him enter the tower. Fortunately Wythe Edwards mounted the stairs to his family's apartment, totally unaware of the plot unfolding only feet beneath him. As he rounded the stairs, Hunt ran down to the jewel room, grabbed Blood and told him they were about to be exposed. The four dashed up the stairs, leaving the half-ruined sceptre and the bleeding Talbot Edwards lying on the floor of the jewel house.

They hustled across the inner ward as quickly as they could without looking too obvious. Just as they rounded the corner of the Byward Tower, they heard loud, confused shouts coming towards them from the rear. Wythe Edwards' mother had told him that his father was showing some friends the Crown Jewels and Wythe had gone to the jewel room to find his father lying in a pool of blood mumbling: 'Treason! Treason! Thief!'

Wythe rushed up the stairs towards the courtyard shouting for the guards, where Captain Beckman, head of the day's watch, quickly joined him. The two rushed towards the Byward Tower and the main gate, calling for help as they ran. In less than a minute there were guardsmen streaming in from every direction. As more and more Beefeaters poured into the yards and alleyways of the Tower, Blood and his companions realised they had been discovered. In an attempt to divert attention from themselves, they pointed to the main gate and began shouting 'Stop! Thief!', running madly as though they, too, were chasing some imaginary thieves.

As they rounded the corner of the Byward Tower, one of the warders blocked their path with his long-handled halberd. Blood drew one of his pistols, aimed and fired, sending the man tumbling to the ground screaming. The chase had escalated into a running gun battle. In the confusion, one of the guards narrowly missed shooting Wythe Edwards who was an unfamiliar face in the close-knit Tower community.

In the forecourt, as the quartet of thieves headed for the main gate, John Kelfy was tackled by a Beefeater who wrestled him to the ground where two more guards held him down. Seconds later Edward Perrot, still encumbered by the orb sloshing around in his breeches, reached the edge of the wharf outside the gate, only to be wrestled to the ground. While three burly warders ripped off his pantaloons, pulled out the orb and pawed through his clothes for more treasure, Thomas Blood and Tom Hunt crossed the drawbridge and headed across the wharf to freedom. As Hunt, the youngest and most agile of the gang, dashed through the outer gate, Captain Beckman caught up with Colonel Blood.

Drawing his second pistol and aiming it at Beckman's head, Blood pulled the trigger; but the gun misfired. Frantically trying to recock his piece and run at the same time, Blood hesitated just long enough for Beckman to land a swift kick in his groin. Even as he was dragged to his feet coughing and gasping, Blood remained defiant. Staring directly into Beckman's face, he smiled and arrogantly said, 'It was a gallant deed, even if it failed. It was, after all, to gain the crown.'

Hunt actually made it beyond the outer gate where he joined the frightened Desborough, who had remained with the horses. The pair jumped on their horses and raced through the narrow streets surrounding the Tower. Hurtling down St Katherine's Lane, Hunt failed to duck in time to avoid a low-hanging barber's pole projecting into the roadway. Torn from his horse, he lay stunned in the gutter where he was recognised as a wanted criminal by a shopkeeper and held for the warders. Only James Desborough managed to escape. Within minutes of leaving the Martin Tower, the other four gang members found themselves being hustled back into the Tower to more permanent accommodations.

In any normal tale of theft and pursuit this would have been the end of the story, but there was never anything normal about the life of Colonel Thomas Blood. Under questioning he arrogantly refused to talk, stating that he would only confess to the king himself. His behaviour was so bizarre that an account of it made its way into the official report of the Lieutenant of the Tower and was duly passed on to the Duke of Buckingham, King Charles's chief minister. By the end of the day, the entire Court was buzzing with the gossip of the daring attempt to steal the Crown Jewels, and the tragic destruction of the crown and sceptre. Trying to lighten the king's mood, Buckingham showed the report of Blood's strange demand to confess to the king. While King Charles was indeed amused, his reaction was not what Buckingham probably expected.

There is little doubt that the king had heard of Colonel Blood through his attempt to seize Dublin Castle and the daring, daylight kidnapping of the Duke of Ormond. Intrigued by the sheer unmitigated gall of this unrepentant rogue, the king ordered that Thomas Blood be brought to Whitehall where he would be given the opportunity to be as good as his word. He could confess directly to his king. Two days later, Blood was bundled out of his cell, locked in chains and carted off to Whitehall for a private audience with Charles II, King of England, Wales, Scotland and Ireland.

When the guards led Blood to a private audience chamber, they were ordered to wait outside. Desperate to know what was happening, they must have pressed their ears to the door in an effort to overhear snippets of conversation, but to no avail. We will never know what passed between the thief and his monarch; but we do know that there were no raised voices, no shouting and no loud pleas for mercy. It would seem that Blood neither begged nor grovelled but apparently was quite calm in placing his life in the hands of the man whose royal treasure he had mangled beyond repair.

Within days of this strange meeting Thomas Blood was ordered released from the Tower with a full royal pardon. Even stranger, he was given the lordly pension of £500 pounds per year for life. In an age when any theft with a value of more than a shilling commonly led to the scaffold, such a thing was unprecedented and unimaginable. Only days later, Blood was spotted by two old friends parading around Tower Green wearing an expensive new suit of clothes, a new hat and an elaborate wig. Within weeks, the rest of the gang was pardoned, including Desborough who had eluded capture.

Inevitably, the strange treatment of Colonel Blood set the gossiping tongues at the royal court wagging furiously. Rumours and theories abounded: chronically broke, King Charles had been in on the plot from the beginning; it was all arranged by the king to check out the security measures at the Tower; the king had made a wager with some of his cronies that he could steal his own Crown Jewels; and on, and on, and on. The truth is probably more prosaic. Being a bit of a rascal himself, King Charles had simply been intrigued by this gutsy man with more balls than brains. Possibly, with his longstanding connections with members of the old Parliamentarian government and knowledge of Irish revolutionaries, Blood could serve as a spy reporting directly to the king. Certainly Blood was adept at spreading rumours, lies and disinformation when it served his own best interests. Whatever the case, Blood quickly became a familiar face around court.

If King Charles had hoped Blood would make an effective spy, it was in vain. With his newfound place at court, Blood's old friends avoided him like the plague and his new associates at court did not think much more highly of him. Although the king seemed to enjoy his company, no one trusted Blood and despite his charm he managed to alienate first one and then another of the royal courtiers. On 10 May 1672, only one year after the incident at the Tower, the famous diarist John Evelyn attended a dinner where Blood was present. His comments make clear the court's general reaction to having this notorious villain in their midst:

> Dined at Mr. Treasurer's house where [I] dined [with] Monsieur de Gramont and several French noblemen, and one Blood, that impudent bold fellow who had not long before attempted to steal the imperial crown itself out of the Tower. How came he to be pardoned, and even received into favour, not only after this but several other bold exploits almost as daring . . . I could never understand. . . . the only treason of this sort that was ever pardoned. The man had not only a daring, but a villainous unmerciful look, a false countenance, but very well spoken and insinuating.

For more than seven years, Blood wavered between being in and out of favour. He would insult someone, or be caught involving himself in some unsavoury plot, and be banished from court. Eventually, he would worm his way back into someone's good graces and be called back. Finally, almost inevitably, he went too far. When he insulted the Duke of Buckingham, the man unintentionally responsible for bringing him to the king's attention, he was sued in open court for libel and ended up in prison. Blood did eventually pay his fine and get out of jail, but his health had been broken in the confines of the dark, damp cell and he was never again welcome at court.

On 24 August 1680, Thomas Blood, sometimes Colonel, sometimes Reverend, sometimes courtier, sometimes revolutionary, but always criminal, died at the age of sixty-two, and was buried in the churchyard at Tothill Fields. But even now, he could not rest. Blood's reputation was so well known among the local villagers that no sooner had the lid been nailed on the coffin than rumours began to spread. He was not dead – the coffin was empty; it was another of his tasteless jokes; there was someone else in the wooden box beneath the sod of the churchyard; it was all a part of one of Blood's bizarre schemes to disappear so that he could carry out some wild plan under an assumed name. Conflicting stories flew so thick and fast that only nine days after the funeral, the local coroner ordered the body exhumed. The rumours were wrong. The grave was one tight spot that even the notorious Colonel Blood could not wriggle out of.

If anything good came of the wasted life of Thomas Blood, it was that security surrounding the Crown Jewels was stepped up. And although they remain in the Tower of London to this day, no one has ever again come so close to pulling off a successful royal heist.

Talbot Edwards lived for more than two years after the brutal attack at the Martin Tower, but never fully recovered from his wounds. His daughter Elizabeth, for whose future Talbot was so concerned, eventually married a Major Beckman, the same Captain Beckman who had been promoted as a result of his daring capture of Colonel Thomas Blood.

Eleven

THE BLOODY ASSIZES

The Duke of Monmouth and Judge Jeffreys
1685–6

Most people are familiar with the saying, 'Power corrupts and absolute power corrupts absolutely.' But sometimes, even constitutionally controlled power can get out of control if a few evil people conspire to subvert the course of justice. When King Charles II died without a legitimate heir in 1685 the struggle for his throne very nearly sparked off another civil war and brought the course of British justice to its knees.

Once the grim, austere, puritanical rule of Oliver Cromwell ended in 1659, the restoration of the monarchy under Charles II must have seemed like a breath of fresh air for the people of England. After ten years without a king, the Stuarts were back on the throne and although, inwardly, King Charles's court was riddled with intrigue aimed at restoring a Catholic monarch, and court life was notoriously debauched, outwardly the realm was peaceful and relatively well ordered. But for all his philandering, a string of mistresses and thirteen illegitimate children, King Charles and his wife failed to produce an heir. Consequently, only two men held any substantial claim to the throne: Charles's brother James, Duke of York, and his eldest illegitimate son, James Scott, Duke of Monmouth.

The king's brother had never been popular, nor does it seem that he made much of an attempt to curry favour in high places. He was secretive, cruel, cowardly and mildly paranoid, in part because he knew his Catholic faith was unpopular among the people, the court, and the Whig-led parliament. To make matters worse, James habitually wore an expression that made people think he had just smelled something nasty. As early as 1697 the largely anti-royalist Whig party attempted to have James removed from the official line of succession, but without ever explaining his reasons King Charles adamantly refused to consider the request.

In stark contrast to his uncle, the king's eldest son, the illegitimate James, Duke of Monmouth, was a young man with a quick wit, an easy smile and just enough arrogance to make him appear completely self-assured. To add to these impressive attributes, Monmouth was, by the standards of the day, very handsome. Small wonder he was popular among the noble classes as well as with members of parliament and the common people – an achievement to be envied by the politically ambitious of any period. But his biggest attraction at court and in parliament was probably not his personal charm, rather it was his status as the Protestant who stood the strongest chance of preventing the throne from reverting to his staunchly Catholic uncle James. Repeatedly, Protestant leaders and members of both political parties tried to convince the king to legitimise his natural son and name him successor to the throne. But just as Charles would not rule out the possibility of his brother assuming the throne, neither would he consent to name his son as legitimate heir.

The Duke of Monmouth's mother was Lucy Walters, a former mistress of Charles II, who had turned to prostitution after the king had tired of her. Despite his neglect of Lucy, Charles saw to it that his eldest son was well cared for. When young James reached the age of thirteen, his father called him to court – a move which should have provided him with the benefits of a fine education and a chance to learn the graces of a courtier. Unfortunately, Monmouth's education turned out to be a bit more comprehensive than it should have been. Charles placed the boy in the care of his latest paramour, Lady Castlemaine, who exposed him to the worst influences of a morally and sexually debauched court. With his natural charm and wit Monmouth quickly became the darling of the court and developed some serious deficiencies of character that were bound to bubble to the surface sooner or later. Even Samuel Pepys, First Lord of the Admiralty and noted diarist, referred to him as 'profligate' – strong words for the time.

Within three years of coming to court, King Charles officially acknowledged the young duke as his son, and arranged a marriage with Anne Scott, Countess of Buccleuch and the wealthiest heiress in Scotland. Following the marriage, James officially adopted his wife's surname, becoming James Scott, Duke of Monmouth. Advancing himself through the political and social ranks of his father's court with astonishing speed, at the tender age of twenty Monmouth was appointed captain-general of all the king's forces, both regular army and cavalry. Amazingly for one so young, he seems to have acquitted himself well. He was admired by common soldiers and senior officers alike and judged to be a fearless and clever commander, who always led from the front. Tragically, the young duke seems not to have been quite as bright as he was charming and bold.

When threats of anti-Catholic riots rumbled across England in 1680, King Charles decided it would be best if his brother James, Duke of York, left the country for his own protection. The wily James agreed but insisted that Monmouth should leave as well. Finally, Charles acquiesced, ordering his son to the court of his Protestant sister Mary and her husband (and cousin) William of Orange, ruler of Holland. Monmouth went as ordered, but in less than two months he returned, uninvited, to England. The king was furious, insisting that the thirty-year-old duke leave the country at once. Monmouth refused. Finally, the two compromised. Monmouth would stay away from court and out of the limelight until he was called for.

So he left court, but he hardly remained out of the public eye. For months Monmouth and some of his closest supporters toured the country on what can only be called an 'image-building' campaign, where his startling good looks and charm won him thousands of ardent fans and supporters. When his father demanded he return to London, a violent argument broke out between the two, which ended with the king stripping his son of his titles. Monmouth insisted it had not been his fault, that he had been led astray by followers who wanted to see him on the throne. It was a poor excuse but Charles believed it (as fathers are wont to do). He forgave his son but ordered the arrest and execution of some of Monmouth's closest followers. The Duke of Monmouth had sent his friends to the block to disguise his own ambition and save his titles.

As part of the reconciliation, Charles insisted that to avoid a conflict with the succession and quell any lingering rumours as to the exact nature of the ill-conceived publicity tour, Monmouth return to the court of the Netherlands and stay there until he was called for. This time, the 35-year-old Monmouth obeyed his father.

Separated by the English Channel, relations between Charles and Monmouth seem to have improved greatly over the next few months. It is even possible that, in time, Charles might have made his son heir to the throne. Unfortunately, on 6 February 1685, just over a year after Monmouth left England, King Charles suffered a stroke and died. When news of his death reached the Netherlands, Monmouth was overcome with grief. His aunt, Queen Mary, reported that he went to his bedroom and mourned so piteously that those in nearby rooms could hear him weeping. Meanwhile, Monmouth's uncle James (Duke of York) hurried to London to claim the throne as King James II.

For all the strange and convoluted plots to return a Catholic to the throne of England, it must have come as a surprise to nearly everyone when James ascended the throne with complete legitimacy. Even less expected was the fury with which he set about ousting Protestants from high office and replacing them with Catholics. As though attempting to make himself unpopular, the new king openly encouraged foreign Catholics and English Catholics in exile to move to England. To Catholics foreign and domestic he handed out important civil and military positions more on the basis of their religious beliefs than on any real qualifications. The move was unprecedented, unconscionable and of highly suspect legality. James had not even had his coronation and he was turning his kingdom on its head. Within weeks of taking the throne, nobles and parliament alike were looking for a way to replace the new king.

Meanwhile, back in the Netherlands, King William and Queen Mary feared their nephew would become a target for his uncle's religious pogroms. His presence at their court might even spark an open war between Holland and England. Consequently, no matter how genuinely fond of him they were, they told Monmouth he had to leave. Seeking advice from his friends and supporters, Monmouth finally came to the conclusion that his best course of action was to go to England, rally his old followers and friends from his time as captain-general of the army, and drive James from the throne. But like so many good plans, Monmouth was plagued by lack of funds. The most he could raise was £9,000, hardly enough to man and equip a mighty insurrection.

On the evening of 11 June 1685, three ships sailed into the English port of Lyme; on board were a mere eighty-three soldiers and a few horses. It was such a strange sight that it drew crowds of spectators. Only when they saw the Duke of Monmouth being rowed to shore did their silent stares turn to cheers and their numbers swell to thousands. People flocked to see him and hear him speak. At Lyme and Taunton he openly claimed that his uncle, whom he referred to as the Duke of York rather than James II, had constantly plotted against the Protestant religion and finally poisoned the king in order to take the throne. In short order Monmouth had attracted more than two thousand soldiers and nearly eight thousand civilian followers. All were anxious to take on the king's army and put their hero on the throne.

Obviously, Monmouth believed that far greater numbers of soldiers would soon desert the crown and take up his banner; but people are fickle, and a known terror is always preferable to an unknown terror. The anticipated wave of followers and trained soldiers never appeared and those already with him slowly ebbed away through desertion and losses in a string of minor skirmishes with King James's troops. By the time Monmouth's army clashed with the royal forces at Sedgemoor on 5 July 1685, he had no more than seven thousand followers, more than five thousand of them untrained civilians.

Despite putting up a brave fight, Monmouth and his troops were no match for the king's army. Within hours the rebels were routed, arrested, or killed. Monmouth himself had remained with the cavalry as long as possible, but in the end was forced to flee the field. At around 7 on the second morning after the battle, a detachment of soldiers discovered the Duke of Monmouth hiding in a ditch disguised in the smock of a common shepherd. As he huddled there, the captain read the arrest warrant: 'James Duke of Monmouth . . . for High Treason in levying war against the King and assuming title to the Crown . . .'

If the outcome of Monmouth's ill-fated coup is no great surprise, we are left with this question: if no one in the government supported the new king, who did he find to issue the arrest warrant for his nephew and force the bill through parliament? Obviously, even before coming to the throne James knew just how unpopular he was and how desperately he would need powerful support to prop up the questionable legality of his radical programmes. He also needed someone in a position of adequate power to keep the populace and parliament in line. The 'someone' who could do all these things was the barbarically cruel George Jeffreys, Lord Chief Justice of England.

Jeffreys' early years had hardly been promising. He had spent most of his time at Cambridge's law school drinking in local taverns where he bought endless rounds of drinks for the best and most influential of his classmates, amusing them with crude jokes and bawdy songs. Eventually, despite his feeble knowledge of the law and failure to complete his degree, his powerful classmates saw to it that Jeffreys was admitted to the Bar. By the time he took his place there in 1668, Jeffreys was either perpetually drunk, in a rage, or both, though it has to be admitted that his constant drinking was partly to relieve the pain of bladder stones that would only grow worse with the passing years. Taller than average, with a heavily pock-marked face and piercing eyes set beneath massive, bushy eyebrows, Jeffreys' furious temper and razor sharp invective made him a master of scathing cross-examination, often reducing witnesses to tears in a matter of minutes by giving them what he called 'a lick with the rough side of his tongue'. In court, Jeffreys harangued juries, twisted the rules and raged at defendants and witnesses whose testimony did not suit him.

Thanks to his peculiar talents, Jeffreys quickly made a name for himself and rose to national prominence towards the end of Charles II's reign. Despite Jeffreys' notoriety, King Charles never trusted him, saying that he had 'no learning, no sense, no manners and more impudence than ten whores'. But Jeffreys served the crown doggedly both to please the king and the Bar and, most importantly, to advance himself. Eventually Charles bowed to pressure from the Bar and allowed Jeffreys to be made Lord Chief Justice of England in 1683. Long before attaining the highest legal post in the land Jeffreys had been busy making enemies in parliament by impeding the implementation of one law after another, and even attempting to prevent parliament from coming into session. As early as November 1680 parliament had passed a resolution stating, in part: 'Sir George Jeffreys, by traducing and obstructing . . . the sitting of Parliament . . . [so] that the king should be requested to remove him out of all public office.'

Once effectively in control of the British legal system, Jeffreys instituted a reign of terror the likes of which had not been seen since the rule of Bishop Bonner under Queen Mary Tudor well over a century earlier. Even members of the nobility went to the block without the benefit of a proper trial. In June 1684, he condemned Sir Thomas Armstrong to the block for treason with no trial whatsoever. When Armstrong demanded a trial to prove his innocence, Jeffreys snapped: 'That you shall have, by the Grace of God.' Then turning to the bailiff, said: 'See that execution be done on next Friday.'

When James became king in March 1685 he undoubtedly recognised a kindred spirit in the vicious Judge Jeffreys and immediately gave him a seat in the House of Lords, making him the first Chief Justice since the thirteenth century to be so honoured and blatantly integrating the power of the judiciary with that of Parliament. With this new honour, Jeffreys' power and access to the king surpassed that of both the Corporation of London and the Lord Mayor, making him the virtual dictator of the capital. Now, anyone who voiced even the mildest criticism of the new Catholic regime would answer to Jeffreys and his production-line justice. In September of the same year, King James appointed him Lord Chancellor, giving him control of the nation's treasury.

To instil a proper sense of terror in defendants and witnesses alike, Jeffreys hung the walls of his court with scarlet tapestries. At his bench there was only one acceptable plea to any charge – guilty. Anything else was a waste of the court's precious time. At criminal trials, there was only one verdict – guilty, and one sentence – execution. Defendants appearing before him were routinely sentenced to death without being allowed to present a defence and sent to their execution without being given time to meet a clergyman, make confession or even say their prayers.

Throughout the country fear and panic rose to a fever pitch as people began to fear a return to the public puritanical witch trials of the Commonwealth. Obligingly, Jeffreys did everything he could to confirm their fears. When the Duke of Monmouth attempted to wrest control of the country from King James, it was Judge George Jeffreys who signed the arrest warrant and forced it through parliament. It was a perfect opportunity to prove once and for all the effectiveness of justice under King James II.

After Monmouth's arrest he was taken to London and locked in the Tower where his wife and three children were waiting for him, having been arrested four days earlier, on 9 July. At his arraignment, Jeffreys informed Monmouth that having attempted to seize the crown negated his right to a trial; his execution would take place in two days. Monmouth begged his uncle for an audience and, amazingly, James agreed. It was a shameful affair. Monmouth attempted to blame the entire rising on those around him, saying, 'my misfortune was such as to meet with some horrid people that made me believe things of your Majesty, and gave me so many false arguments that I was fully led to believe it was a shame and a sin before God not to do it.' He added that if his life were spared he would show James 'how zealous I shall ever be in your service'. He even offered to convert to Catholicism. For all his own cruelty, the king was disgusted by this display of cowardice. The execution would take place in two days' time.

At 10 a.m. on 15 July 1685, an armed guard escorted the Duke of Monmouth from the Tower to Tower Hill where he was to mount a scaffold draped in black bunting especially for the occasion. Along the route, more than three thousand of the young duke's supporters had gathered to witness the grisly spectacle. So fearful was the king of an attempt to rescue his nephew that he had ordered the guard to shoot Monmouth dead if there were any disturbances in the crowd before the execution was complete. For a man about to die, the duke's manner was unnervingly calm and composed. When the

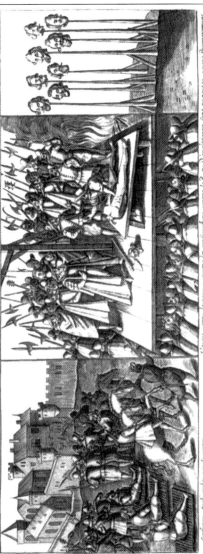

Broadsheet of the Gunpowder Plot showing eight of the thirteen conspirators: missing are Digby, Grant, Keyes, Rookwood and Tresham. (*Bodleian Library, Oxford*)

Divine Discovery, an artistic interpretation of Guy Fawkes entering Parliament, drawn in 1605. (*Ashmolean Museum, Oxford*)

Portrait of Colonel Thomas Blood taken from a near contemporary account of his life. (*Authors' collection*)

The arrest of Judge Jeffreys at Wapping while attempting to escape disguised as a common sailor, December 1688. The words coming out of Jeffreys' mouth read, 'Tear me to pecces'. (*The Mansell Collection*)

A Dutch broadsheet depicting the execution of the Duke of Monmouth. (*Authors' collection*)

The escape of Lord Nithsdale from the Tower, 1716 (engraving by F. Fraenkel from the picture by E.M. Osborn). (*Authors' collection*)

An eighteenth-century engraving of Henry 'Tower' Laurens, the only American citizen to have been imprisoned in the Tower. (*Authors' collection*)

Roger Casement, 1916.

Sir Roger Casement in court, 16 May 1916. (*Daily Mirror Picture Library*)

Photograph of Josef Jacobs taken
shortly before his execution.
(*The National Archives*)

The makeshift shooting range which served as the site of execution for Josef Jacobs in the
Second World War. (*The National Archives*)

entourage mounted the scaffold, the two bishops who accompanied the condemned man began a prayer. Although Monmouth dutifully repeated their words, he refused to pray for the salvation of the king, only muttering 'amen' when they had finished. In a break with established custom, he refused to make a final speech, handing a prepared statement to one of the bishops to read to the crowd. As he approached the block, he also refused the customary blindfold.

Before kneeling to place his head on the block, Monmouth calmly bent down and pulled the executioner's axe from under a pile of straw. Lifting it up, he ran his finger along the edge and turned to the headsman, the notorious Jack Ketch, asking if he thought it was sharp enough to do the job properly. Staring at his victim with disbelief, Ketch was even more astonished when Monmouth handed him the exorbitant sum of 6 guineas, saying: 'Pray, do your business well. Do not serve me as you did my Lord Russell. I have heard you struck him four or five times; if you strike me twice, I cannot promise you not to stir.' He then turned to one of his servants and told him that if Ketch did a clean job he was to receive 6 more guineas. With that, he knelt down and placed his head on the block.

Ketch, unnerved by Monmouth's calmness and casual attitude, completely bungled the job. When the first blow only grazed the back of the duke's head, he turned his blood-covered face upward, staring directly into Ketch's eyes. Two more blows had still not finished the horrid job and in anger and frustration Ketch threw down the axe, declaring that he would pay 40 guineas to anyone in the angry crowd who could do the job better. It was only when the Sheriff of Middlesex, who was standing on the platform, demanded that Ketch finish his job or be killed on the spot, that he retrieved the axe and struck another ill-aimed blow. According to an eyewitness, 'the butcherly dog did so barbarously act his part that he could not, at five strokes sever the head from the body'. Finally, in exasperation, Ketch used his belt knife to sever the duke's head from his body and put the condemned man out of his misery.

By now, the crowd's anger had turned to fury. Their young hero had been butchered like a hog. Pushing and shoving their way past the ring of guards, they stormed the scaffold, dragging Jack Ketch to the ground, threatening to tear him limb from limb. Before the guards could control the situation and rescue the executioner, dozens of people had dipped their handkerchiefs in Monmouth's blood as though he were a holy martyr to the Protestant cause. To make the already grotesque situation even worse, Monmouth's family now realised that the duke had never had his portrait painted. After retrieving the body, they had the head sewn back on the stump and propped up long enough for an artist's rendering to be made. Only then was the body returned to the Tower for burial in the chapel of St Peter ad Vincula.

Undoubtedly the anger of the crowd and the horrible scene at the execution led King James to fear a general insurrection even more than he had before. In council with his enforcer, Judge Jeffreys, the king decided to make an example of Monmouth's followers and put the fear of God into anyone else who might contemplate driving him from the throne. If the job could be done effectively enough, it might even enable him to disband parliament and re-establish an absolute monarchy. The plan so appealed to James that he promptly ordered the Royal Mint to strike a medal celebrating his nephew's execution.

Even before Monmouth's execution, George Jeffreys had begun working hard to rout out Monmouth's supporters and everyone however remotely associated with them. Even by the harsh standards of the seventeenth century, he fulfilled his task beyond all limits of sanity, and did so with ghoulish delight. The next assize (the name given to any particular, periodic session of court) would be dedicated entirely to the trials of Monmouth supporters.

Conducting his proceedings with such blatant disregard for legal procedure that they became known as the 'Bloody Assizes', Jeffreys condemned three hundred and twenty men to execution and sentenced another eight hundred and forty-one to be sent to the West Indies where they would be sold as slaves. Even a group of schoolgirls who had once handed Monmouth bouquets of flowers were sentenced to a near lethal flogging. The trials were conducted like some nightmarish production line, with the first hundred victims having been put to death within a week of the uprising's collapse. To make all this effort worth his while, Jeffreys extorted a small fortune from the families of his victims with false promises of leniency. On many occasions he claimed the entire estate of his victims for himself even before they had been sent to the block or the gallows. By the end of the Bloody Assizes, Jeffreys boasted that he had sentenced more men to execution than all his predecessors combined since the Norman Conquest.

While the Bloody Assizes held England in terror, the king delighted in following Jeffreys' adventures in court; insisting that he write a brief account of each day's proceedings and have them couriered to the palace so that James could use them to entertain his dinner guests. Thanks to his ruthless administration of the 'law', Jeffreys gathered quite a list of honours: to his existing titles of Lord Chief Justice of England and Lord Chancellor were now added Member of the Privy Council and Baron Jeffreys of Wem.

Obviously, all this did not go unnoticed in high places. When a member of the House of Lords spoke out against Jeffreys' blatant disregard for the law and the king's support for his methods, he was rewarded by having a corpse chained to the front gate of his house. By the beginning of 1687 objections to the king's and Jeffreys' medieval tactics had risen to the level of political uproar. Without hesitation the king addressed the charges in the simplest way possible. He dissolved parliament. Not surprisingly, the Lord Chief Justice ruled that his action had been well within the bounds of the law. King James had effectively re-established the absolute monarchy he wanted so badly.

Now ruling virtually by decree, James's rearrangement of the country to suit himself accelerated at an ever faster pace. In the spring of 1688 he appointed a Roman Catholic as President of Oxford University; and when the Archbishop of Canterbury and six other bishops protested at the move, he had them arrested and sent to the Tower. As the barge carrying the prisoners of faith moved slowly up the Thames, the riverbanks were crowded with cheering, seething masses of Londoners. When the bishops were marched up the steps at Traitors' Gate, even the tower warders knelt in respect. Every day during their incarceration, the banks of the Tower moat were ringed with cheering crowds that refused to leave. The case had aroused so much public indignation that the king and Judge Jeffreys had no choice but to set aside their usual summary justice and arrange for a jury trial.

The trial of the seven bishops lasted only one day, but to the surprise of the king and the judge, the jury's deliberations went on all night. The next morning, 30 June, the jurors delivered the unanimous verdict of 'not guilty'. To the frustration of king and judge, the bishops were released. Now that someone had found the courage to stand up to the dreaded judge and the tyrannical king, a few members of the dissolved parliament also seemed to rediscover their manhood. Within hours of the bishops' release, a group of Lords drafted a letter to James's daughter and her husband, Queen Mary and King William of the Netherlands, with the unprecedented request to mount an army and invade England with the express purpose of driving the king from the throne.

Obviously it did not take as long for word of this potential disaster to reach King James as it did for King William to reach his decision. Despite frantic attempts at political back-pedalling and trying desperately to make some sort of weak amends for more than two years of tyranny, no one seemed to be in the mood for an apology. On 5 November 1688, William of Orange landed with his army at Torbay and within hours all hint of support for King James had vanished. The army deserted in swarms to join William and spontaneous uprisings in support of 'Dutch William' broke out all over the country. Even James's younger daughter Anne (later Queen Anne) deserted her father and sided with her sister and brother-in-law. Five weeks later, on 11 December, James gathered a few possessions in a small chest, put on the clothes of a servant and rowed down the Thames to catch a boat to the continent where he would spend the rest of his life as an exile at the court of Louis XIV of France. In a last act of petty defiance, as he rowed away from London, King James II tossed the Great Seal into the water, knowing that without it parliament could not legally enact emergency measures into law.

With his protector gone, there was nothing left for the hated Judge Jeffreys to do but flee for his life. The day after the king fled London, Jeffreys disguised himself as a common sailor and trimmed his massive eyebrows to alter his face. Next, he hired a cart into which he loaded several small chests and headed through London towards the docks at Wapping where he had arranged passage to the continent aboard a coal barge scheduled to sail on the morning tide. Dragging his chests aboard the barge, Jeffreys settled himself out of sight to wait till morning. But George Jeffreys was an alcoholic and it was only a matter of hours before his rampant thirst and shattered nerves got the better of him. Creeping silently from the barge, he stole up Wapping steps and headed directly to the nearby Red Crow Tavern.

Seated alone at a corner table, the judge attempted to drink himself into a stupor, but was interrupted by a well-dressed young man who approached him and asked if he was Judge Jeffreys. Keeping his face in the shadows, Jeffreys mumbled that he didn't know what the man was talking about. But the man did know. He was a copy clerk who had once been hauled before Jeffreys' bench and received a 'lick from the rough side of the judge's tongue'. There was no doubt this was the same man. In seconds, everyone in the tavern had started shouting and throwing food and beer at Jeffreys who scurried into a corner in an attempt to keep from being beaten to death or lynched on the spot. Fearing a riot, the landlord sent a runner to fetch the local militia, known as the 'trained bands'.

By the time the militia arrived, a crowd had gathered at the door and joined the drunken chorus of customers hurling beer and invective at the figure cowering in the back corner of the inn. Fighting their way through the mob, the watch dragged Jeffreys through the screaming crowd, grasping and clutching at the most hated man in London. As the judge was pulled and pushed into the street he shouted at the watch: 'Keep them off, gentlemen! For God's sake, keep them off.' While most of the watch remained behind to quiet the seething crowd, the remainder flagged down a passing carriage and pushed George Jeffreys inside, telling the coachman to drive as fast as he could to the home of the Lord Mayor. To protect their prisoner from the rocks and mud being flung into the coach from all sides, one of the soldiers was forced to straddle Jeffreys' body to cover him.

Passing near the house of Sir John Chapman the Lord Mayor was Sir Edmund King, physician to the late King Charles II. In his diary, Sir Edmund wrote, 'I was in Cheapside when the Chancellor was brought to my Lord Mayor. . . . There never was such joy, not a man sorry that we could see. They longed to have him out of the coach, had he not had a good guard.' The guards roused the sleeping Lord Mayor from his bed, insisting they had a prisoner who could not wait till morning. Stumbling, half asleep and in his nightclothes, to his reception hall, the Lord Mayor took one look at the cowering figure of George Jeffreys and instantly suffered a massive coronary. He died a few days later. Before the militia could decide what to do with either Jeffreys or the dying Lord Mayor, the sound of hundreds of screaming voices came floating through the narrow streets. The mob was hot on the trail of George Jeffreys. Frantic not to be turned over to justice even more crude and barbaric than his own, Jeffreys begged the watch to take him somewhere safe; and the only place anyone could think of that might be safe enough was the Tower of London. He even offered to draw up, and sign, his own arrest warrant. The watch happily agreed and bundled him off to the one place in London where Jeffreys was safe from the people and the people were safe from Jeffreys.

Meanwhile, the contingent of the night watch remaining at the Red Crow had searched the boats and barges at the nearby docks. There, on board a coal barge scheduled to sail for the continent, they found what was officially described as: '35,000 gold guineas . . . besides a great amount of silver, which he had set on board . . .'

By morning parliament had received word of the Tower's latest guest. They immediately issued a warrant to the Lieutenant of the Tower, which read, in part: 'We, the peers of this realm . . . do hereby . . . require you to take into your custody . . . George, Lord Jeffreys . . . and to keep him safe prisoner until further order . . .'.

But even the Tower proved insufficient to keep Judge Jeffreys safe from the hatred of the people. Many of those who had been victimised in his court came to jeer and laugh through the bars of his cell door, throwing rotten food and spitting on him. One day when a barrel of oysters arrived at his cell, Jeffreys commented to one of the guards: 'Thank God, I still have some friends left.' But when he opened the cask, it contained only empty oyster shells with a length of rope tied into a noose lying on top. On one occasion, Jeffreys talked to a visiting clergyman about his role in the Bloody Assizes. Like so many men complicit in mass crimes, Jeffreys insisted he was only following orders. But then he added, 'and I have this further to say for myself, that I was not half bloody enough for him that sent me thither.'

In an act that could be seen as either leniency, or simple expediency, parliament allowed Jeffreys to purchase brandy – as much of it as he wanted so long as his money held out. Four months later, on 18 April 1689, the 41-year-old George Jeffreys, once Lord Chief Justice of England and Lord Chancellor, died in an alcoholic stupor from complications brought on by bladder stones.

As Jeffreys had not been convicted of any crime, parliament felt free to offer his body to anyone who wished to claim it for proper burial. There were no takers. Consequently, Jeffreys was interred in the chapel of St Peter ad Vincula within the grounds of the Tower where so many of his victims had found their final rest. In a bizarre and ironic twist of fate, the grave of George Jeffreys lies immediately alongside that of James Scott, Duke of Monmouth.

Twelve

THE KING OVER THE WATER

William and Winifred Maxwell,
Lord and Lady Nithsdale
1715–16

When James Stuart (James II) was driven from the throne in 1688, his successors, William and Mary, and their successor, Queen Anne, were all technically Stuarts, but the royal family itself was pushed further and further from the line of succession. When Queen Anne died in 1714 with no surviving children, parliament had to decide between returning to the direct Stuart lineage – populated with staunch Roman Catholics – and offering the crown to some other, comfortably Protestant relative of the late queen. It seems to have been a fairly unanimous decision. The new king would be Anne's distant cousin George, Elector of Hanover.

Apart from the fact that George couldn't speak a single word of English, his elevation to King of England was generally acceptable, at least among the more progressively minded. Hardcore conservatives and the Scots in general were outraged. Within weeks they raised the banner of James Edward Stuart – exiled son of the late James II – insisting they would drive the German usurper from the throne.

Predictably, the uprising ended unhappily and was of little historical consequence; but it did spawn the most daring and amazing escape attempt in the history of the Tower of London.

Since before the Norman invasion, the Maxwell family had played an important role in Britain's political arena. The earliest recorded member of the family was a Saxon named Undwin who fled to Scotland to escape persecution at the hands of William the Conqueror. Within a century, Undwin's descendants had picked up a Scottish knighthood, and a century after that they had adopted the surname Maxwell and risen to the rank of Chamberlain of Scotland.

From their meteoric rise in society it is reasonable to assume that the Maxwells were a family of outstanding fighters. They fought and died heroically at Falkirk in 1298 and in many other battles before and after. By 1346 the sire of the most honoured branch of the family was granted the title 'Lord' Maxwell, which made him and his descendants the official heads of the Maxwell clan. They were also Lords of Caerlaverock, Pencaitland and Mearns, and kept their family seat at Lochmaben Castle. Enriched with all these lands and titles, the lord of the Maxwell clan became one of the three dozen most powerful men in Scotland. Despite the fact that Sir Herbert Maxwell was even made a lord of the Scottish parliament in 1440, the family seems to have clung to their tradition of fighting at any, and every, opportunity. Sometimes they fought heroically in battle and sometimes they just fought. A son of the 2nd Lord Maxwell was killed by the Lord of Cockpool in a violent argument over a football game and the 9th Lord was beheaded for having murdered the Lord of Johnstone and a litany of other crimes.

In 1545 Lord John Maxwell and his private army of two thousand soldiers held the family castle of Lochmaben against an entire English army while the English held his father and brother prisoners. The argument seems to have centred around the Maxwells' support for Mary Stuart, Queen of Scots. It was a stand that made them few friends at the English court, but Mary granted them the additional title Lords of Herries.

When Mary Queen of Scots' son, James VI, inherited the English throne in 1603 and became James I of England, the Maxwell fortune seemed secure. They even picked up a new title, Earls of Nithsdale. By the time the Stuart line was replaced by the House of Hanover in 1714, the Maxwells' day in the sun appeared to be over, but the new head of the Maxwell clan, William Maxwell, 5th Earl of Nithsdale, didn't seem to mind. The formerly violent Maxwell clan had settled into the refined life of the country gentry and fighting was seen as a thing of the past.

William Maxwell was born in 1676 at the family seat of Terregles in Dumfriesshire and inherited his titles at the tender age of seven on the death of his father. His mother raised him to be a devout Catholic and a loyal servant to the Stuart monarchy. In his early twenties, the young Lord Nithsdale travelled to France to swear his loyalty to the now exiled King James II. While there he met Lady Winifred Herbert, daughter of the Marquess of Powys, who had followed King James into exile in 1688. William Maxwell and Winifred Herbert fell in love and were married on 2 March

1699. A few months later, they returned to Terregles, Scotland, to take up the duties of lord of the manor. Their story would have probably ended there except for the fact that in 1715, after the couple had enjoyed sixteen years of quiet married life, George I was offered the British throne.

In September of that year, a group of powerful Scottish lords began plotting to overthrow King George and replace him with the exiled heir to the throne, James Edward Stuart – son of the now deceased James II – known to the Scots as 'The King Over the Water' and to the English as 'The Old Pretender'.

The rebels called themselves 'Jacobites' after the latinised form of James, the Christian name of nearly all males in the royal Stuart line. The most noble and powerful men in Scotland joined the cause, applying ever-increasing pressure on their peers to join them. William Maxwell could hardly refuse the call; he had, after all, personally sworn to uphold the Stuarts in front of King James II. With the Maxwells on board, the lords raised their army and sent word to James Edward Stuart to come to Scotland in anticipation of assuming his throne.

The rebellion of 1715, or 'The 15' as the Scots called it, never really got off the ground. The rebels fought a few half-hearted engagements but by the time James Stuart arrived in December the entire enterprise had collapsed. Among the hundreds of prisoners rounded up by the English was William Maxwell. He had been captured at the Battle of Preston and, along with other noblemen and high-ranking officers, taken to London and thrown into the Tower.

Neither King George nor parliament wanted to instigate a pogrom against the Scots. Parliament wanted to keep relations with England's northern neighbours on an even keel and King George was anxious not to get off on the wrong foot with his new subjects. The vast majority of the captured Scottish prisoners received a blanket reprieve and were released to return home. But to satisfy the law, someone had to be held accountable for the rebellion. In the end, only the seven most powerful leaders of the uprising were held for trial. Among these seven was William Maxwell. It was only a few days before Christmas, 1715, when Winifred Maxwell received news that her husband had been captured at Preston and taken to London as a prisoner of the crown. She was understandably frantic, and could hardly bear to sit placidly for word of what would become of Lord Maxwell. It was important that whatever she did, Winifred secured the family titles and estates for her son. William Maxwell had already made arrangements for their son to inherit the family lands and titles three years earlier and it was now Winifred's job to ensure that inheritance. After telling her maid to pack the absolute minimum necessary travelling clothes for both of them, Winifred hid the family papers in the walls of her house.

The winter of 1715–16 was one of the worst in living memory. Heavy snows had left the roads in and around Dumfriesshire impassable and it was impossible to travel in the family carriage. Undaunted, Winifred and her maid saddled two of their best horses and set off through howling winds and deep snow towards Newcastle on the English side of the border. Once there, it might be possible to take the stagecoach to London, but London was more than 400 miles away. On Christmas Day, Lady Maxwell and her maid took rooms at an inn just north of Newcastle. There, she wrote a letter to her sister describing the first leg of their desperate journey. 'Such a journey, I believe was scarce ever made, considering the weather, but with God's help, an earnest desire achieves a great deal.'

From Newcastle, the women boarded the stagecoach for York nearly 100 miles to the south-east. From there, they should have been able to catch the mail coach that would take them all the way south to London. But again, howling winds and heavy snow had closed in, blocking the roads south of York. Terrified that she would be too late to intercede with parliament on her husband's behalf, Winifred Maxwell purchased two horses and again set off with her maid through bone-chilling weather on a frantic 250-mile ride. In total, it took the women fifteen arduous days to make their way from Scotland to London.

Once in London, Lady Maxwell took rooms with a Mrs Mills, a woman known to be among the many Londoners who were sympathetic to the Scottish rebels. Having settled in and visited her husband in his cell at the Lieutenant's Lodgings at the Tower, she began preparing an appeal to the House of Lords on Lord Maxwell's behalf. Tragically, her plea came too late. The rebels were scheduled to go to trial within days and the machinery of justice, once set in motion, could not be stopped. Increasingly anxious and distraught, Winifred visited her husband in the Tower almost continually and waited nervously for the verdict. When it came, it was what everyone had feared. Although one of the seven defendants was found innocent and released, the remaining six, including Lord Maxwell, were found guilty of inciting rebellion and condemned to the block.

Thanks to the pleas of Lady Maxwell and others like her, the House of Commons nearly granted a pardon to the condemned men, but the bill failed to pass by seven votes. In an attempt to calm both sides in the now all-too-public debate over the fate of the Scottish rebels, King George granted a royal pardon to three of the men but the remaining three were left to satisfy the demands of the law. Tragically for the Maxwells, William's name was not on the list of those being pardoned. He, along with the Earl of Derwentwater and Viscount Kenmore, was to go to the block on 24 February – now less than three weeks away. Refusing to believe that nothing could be done to save her husband, Lady Maxwell decided to go to the king personally, present her case and give him a copy of the written petition she had previously submitted to parliament. The king had already freed three of the six condemned men; surely he would release her husband.

Dressing in servant's clothes, Winifred Maxwell managed to inveigle her way through the back door of St James's Palace. Then, pretending to be dusting the furniture, she moved from one room to another until she found the king. He was alone in a small anteroom just off one of the palace's main drawing rooms. According to her own account of the event, written some years later, 'I threw myself at his feet and told him in French [since King George spoke no English] that I was the unfortunate Countess of Nithsdale . . . but seeing that he wanted to go off without taking my petition, I caught hold of the skirt of his coat, that he might stop and hear me. He endeavoured to escape out of my hands, but I kept such a strong hold, that he dragged me on my knees, from the middle of the room to the very door of the drawing room. At last one of the [servants] who attended his Majesty took me round the waist, while another wrestled the coat from my hands. The petition which I had endeavoured to thrust into his pocket fell to the ground in the scuffle, and I almost fainted away from grief and disappointment.'

Having exhausted every conceivable tactic to free her husband, Winifred Maxwell was devastated; worse, she had to tell her husband that all her efforts had failed. Stoically, Lord Maxwell prepared himself for death. As all condemned men were entitled to address the crowds which inevitably gathered to gawk at the grisly spectacle of public executions, Maxwell spent his last days preparing his 'Dying Speech' and wrote letters to his relatives in Scotland pleading with them to ensure that his money, land and titles were not revoked by the crown, but were duly passed on to his son. He also asked them to take care of his beloved Winifred who had tried so hard to free him. He wrote 'There cannot be enough said in her praise. Everyone admires her, everyone applauds her and extols her for the proofs she has given me of her love.'

If Lord William Maxwell, 5th Earl of Nithsdale, had come to accept his fate, his wife had done no such thing. With a courage born of desperation, Winifred Maxwell became more determined than ever to save her husband; this time, however, she would simply have to take a more direct approach. As the days and hours ticked away a plan began to take shape in her mind. It would require at least two accomplices, some rather unfashionable clothes, her cosmetics and a bottle of the best French cognac.

After taking her maid into her confidence, Lady Maxwell sent her out to purchase five nearly identical and completely nondescript hooded cloaks. She then arranged to dine with her landlady, Mrs Mills, and a mutual friend, Mrs Morgan. Over dinner, she laid out her plan. It sounded so impossible to the women that they must have thought she was either joking or had completely lost her wits with grief; but Winifred insisted she was completely serious. There was no doubt it would be dangerous and if they were discovered they would surely go to prison. Now, would they help her save her husband's life? Finally after much cajoling and pleading, they both agreed.

On 23 February, the afternoon before the scheduled executions, Lady Maxwell ordered a coach to carry her and her three accomplices to the Tower. As they dressed for their visit, Mrs Morgan, the tallest and slimmest of the women, put on two gowns, one over the top of the other, and then donned two identical brown cloaks. Mrs Mills, Lady Maxwell and her maid each dressed and put on their own cloaks. Lady Maxwell also carried her cosmetics bag and the bottle of cognac. When they arrived at the Tower it was already late in the afternoon and dusk was settling over London. In only a few hours the gates of the Tower would be locked.

Fortunately, the condemned men were being held in the Lieutenant's Lodgings, which were situated near the main gate and the massive drawbridge that would be closed after all the visitors had left. Together, the four women left the carriage outside the gate and walked to the Lieutenant's Lodgings. When Mrs Mills, Mrs Morgan and Lady Maxwell went inside, her maid waited in the cold, snowy yard.

In the wake of the rebellion, regular soldiers specifically assigned to keep a close watch on the condemned men had augmented the normal complement of Tower warders. The troops were garrisoned inside the Lieutenant's Lodgings so they were never far from the prisoners. But, as Lady Maxwell had observed on her many previous visits, the guards spent most of their time in the wardroom with their wives and girlfriends, leaving the prisoners' day-today needs to the servants. There was also an almost continual coming and going of grieving friends and relatives. The guards' constant preoccupation with their ladies and the visitors would be Winifred Maxwell's greatest ally.

When the women reported to the wardroom, Lady Maxwell swept in as though she was entering a grand ball, and happily – nearly hysterically – announced that parliament had agreed to hear a last-minute appeal on behalf of her husband. With that, she produced the bottle of cognac and invited the guards to toast her good fortune and the benevolence of parliament and the king. With half of the condemned men already having been pardoned, it was a plausible enough lie. The guards were happy to share in a drink, but they told the countess that because of the heightened security only two visitors would be allowed into a prisoner's cell at a time. The women would have to take turns visiting the earl. Lady Maxwell insisted it would be no problem since in the morning her husband would be a free man and they could spend all the time together that they wanted. The guards undoubtedly noticed how nervous and flustered Lady Maxwell's friends were. The one introduced to them as Mrs Mills seemed to spend most of her time with her face buried in her handkerchief weeping. But under the strained circumstances, it would hardly have seemed unusual.

The first to be shown upstairs to Lord Maxwell's cell were Lady Maxwell and Mrs Morgan. Once they were ushered inside, the guard quickly returned to the wardroom and the rapidly diminishing bottle of cognac. As Winifred Maxwell hurriedly explained her plan to her incredulous husband, Mrs Morgan began removing her clothing. First one cloak, then another and finally the outermost of her two gowns. If the Earl of Nithsdale baulked at the flurry of instructions and strange goings-on, his wife insisted there was no time for explanations and this was not nearly as undignified as kneeling in front of a jeering crowd who were waiting to see his head roll across a scaffold. She would explain everything later. Right now, he had to take off his clothes and put on Mrs Morgan's extra dress.

As Maxwell numbly did as he was told, his wife led Mrs Morgan back down to the wardroom, where she loudly instructed her to run as quickly as she could and tell her maid to come and help her dress for her meeting with parliament. As Mrs Morgan left, Lady Maxwell escorted the still weeping Mrs Mills up to her husband's cell, constantly reassuring her that everything would be all right, that Lord Maxwell was sure to be released. They arrived just in time to help the now thoroughly flustered man lace up his gown. With the dress in place, Lady Maxwell began applying enough heavy make-up to conceal his thick eyebrows and week-old growth of beard. Finally, she replaced his white periwig with another wig that matched Mrs Mills' bright red hair.

She now escorted Mrs Mills back downstairs, through the wardroom and towards the door, telling her to 'Send my maid with all haste, for if I can not press my petition tonight, I am undone; tomorrow will be too late. Hasten her as much as possible, for I shall be on thorns till she comes.' Only minutes after Mrs Mills left, Mrs Morgan re-entered the building, ran through the wardroom and up to Lord Maxwell's cell. By this time, so many hysterical women had run back and forth between the wardroom and the cell that the guards had completely lost track of who had come in and who had gone out. Liberal doses of cognac had no doubt helped take the edge off their senses.

When Mrs Morgan arrived at Maxwell's cell, the transformation was complete. Dressed in women's clothes and with his head covered with the hooded cloak, Lord Maxwell may have looked embarrassed, but at least he looked completely unlike himself. Lady Maxwell now handed her husband her handkerchief and told him to hold it to his face and weep as loudly as he could. Leaving Mrs Morgan alone in the cell to talk loudly to herself, Lady Maxwell led her weeping husband out of his cell where, by her own account, 'The guards opened the door and I went downstairs with him still conjuring him to make all possible dispatch [to fetch my maid]. As soon as he had cleared the door, I made him walk before me, for fear the sentinel should take notice of his walk. . . . Everybody in the [ward]room, who were chiefly the guards' wives and daughters, seemed to compassionate me exceedingly.'

As Lady Maxwell led her husband through the outside door, she turned him over to her maid who had been waiting there the entire time. As the maid hustled the 'weeping' Lord Maxwell through the main gate and into the waiting carriage, Lady Maxwell returned to the cell where Mrs Morgan had been keeping up a one-sided conversation. Now it was Mrs Morgan's turn to make a hurried exit from the Tower. This left Lady Winifred Maxwell alone to keep up a steady stream of nervous chatter with her now absent husband.

A few minutes later, Lady Maxwell opened the cell door just enough to allow her to slip through, saying her goodbyes to the empty room, insisting that she had to go and find her maid. If she was detained too long at parliament to come back that evening, she would return first thing in the morning with news of his pardon. As she slipped out of the room, Winifred reached down and jerked the latch cord on the door handle so hard that the knot snapped and the cord dangled uselessly on the inside. When she slammed the door, it became impossible to enter the room without breaking it down. Walking towards the stairs, she saw one of the servants heading for her husband's room with a handful of candles. According to her account of the affair, she never hesitated but, 'I said to the servant as I passed by, that he need not carry in candles yet as my Lord wanted to finish his prayers first.'

By the time Winifred Maxwell reached the outer gate of the Tower, her friends had all made their way home and her husband had been taken by their maid to the safety of a friend's home. Within half an hour, she joined him there.

At dawn on 24 February, the guards came to escort the Earls of Derwentwater and Nithsdale and Viscount Kenmore to their execution. Only then did they discover that Lord Maxwell, Earl of Nithsdale, was nowhere to be found. Frantically they sounded the alarm. The Tower was scoured from top to bottom, but there was no sign of William Maxwell. As the search continued, ghoulish crowds were gathering on Tower Hill awaiting the day's 'entertainment'. Only a few streets away, two more spectators watched the scene with horror. Lord and Lady Maxwell were watching the horrific drama unfold from an attic window in their safe house.

Viscount Kenmore, commander of the rebel army, went to the scaffold first. Before kneeling down to put his head on the block, he apologised to the crowd for the fact that his clothes did not suit such a sombre occasion, but he had not been allowed to change into something more appropriate. By the time the Earl of Derwentwater mounted the scaffold, a general alarm had been sent out across London. The Earl of Nithsdale must not be allowed to escape. A twenty-four-hour guard was stationed at every road and gate leading out of the city.

But only two days after the executions, a magnificent coach bearing the arms of the ambassador of the Venetian Republic rolled out of London. Inside were the ambassador and two servants in brightly coloured livery. One of them was Lord Maxwell. Through the good graces of the exiled Stuarts, now living in Rome, the ambassador had agreed to escort Maxwell out of England, through the port of Dover, and safely to France.

Although her husband was well on his way to safety, Lady Maxwell's odyssey was not yet over. Defying the general alarm that had been sent out to apprehend Lord Maxwell, his wife and her unidentified accomplices, she rode back to the family seat in Scotland to secure the family papers she had hidden away in the event that her plans to free her husband had failed. Once the papers were safely in the hands of her husband's powerful friends, their son's inheritance would be safe.

In an ironic twist of fate, there is some historical evidence that King George may actually have ordered a reprieve for Lord Maxwell on the same afternoon that his wife was busily helping him escape from the Tower. Even if the king was happy to see Maxwell go free, the jailbreak had made both the earl and his wife fugitives from an entirely new set of charges. So frustrated was the king that he declared the Countess Nithsdale had caused him 'more mischief than any woman in Christendom'.

Against all the odds Winifred Maxwell finally sailed from Scotland to join her husband in France. Together, they moved to Rome to be near James Edward Stuart, the King Over the Water, whom they had lived, and nearly died, to serve. The rest of their lives were spent in obscurity and near-poverty, but their bravery and devotion to each other left a legacy rich in love. Lord Maxwell died in 1744 at the age of sixty-eight. Five years later, Winifred Maxwell was reunited with her husband in death.

The letter in which Lady Maxwell laid out the harrowing rescue of her husband, along with the brown cloak in which he escaped from the Tower, still survive in the collection of the Duchess of Norfolk, a descendant of Winifred Maxwell.

Thirteen

THE AMERICAN (P)RESIDENT

Henry Laurens
1780–1

Few individuals can claim to have significantly changed the course of their nation's history. Fewer still have inadvertently started one war while attempting to end another. Henry Laurens could legitimately have made both these claims as well as holding the unique honour of being the only American ever imprisoned in the Tower of London.

Henry Laurens was born in Charleston, South Carolina, on 6 March 1724. His French Protestant parents had emigrated to the New World some years earlier to escape the deprivations imposed on all Protestants by the Catholic French crown. Henry's father was a saddle-maker who prospered well enough to provide his son with the best education the colonies had to offer. By the time Henry was twenty years old, his father realised that if the boy was going to climb the ladder of society and business he would have to go abroad to further his education and make whatever social contacts he could.

For three years, beginning in 1744, Henry Laurens lived in London, serving an apprenticeship in the mercantile shipping business. Evidently the lad showed promise. As he was preparing to return to America, a London commercial house wrote to him with the offer of a partnership in their growing business. The letter followed Henry through London to Portsmouth, only missing the ship on which he had booked passage back to the colonies by five hours. Had the letter reached him, the course of his life and the history of three nations would have been irrevocably altered.

Back in Charleston, Henry went into partnership with two other men in a general mercantile partnership, acting as middlemen who arranged to ship their clients' goods from America to England, bringing British and European goods back to the colonies on the return run. Exporting predominantly raw materials such as unprocessed rice, deerskins, indigo and rum, and importing luxury items including wine, indentured servants and slaves, the firm prospered to the point where, by 1750, Laurens had married Eleanor Ball, started a family and begun to buy sizeable tracts of plantation land around Charleston. If he was to supply rice and indigo to the European market, it made good business sense to produce them himself.

For a decade, Laurens' business and family prospered, but by 1760 Henry's conscience and religious convictions brought him to the conclusion that the slave trade was immoral. When his partners objected to the idea of forgoing their most profitable cargo, there was a terrible row. Finally, Henry left the firm, taking with him three ships that were registered in his name. He would continue trading, but now it would be mostly the produce of his own plantations. At thirty-eight years of age, Henry Laurens owned eight plantations covering more than 20,000 acres, three ships and a part-interest in two more vessels.

He now devoted his time to his family and his own enterprises with a staunch morality that brought him an unassailable reputation for honesty, and made numerous enemies in the business world. On three separate occasions Laurens was forced into duels to defend his honour, but on each occasion he refused to fire his pistol.

In 1770, Henry's wife Eleanor died, leaving her husband to look after the four surviving children of the twelve she had borne him. To escape his grief and provide his two sons with the same advantages that his father had given him, Henry took the boys, Henry Jr and John, to London where he enrolled them in university. After taking a house in Westminster, Henry looked after his shipping business, corresponded with his plantations and cared for the boys and their education. He also took advantage of his extensive business, political and social contacts to argue the case for the American colonies' growing list of grievances against the crown.

Always a political moderate, Laurens firmly believed the problems between the colonies and the mother country could be solved amicably. Many of his British opposite numbers held the same opinion, and he and his friends petitioned the House of Commons, the House of Lords and the crown itself to do everything possible to ease the increasingly tense political situation in America. Always, Laurens believed the best course of action was not confrontation, but a negotiated settlement that would benefit both Britain and America. If such a solution could be reached, the ties between the two countries would be stronger than ever; if not, the economic damage to both sides could be devastating.

Henry Laurens understood all too well the revolutionary fervour that had already gripped a minority of his countrymen. During the Stamp Act crisis in 1765, mobs incensed at England's imposition of a tax on imported goods stormed through Charleston, ransacking Laurens' home in the mistaken belief that he was a royalist agent. In Henry Laurens' words, these revolutionaries 'seem forced and impelled to do very improper acts to support a very good cause'.

If Laurens had ample reason to fear America's revolutionary mob mentality, he also had personal experience of the arbitrary manner used by English bureaucrats when dealing with their colonial subjects. While Laurens was living in England with his sons, the Royal Navy seized two of his ships for a frivolous breach of maritime law. Dutifully running the maze of legalities imposed by the maritime courts, when his case finally came to trial Laurens was so incensed by the court's rude and insulting behaviour that he leaned across the bench and twisted the judge's nose. Eventually he managed to get his ships back, and avoid being sent to jail for contempt of court, but the incident probably hastened his return to America. In the autumn of 1774 Henry Laurens and his son John left England, while Henry Jr remained behind to continue his education.

Two weeks before Christmas 1774, Henry Laurens arrived in Charleston, only to discover the story of his altercation with the maritime judge had preceded him. In the super-heated revolutionary atmosphere that now pervaded America, Henry Laurens had become a local hero. Within less than a month of his return, Laurens found himself elected to the First Provisional Congress of South Carolina, established when the old royalist government had been ousted from office only months earlier. Despite his continued advocacy of a negotiated settlement, within six months Laurens was promoted to President of the Congress and appointed President of the twelve-member Council of Safety, charged with overseeing South Carolina's defences in case of a British attack. The international situation now deteriorated at an ever-accelerating rate. Within six months the war of words spiralled into open fighting. Britain and America were at war and Henry Laurens, along with every other American politician, had been branded a rebel and traitor to the crown. On a personal level, Laurens' family, like those of so many of his countrymen, was torn apart by war. Henry Jr could not return to America and Henry Sr could not go to England. But for the moment, Laurens had more pressing problems than his own family.

With most of the colonies' fledgling army and navy scrambling to defend the northern ports of Boston, New York and Philadelphia, the port of Charleston was left dangerously exposed to attack. No troops could be spared from the continental army and South Carolina did not have the money to raise an effective militia of its own. Making the situation worse, many of the able-bodied white men in South Carolina feared that if they left their plantations their slaves would escape or break into open revolt.

Faced with the imminent threat of blockade, Charleston called on Henry Laurens, as the President of the Council of Safety, to oversee construction of fortifications and raise whatever military force he could to defend the city. Laurens agreed, but insisted on a free hand in organising the regiment as he saw fit. Everyone agreed, but they were hardly prepared for Henry Laurens' proposal. In letters to the South Carolina Congress and the Continental Congress, Laurens envisioned a militia comprised entirely of free blacks and volunteer slaves.

Considering the radical nature of the idea, the amount of high-level support was probably more than Laurens could have hoped for. South Carolina's representative to the Continental Congress took the idea one step further, suggesting that because plantation owners and overseers 'must remain at home to prevent revolts among the Negroes . . . [All] the thirteen states should arm three thousand of the most vigorous and enterprising Negroes under the command of white officers.'

Further support came from young Alexander Hamilton, then acting as aide-de-camp to General George Washington. Hamilton wrote, 'The Negroes will make excellent soldiers . . . [but] this project will have to combat prejudice and self-interest. Contempt for the Blacks makes us fancy many things that are founded neither on reason or experience. . . . Give them their freedom with their muskets; this will secure their fidelity, animate their courage, and have a good influence upon those who remain, by opening the door for their emancipation . . .'

While many slave owners were understandably opposed to the plan, the strongest objection came from George Washington. Washington insisted that Negroes simply could not handle such a complex job of soldiering and threatened to remove Laurens from command of the Charleston defensive project if he persisted with his plan. Although a slave owner himself, Laurens was outraged at Washington's attitude. Armed with the letters from South Carolina's congressional representative and Alexander Hamilton, Laurens set about building his black militia as quickly as possible. Charleston was running out of time.

By May 1776 the British had overrun neighbouring Georgia and most of the territory between Savannah and Charleston was seething with red coats who were busily confiscating slaves or urging them into open revolt against their owners. Weeks later, in early June, the British attempted a sea-borne assault on Charleston, but thanks to Laurens and his black soldiers, it was impossible for them to land any troops. Before the end of the month the British gave up and sailed out of Charleston harbour. Henry Laurens was again a local hero, but Washington and his supporters in Congress would never forgive his insubordination.

Had Laurens ever given the matter a second thought, he might have assumed he could escape Washington's ire simply by staying in South Carolina and continuing the defence of Charleston. If so, he would have been wrong. Swept along on a tide of popular approval, Laurens was elected to the Continental Congress in January 1777. By July of that year Laurens had taken his seat in Congress, then meeting in Philadelphia, and began serving on several important committees despite the opposition of the strong Washingtonian party. At least Laurens had a powerful supporter in the person of John Hancock, author of the Declaration of Independence and President of the Congress. When Hancock stepped down as president in November 1777 his hand-picked successor was Henry Laurens.

Now saddled with the awesome job of holding the radically factionalised congress together, Laurens continued to petition the English government to recognise America as a sovereign state while simultaneously supporting the continental army in its war against Britain. It was a no-win situation and even Congress could not form a consensus on the best course of action. Political infighting and personal interests kept congressmen continually at each others' throats and the majority of them refused to cooperate with Henry Laurens simply because he had defied General Washington.

To be fair to all concerned, the American Congress of 1777 was operating against impossible odds. As Washington's army met with one defeat after another, congressional membership sometimes dropped as low as fifteen and political allegiances shifted almost daily. Still, Laurens did his best to make some kind of progress, often working twenty hours a day. Always personally sensitive and moral to the point of being stiff-necked, as tempers frayed on all sides, Laurens' contentious relations with the congressmen continued to deteriorate. When Congress proposed an alliance with England's enemy, France, Laurens insisted that the Dutch would make better allies. He referred to the French as 'artful, specious half-friends', and pointed out that Holland, although Britain's ally, had continually expressed its disapproval over the handling of the American colonies. Furthermore, the Dutch were wealthy, had a far stronger naval power than the French, and (like America) were also largely Protestant. But Laurens' arguments fell on deaf ears. Either because they firmly believed the French would make better allies than the Dutch, or simply to spite Henry Laurens, Congress would not back a Dutch treaty. If Henry Laurens wanted to strike a deal with the Dutch, he would have to shoulder the entire affair himself.

After a year of battling and backstabbing, Henry Laurens could no longer hold up under the pressure of his job. In December 1778 he resigned as President of the American Continental Congress. In a letter, he stated that he did not approve of the manner in which business was transacted in Congress, accusing his fellow congressmen of 'venality, peculation and fraud'. He did, however, retain his seat as South Carolina's representative and began making cautious overtures to the Dutch for aid in America's war with the British. After more than two years of delicate manoeuvring, the Dutch agreed to resume trade with the United States and provide a $10,000,000 war loan. It was a major coup, but congress remained unimpressed. Laurens had negotiated the deal, now he could work out how to get the treaty to Holland for ratification.

In an emergency session of Congress, Henry Laurens was appointed the United States' first Ambassador to The Netherlands. The appointment was hardly an honour. He had no choice but to try to run the naval blockade that choked off America's Atlantic coast and get the treaty ratified by himself. For their part, fellow members of Congress were glad to be rid of Henry Laurens.

On 30 August 1780 Laurens boarded the *Mercury*, a merchant brigantine based in Philadelphia. With him was a waterproof briefcase containing a draft of the Dutch–American treaty and papers identifying him as the US Ambassador to The Netherlands. As the ship slipped out to sea, Laurens was under no delusion as to his chances of making it across the Atlantic without running into Britain's Royal Navy. Up and down the coast and all across the ocean the American navy had been subjected to the same trouncing at sea as the continental army had been taking on land. Only pure luck would see the *Mercury* safely to Holland.

Clinging to the coast as long as possible, the *Mercury* sailed north along New England, creeping slowly towards Canadian waters. Once in the cold, fog-bound sea around Newfoundland the ship broke away from land and headed into the vast ocean – directly into the path of the British naval frigate *Vestal*. As the heavily armed gunboat bore down on the unarmed merchantman, Laurens was torn as to what to do. If he destroyed the treaty, his mission was ruined even if the *Mercury* was not seized; on the other hand, if the ship were taken and the papers discovered, it would almost certainly mean his life. Only when it became obvious that the *Mercury* was being forced to 'heave-to' did Laurens toss his diplomatic pouch overboard. But it was too late. As the *Vestal* eased alongside the American ship a British sailor spotted the oilskin pouch bobbing in the water. As British sailors swarmed over the railings of the *Mercury* the pouch was fished out of the water with a boarding pike. The papers were all the evidence the British needed. The *Mercury* was an enemy ship on a mission of war. Henry Laurens was taken into custody on 'suspicion of high treason'.

When the *Vestal* reached London, Laurens was immediately taken to Whitehall to be interrogated and formally charged. The contents of the diplomatic pouch made the British authorities fully aware of the importance of their prisoner and his mission. The joint Secretaries of State would carry out questioning and, in deference to his high office Laurens would not be subjected to a public trial. He was, however, mercilessly grilled for more than three weeks. Throughout the questioning, Laurens steadfastly insisted that his title as Ambassador and former President of the Continental Congress gave him diplomatic immunity from prosecution. Even in the face of repeated threats of hanging, Laurens refused to answer any questions about his mission, the interim American government or any other questions – the exact intent of which seemed unclear. The British, however, saw the matter differently. Since there had been no formal recognition of the new American government, Henry Laurens was a rebel, pure and simple. He was still officially a subject of the British Crown and therefore guilty of high treason.

Still, Laurens refused to cooperate. No matter. The draft of the treaty was all the evidence the court needed. The rebels were negotiating with Britain's Dutch allies. This was a clear act of treason on the part of the colonials and a betrayal of loyalty tantamount to an act of war by the Dutch.

On 6 October, Henry Laurens was convicted of high treason and told that his status as a convicted traitor made it impossible for him to be exchanged as a prisoner of war. He was sentenced by the Secretary for State who, in consideration of Laurens' diplomatic status, told him, 'You are to be sent to the Tower of London, not a prison, you must have no idea of a prison.' Laurens may not have understood the difference between the Tower and a common prison, but to the English authorities it was clear; the rebel American was being treated as though he were nobility.

If Laurens' sentence was more than equitable by eighteenth-century standards, the punishment meted out to the Dutch was both swift and brutal. The combined might of the Royal Navy on the eastern shores of the Atlantic, along with thousands of regular army troops fighting in nearby France, descended on Holland with a fury. Within weeks Dutch defences were broken and their navy was left a burning wreck. American relations with Holland were nearly destroyed and there would be no monetary aid for the colonies. And both America and Holland blamed the débâcle on Henry Laurens.

As Holland and the proposed alliance went down in flames, Henry Laurens was transferred from his temporary quarters to the Tower of London. In what must have been one of history's most peculiar displays of good will, when Laurens' carriage pulled through the outer gates and on to Tower Green, it was greeted by dozens of armed wardens merrily singing 'Yankee Doodle'. He dismounted from the carriage stone-faced, to be led to the Lieutenant of the Tower. The Lieutenant General, Mr Vernon, told Laurens that rather than being placed in one of the damp, ancient cells he would be quartered in a warden's house located on the Parade, one of the most public areas of the Tower complex. Unimpressed, Laurens was even more disheartened when he was shown to his rooms.

According to a letter written to a friend in London, Laurens was 'shut up in two small rooms . . . a warder my constant companion; and a [guard with a] fixed bayonet under my window'. Laurens' situation seemed to worsen when, according to the same letter, 'I discovered I was to pay rent for my little rooms, find my own meat and drink, bedding, coal, candles &c.' However awful Laurens thought his punishment was, he could not have known that such treatment was normally reserved for respected political prisoners of the highest calibre.

Certainly the conditions of Laurens' captivity were more lenient than a convicted spy and traitor had any right to expect. He was allowed frequent visits from his son, Henry, whom he had not seen for six years, along with any other guests who chose to visit him. Old friends, business associates and members of the government sympathetic to the American cause flowed in and out of the Tower in a constant stream. With them they brought gifts of food and good wine, which Laurens dutifully shared with his guards and Lieutenant Vernon and his family. The notoriety of the Tower's latest guest also brought the curious and bored aristocratic glitterati that constantly sought out new and novel diversions – a category into which Henry Laurens definitely fell. Among the more scandalous characters to frequent his rooms were Selina, Countess of Huntingdon, and her lover Lady Ann Erskine.

Whenever possible, Laurens plied his visitors with the cause of American independence. He urged influential businessmen and politicians like Edmund Burke to urge the king and government to bring the hostilities to an end. The sooner the war ended, he argued, the sooner relations between the two countries could return to normal – and if the conflict did not stop soon, the economic and political damage to both sides could be irreparable.

Word of Laurens' pleas evidently spread and found fertile ground. Both Edmund Burke, in England, and Benjamin Franklin, in America, began petitioning the crown for Laurens' release. Despite his advancing age and deteriorating health, the government twice refused to grant a pardon – insisting that pardon would come only if Laurens agreed to help the British win the war in America. The price was unacceptable. Laurens would remain in the Tower and continue petitioning anyone who would listen to him.

To support his position, and that of America, Laurens began turning out a stream of letters and articles for what was called 'the rebel press': a chain of London underground newspapers sympathetic to the American cause. To get the letters out of the Tower and into the right hands, Laurens enlisted the aid of Elizabeth Vernon, the teenage daughter of the Lieutenant General of the Tower. Week after week, Elizabeth smuggled Laurens' manuscripts past the eyes of her father's guards. Swept up in the thrill of clandestine meetings, spy games and secret messages, the impressionable girl soon found herself passionately involved with the middle-aged revolutionary. Inevitably, the all-too-frequent meetings aroused the guards' suspicions and the situation was reported to Vernon. Overnight, Laurens' privileges and lenient treatment disappeared. He was subjected to random searches for paper and ink, and periods of harsh deprivation followed even minor infractions of the rules. Even the occasional walk through the Tower grounds was now prohibited.

On 19 October 1781, one year and two weeks after Henry Laurens entered the Tower, Lord Cornwallis surrendered his contingent of the British colonial forces in America to General George Washington at Yorktown, Virginia, effectively ending the American Revolutionary War. Ten weeks later, the pleas of Edmund Burke and Benjamin Franklin were answered; Henry Laurens was released on parole, ostensibly for health reasons, pending final settlement of the war. On his release, he was presented with a bill for £100 to pay the cost of maintaining a guard on his rooms for the past fifty-four weeks. Insisting he had not personally employed the guard, Laurens declined to honour the bill.

With the dawn of the new year, Laurens travelled to Bath to take the spa waters for his health. While there he took time to have his portrait painted by John Singleton Copley, the most famous portrait painter of his day and an expatriate American. By June 1782 word came that Henry Laurens was to be unconditionally released in exchange for none other than Lord Cornwallis who, ironically, had long held the title of Constable of the Tower.

As Laurens prepared to return to the newly independent United States, a letter arrived from Benjamin Franklin requesting that he join the American peace delegation in Paris. The diplomatic mission already included Franklin, John Adams and John Jay and while they were capable of negotiating a treaty between America and Great Britain, Laurens was the only American diplomat who had spent any significant amount of time in England. His insights into the British character would be an invaluable asset. Laurens dutifully changed his plans and attended the negotiating sessions and the signing of the preliminaries of the Treaty of Paris in September 1782. But before the final draft could be signed, Franklin had yet another assignment for Laurens. He was to return to London where he would serve as America's first, if unofficial, ambassador to the Court of St James. The war was over, Laurens had been released from the Tower, but he just could not escape the British.

For the next eighteen months Henry Laurens shuttled back and forth between Paris and London carrying out the tasks of an ambassador, trying to rebuild the shattered relations between the two countries. Whenever his duties allowed, he spent time with old friends like Edmund Burke and his former trading associates, but records indicate that he also visited Lieutenant General Vernon, his wife and daughter Elizabeth at the Tower. Finally, in 1784, Henry Laurens was given permission to return home. His ship landed in New York on 3 August and by January he was back in Charleston – but it was not to be a joyous homecoming.

The war had ravaged Laurens' plantations with a loss estimated at more than £45,000. If more bad news were possible after already having suffered so much, Laurens now learned that his son John had been killed in the closing days of the war. Bitter and despondent, Laurens occupied his time writing a book about his adventures entitled *A Narrative of the Capture of Henry Laurens, of his Confinement in the Tower of London.* It was not particularly complimentary. But evidently there were a few good memories to compensate for all the pain and suffering. Somewhere along the way, friends and associates on both sides of the Atlantic had taken to calling him 'Tower' Laurens and the nickname seems to have genuinely amused him.

When Henry Laurens died in 1792, seven years after his return to the United States, his will instructed that two endowments be left to people he had known in England; one to Mrs Vernon, wife of the Lieutenant General of the Tower, and another to the Vernons' daughter Elizabeth, who had befriended, and loved, an ageing rebel and convicted traitor.

PART IV
A Home for Spies and Tourists

Fourteen

THE BLACK BOOK

Sir Roger Casement
1914–16

I ntrigue, sexual betrayal and cloak-and-dagger deception somehow seem most at home amid the romance of the Middle Ages and renaissance. But where love of country and people's private lives collide with politics and war, time and place become irrelevant. When Sir Roger Casement's divided loyalties were put to the test during the turbulent years of the First World War, the results were as harrowing for him and his nation as anything in a medieval chronicle.

England's rule of Ireland dates back to the reign of Henry II who invaded his island neighbour in 1171 and subdued the Irish kings to extract tribute from them. As much as the Irish resented foreign rule, their ire increased after Henry VIII reformed the church, replacing traditional Catholicism with his new Church of England. The staunchly Catholic island nation now had two enemies, the English and their church, and the tension more than once pushed the two nations over the brink of war.

By 1800 Ireland had gained representation in Great Britain's House of Commons and by 1900 the British government was seriously considering allowing them to govern themselves under the Home Rule Bill. According to the terms of Home Rule, Ireland would govern its own internal affairs with the English government retaining control of foreign policy and the military. With its protectorates Canada, Australia and South Africa already governing themselves, it seemed a logical step to grant Ireland the same autonomy. It was, however, a step that deeply divided the Irish people. The 75 per cent of Ireland's population who were Catholic desperately wanted autonomy, but the Protestant minority, concentrated mostly in Ireland's six northern counties, demanded a continuation of full ties with Great Britain. On 25 May 1914, the *Irish Times* reported that 'The Home Rule Bill is carried in the House of

Commons for the third and last time, provoking Unionist [sic, Protestant] attacks on Catholic property in Belfast.'

But a mere three months after the above report, Great Britain (along with the rest of Europe) was dragged into the hell of the First World War. With the entire continent going up in flames and German submarines destroying millions of tons of British shipping, the Irish question was laid aside.

In Ireland it was a time of desperate soul-searching. The vast majority of the people understood the necessity of supporting England in its struggle against imperial Germany and the Austro-Hungarian Empire. Over the course of the war more than two hundred thousand Irishmen would volunteer to serve in Britain's armed forces. There were some, however, who were so desperate for independence that they actively supported Germany, hoping that a pro-German stance would entice the German Kaiser to take an active part in Ireland's fight for independence. In the ensuing confusion, Ireland tore itself apart in a series of devastating strikes and riots. Simple reason, along with religious and political loyalties, became blurred by anger and hate. Into this maelstrom of controversy walked Sir Roger Casement, a retired consular official with more than twenty years of distinguished service in the British Foreign Office.

Casement had come from a wealthy Irish family, his father a Protestant and his mother a Catholic, but Roger had been raised in his father's church and educated at the best schools in England. In 1884, at the age of twenty, Roger went to work for the African International Association but left seven years later when he began to suspect that the association was involved in the exploitation of the native African labour force. The following year, 1892, he went to work for the British Foreign Service, serving as consul to Portuguese East Africa. Cited in government dispatches as 'brave, diplomatic and unusually observant', Casement was chosen to investigate reports of extreme racial oppression in the Belgian Congo. While there, he exposed some of the most horrific working conditions on earth and tied them directly to King Leopold II of Belgium. The work drew such international criticism of Belgian policies that American author Mark Twain demanded the overthrow of King Leopold.

With a worldwide reputation for humanitarianism, Casement was sent in 1910 to the Putumayo region of Peru to investigate conditions similar to those he had uncovered in the Congo. His reports on the systematic exploitation of Indian labourers at the hands of international rubber conglomerates were so well documented that international laws could be instituted to halt such atrocities. Within a year, Casement's work in Peru had earned him a knighthood and the thanks of a grateful British nation. In 1913, at the age of fifty, Casement retired from the Foreign Office on the grounds of health problems dating from his years in the tropics. In retirement, he returned to Northern Ireland.

But Casement's relocation to Ireland ran far deeper than nostalgia for his childhood home. As early as 1902 he had become fascinated by the issue of Irish independence and began donating money to various Republican causes. Soon, he became a devoted advocate of a free Ireland and although his position in the British government forced him to work anonymously, he began writing articles for the *Irish Review*. In 1912, the year before his retirement, he wrote an article in which he said that should war break out between Great Britain and Germany, the situation could be used to Ireland's advantage. If the Irish people refused to support Britain, it might induce Germany to aid them in their struggle for independence. The following year he helped organise the Irish Volunteer Force (IVF), a paramilitary group dedicated to driving the English out of Ireland. He also joined the Irish National Volunteers (INV) and helped them organise a London committee to raise funds from London's Irish immigrant population.

It must have been an odd association. Most of the Irish rebels were working-class Catholics with few of the social graces of a trained diplomat. In contrast, the tall, almost emaciated Casement was well spoken, well dressed and a career diplomat. Because of his long association with the British government, the Irish Nationalists never quite accepted, nor trusted, Casement, but if he were sincere, they were more than willing to use his services and connections in high places.

When the First World War broke out in August 1914, Casement was in the United States addressing a pro-Irish rally in Philadelphia in support of the Irish National Volunteers and their radical political wing, Sinn Fein. Obviously, news of the war changed Casement's plans dramatically. With Britain now embroiled in a war with Germany, Casement's plan to enlist German help in securing a free Ireland could be put into action. In a letter to his comrades back in Ireland, he insisted that Ireland was not strong enough to gain its own independence without outside help. Any move towards an uprising without foreign aid would be doomed to disastrous failure, but he would support the 'cause' no matter what course of action they chose. He wrote 'if you are bent upon this act of idiocy, I will come and join you [although] . . . I . . . regard it as the wildest form of boyish folly . . . I . . . have always stood for action, but not this action and not under these circumstances . . .'

Hoping to convince the INV and Sinn Fein that his plan could work, Casement hurried to Washington DC, where he arranged a meeting with the German military attaché. The Germans seemed interested, but with the war only a month old it was impossible to commit themselves to any such radical deviation from their original plans. They would, however, arrange for Casement to go to Germany and meet members of the High Command and make his case personally. In October 1914, Roger Casement booked passage to Germany on a neutral Norwegian freighter. Travelling with him was a man named Adler Christensen, an out-of-work Norwegian seaman who Casement claimed was his butler.

Once in Berlin, Casement held a series of meetings with members of the Military High Command, up to and including Germany's Foreign Minister Count Arthur von Zimmerman, who was always eager to gain new allies for the German cause. Casement laid out his plans carefully and clearly. If Germany would agree to supply the Irish rebels with two hundred thousand guns and ammunition, along with a substantial war loan and an invasion force of fifty thousand German troops with orders to land in Ireland, the Germans and the Irish people could force the English to fight a two-front war, dividing British forces, and pulling tens of thousands of men off the Western Front. This would allow Germany to push through France clear to the English Channel. The Germans may have had no interest in Irish independence, but anything that would help weaken English forces on the continent seemed like a good idea. To test Casement's sincerity and his organisational abilities, the Germans suggested he visit prisoner-of-war camps and try to recruit a fighting unit from among the thousands of Irish PoWs being held by the Germans. Casement readily agreed but, as he would soon discover, the Irish were less enthusiastic.

For more than a year, from late 1914 till spring 1916, Roger Casement travelled from one PoW camp to another talking to every Irish internee he could find, in an attempt to convince them that the cause of a free Ireland outweighed any loyalty they may have had to the British Empire. Although he did convince nearly two thousand men to begin training, only fifty-five of them openly supported the idea of siding with the hated Germans – even if it meant gaining national freedom.

Trading English domination for autonomy might have been desirable, but betraying King George to the Kaiser was quite another matter. Besides, they argued, if Germany won the war, what assurance did they have that Ireland would not become a vassal state of the German Empire just as it now was to England? Casement tried to convince them by providing encouraging dispatches from Irish Nationalists back home, but all communiqués had to be routed from Berlin, through Germany's American Embassy and back to Ireland – it took forever and too often the answers simply never came.

Casement's ultimate failure to raise a fighting force of Irish volunteers did nothing to convince Germany that supporting Ireland was in the Fatherland's best interests, and Casement's own growing frustration led many in the High Command to conclude that he was either a crackpot or simply a man on a fool's errand. Casement's position was not strengthened by the fact that his close association with his companion Adler Christensen caused many in the German government to whisper.

In early April 1916, the Germans finally agreed to provide Casement with twenty thousand Mauser rifles and one million rounds of outdated ammunition. There would be no monetary loan and no invasion force. Casement would be returned to Ireland by submarine and the arms would be delivered shortly thereafter by the German navy. It was only one-tenth the number of arms he had requested, and lacked the badly needed money and military back-up, but it was the best he was going to get. Reluctantly, Roger Casement accepted the offer.

Casement knew that the great uprising, scheduled to take place on Easter Sunday – now less than two weeks away – could not hope to succeed. The Irish could not win their independence without help and he had to persuade them to call off the insurrection. If they went ahead without help the cause was doomed and they would probably all be slaughtered. Casement was devastated. But had he known the full extent of his problems, he would have been even more disheartened.

Since the beginning of the war British Intelligence (MI5) had been monitoring messages between the German ambassador in Washington and his superiors at home as well as with Sinn Fein. At least thirty-two messages had been intercepted and London knew all about the planned uprising. To make matters worse for Casement, his lover, Adler Christensen, was on the payroll of MI5. His companion had duly reported every move Casement had made since he left New York over a year earlier. The only thing the British were unsure of was whether the Germans were actually going to support the expected Irish rebellion.

With the cache of arms and ammunition stowed aboard the German ship *Aud* (which had been disguised as a Dutch trawler) Roger Casement climbed into a U-boat and headed for Ireland for the first time since before the war broke out. On Good Friday, 21 April 1916, the German submarine surfaced off the coast of County Kerry. Casement, who had shaved off his beard so he would not be recognised, was provided with an inflatable rubber raft and began paddling towards the shore as the submarine disappeared beneath the waves of the Irish Sea.

When he landed at Banna Strand, Casement walked through the driving rain towards an ancient, abandoned fortress where he took shelter to wait for the *Aud*. Six hours later a local policeman found him there, exhausted and soaking wet. When he asked what the bedraggled man was doing, a rather disoriented Casement muttered that he was an author out exploring the countryside. Considering the weather, the story seemed a little strange. When the policeman asked for identification, Casement fumbled through his pockets, accidentally allowing a soggy German train ticket to fall to the ground. His suspicions now on high alert, the officer made a quick search of Casement's suitcase where he found a cargo manifest from the *Aud* revealing details of twenty thousand rifles and ammunition. Roger Casement was arrested on suspicion of spying and taken to nearby Ardfert barracks for questioning by the military.

Even as the hapless Casement was being taken to Ardfert, the Royal Navy intercepted the *Aud*. The information provided by Christensen and intercepted German transmissions had conveniently provided the exact time and place of its arrival. Rather than have his cargo of contraband confiscated by the British, the captain scuttled his ship, sending the rifles and all hopes for Irish independence to the bottom of the Irish Sea.

During his interrogation at Ardfert, Casement asked to see a priest. Had his captors known that Casement was a Protestant, it might have seemed strange, but in predominantly Catholic Ireland it seemed a perfectly normal request. When Father Francis Ryan arrived, Casement told him who he was and explained the urgency of getting word to the Irish National Volunteers and Sinn Fein that there would be no aid from the Germans. The rebellion must be called off. Whatever his politics might have been, Father Ryan was dedicated to saving lives and agreed to deliver the message.

Beyond his brief meeting with Ryan, Casement seemed completely willing to cooperate with the authorities. He duly answered all their questions, saying, 'I am not endeavouring to shield myself at all. I face all the consequences. All I ask you is to believe I have done nothing dishonourable . . . I have done nothing treacherous to my country. . . .' It seemed a very odd statement for a man carrying German armament manifests, but it certainly convinced the authorities that their prisoner was a traitor. The next day Sir Roger Casement was escorted to London under heavy guard, arriving at Euston station on Easter Sunday morning. From the station he was whisked to Scotland Yard and more questioning by Basil Thompson, head of CID, and Captain Reginald 'Blinker' Hall, chief of Naval Intelligence.

As in his previous round of questioning, Casement was more than happy to cooperate so long as his testimony did not implicate anyone other than himself. Yes, he had attempted to obtain arms from Germany; yes, they were intended to aid in an Irish rebellion and yes, he knew that it was a treasonable offence. But, he insisted, he had not been disloyal to Great Britain, insisting that 'loyalty is a sentiment, not a law'. Obviously, it was a sentiment he did not share. According to Thompson, Casement's answers were 'very vivacious and at times histrionic in manner'. After hours of questioning, Sir Roger was moved from Scotland Yard to the Tower of London where several German spies were already being held. After long years of non-political use, the Tower had been brought back into service during the early years of the war, mostly for its psychological effects both in reassuring citizens that captured spies were being securely detained and for the effect the Tower's reputation would have on would-be spies.

While Casement was being grilled in London, Ireland was descending into chaos. Even before the rising began its leaders had fallen out among themselves. Because there had been word that Casement's plan to smuggle arms had failed, some wanted to call the whole thing off, others wanted a postponement to verify where Casement, and Germany, stood, and still others wanted to proceed as planned. In all the confusion, the number of men who actually took part in the Easter morning rising plummeted from the hoped-for five thousand to just over a thousand. This small band of rebels stormed through the streets of Dublin, rushing past startled knots of people on their way to Easter morning church services. By the time the rebels smashed their way into the General Post Office, the law courts and a few other public buildings to declare a free Irish Republic, the crowds had turned from wondering confusion to outright hostility. Most of them simply shook their heads in derision but a few openly faced the rebels down, jeering at them. It was hardly the reception they had hoped for.

The following day, Monday 24 April, the Lord Lieutenant of Ireland placed the entire country under martial law. Since there was no way of knowing how many rebels there actually were, and whether they would be receiving support from a German invasion force, the Irish police were told to expect significant back-up from the military.

Under less harrowing conditions than the middle of the First World War, the British might have reacted differently to the crisis. As it was, Whitehall was in no mood to chance either a German invasion or a civil war in Ireland. Rather than simply protect public and private property and wait for the revolutionaries to exhaust themselves, the full force of Great Britain's military might was brought to bear. Five thousand battle-ready troops, along with armoured cars, machine guns and field artillery descended on Dublin to contain the situation. To 'soften up' rebel positions before the troops arrived, the Royal Navy's *Hielga* steamed up the River Liffey and began shelling all known rebel locations. In a week of absolute anarchy, more than two hundred civilians and one hundred and thirty British soldiers and Irish police were killed.

News of both Casement's arrest and the Dublin uprising hit England's newspapers on Monday morning, Casement receiving almost as many column inches as the uprising itself. Not since the Scottish uprising under Bonnie Prince Charlie 170 years earlier had there been such an internal threat to Great Britain. And at the centre of it all was Sir Roger Casement, one of the most honoured British civil servants of the age. The crown and government felt completely betrayed. Home Office legal adviser Sir Ernly Blackwell said, 'It is difficult . . . to imagine a worse case of High Treason than Casement's. It is aggravated, rather than mitigated, by his previous career in the public service.' In the six days before it collapsed, the Irish rebellion transformed Roger Casement from a revered public figure into the most vilified man in Britain.

On 29 April the Dublin rebels surrendered to the military. Of the hundreds that were arrested, fifteen were tried by court martial and sentenced to death. The vast majority of Irishmen and women wholeheartedly supported the verdict.

Following his move from Scotland Yard to the Tower of London, Roger Casement was held incommunicado for more than two weeks. Even the soldiers who guarded him were ordered not to speak to him. Had it not been for one Welsh guardsman who whispered the news of the uprising and its calamitous results, Casement might never have known the outcome of his hurried plea to Father Ryan. Depressed and discouraged, Casement twice tried to kill himself; once by swallowing a bent nail he had pulled out of the wall of his cell and once by swallowing a tiny flask of curare that he probably kept hidden in his clothes. Now under a constant suicide watch, Casement was forced to have two guards inside his cell at all times, as well as a third stationed outside his door. The single bulb in his cell burned twenty-four hours a day. In this paranoiac atmosphere, and unable to sleep with guards watching him, Casement's mental condition deteriorated rapidly.

By the time his case came to court a few weeks later, the preponderance of evidence, not least of which was Casement's own confessions, offered little doubt as to what the outcome would be. Somehow, the seriousness of his situation either never dawned on Casement, or his deteriorating condition simply blocked out reality. Day after day, as he stood in the dock, Casement seemed completely unmoved by the proceedings and the mounting pile of evidence being presented against him.

As the trial proceeded, a routine police investigation of his Ebury Street flat in London turned up new, and completely unexpected, revelations about Sir Roger. A series of small journals, dubbed by metropolitan police 'the Black Diaries' were ostensibly accounts of his time in the Congo in 1903, and in Peru in 1910–11. On closer examination, they revealed a secret life of almost constant, casual sexual encounters with young men, most of them black and nearly all of them for money. In a separate account ledger were records of how much he had paid each of the young men for their services. Shocked and disgusted, the police passed the diaries over to the prosecution team headed by King's Counsel F.E. Smith.

Knowing that regardless of how shocking the diaries were they had no bearing on the charge of treason, in what seemed a gesture of good will Smith passed the diaries on to Casement's defence counsel. To barrister Alexander Sullivan, Smith suggested that while they had no direct bearing on the case, the diaries might convince the three-judge panel hearing the case to accept a plea of insanity. It would be an unspeakable humiliation for Casement, but it was probably the only way to save his life.

When Sullivan confronted his client with the diaries, he was completely taken aback with Casement's reaction. According to Sullivan, 'He instructed me to explain to the jury that the filthy and disreputable practices and the rhapsodic glorification of them were inseparable from the true genius; moreover, I was to cite a list of all truly great men to prove it.' Sullivan pondered long and hard as to what to do about the diaries and his client's inexplicable behaviour. If he failed to make them public, his client was doomed, if he offered them in evidence, it would certainly rob Casement of the public sympathy that would be necessary to obtain an appeal. In the end, Sullivan decided the Black Diaries would do his case more harm than good and they were quietly laid aside.

After closing arguments by both sides, Casement was brought back into court to hear the verdict. As he took his place in the dock, he looked around, smiled at the audience and waved at distraught friends in the public gallery. Even when the judges announced the verdict of guilty and placed the traditional black caps over their wigs for the pronouncement of the death sentence, Casement seemed not to understand the significance of what was happening. In fact, he seemed amused at the sight of the three bewigged judges wearing little black cloth caps on their heads. The day after the trial closed, Sir Roger Casement was formally stripped of his knighthood, the first such disgrace in nearly three centuries.

While no one could argue that the trial had been anything but fair, and the loss of his knighthood was certainly no more than Casement deserved, the sentence of death seemed somehow too severe for a man who had dedicated two decades of his life to humanitarian causes. The matter began gnawing away at the conscience of the international community. From both sides of the Atlantic appeals began pouring into British government offices pleading for the life of Roger Casement. The Archbishop of Canterbury met the Lord Chancellor and the Home Secretary in the hope of having the death sentence commuted. Sir Arthur Conan Doyle insisted that Casement's mental and physical health had obviously been broken by his years in the tropics and that he was not responsible for his actions. Colonel T.E. Lawrence (of Arabia) described Casement as 'a broken archangel' and begged the government to take pity on him. In the United States, letters and petitions flooded the British Embassy in Washington. The American Negro Fellowship League asked for clemency on the grounds of 'the revelations he made while the British Consul in Africa, touching [on] the treatment of natives in the Congo. . . . Because of this great service to humanity . . . we feel impelled to beg for mercy on his behalf.'

But it was Irish playwright George Bernard Shaw who most concisely stated the real danger in the situation when he wrote to the *Manchester Guardian* on 22 July. Shaw accepted the validity of the verdict, saying, 'There need be no hesitation to carry out the sentence if it should appear, on reflection, a sensible one,' and agreed 'that Casement's treatment should not be exceptional'. But he also insisted that if Casement were executed, the reaction in Ireland would effectively hand Ireland over to Sinn Fein and the revolutionaries, saying, 'In Ireland he will be regarded as a national hero if he is executed, and quite possibly a spy if he is not.' It was a double-edged danger of which the government was fully aware. Worse still, Whitehall feared that an American backlash of pro-Casement sentiment might slow any possible US entry into the war – a risk that Great Britain could no longer afford to run.

On 15 July 1916, Home Office legal adviser Sir Ernly Blackwell proposed a solution. In a memorandum, he wrote, 'Public sentiment must not be allowed to influence the execution of the law and nothing is to be gained by reprieving [Casement] on one ground and pretending to have done so on another. So far as I can judge it, it would be far wiser from every point of view to allow the law to take its course. In closing, he added that although the Black Diaries were irrelevant to Casement's trail they might be an effective tool to stop the public outcry against his execution and prevent a traitor from being transformed into a martyr. The government agreed. To release Casement to appease his supporters would make a mockery of justice but to execute him could well transmute him into a martyr for Irish independence. The best option would be to use the diaries to discredit him and then let the law take its course.

There was little doubt that the Black Diaries' revelations about Casement's private life would destroy his reputation. If his sexuality were not enough, his predilection for young, hired, black men and his statements alluding to his preference for the submissive role in sex would lead almost everyone to believe that he was at best unhinged, or at worst a sinner beyond redemption. Casement had, in Blackwell's words, 'completed the full cycle of sexual degeneracy'.

To facilitate the plan, selected extracts of the diaries were typed up and circulated privately to various influential parties most concerned with the case. The prime minister, the Archbishop of Canterbury, the American ambassador and even the head of the outlawed Irish National Volunteers were all given copies. Walter Page, the US ambassador, had been warned that the diary extracts were 'of an unspeakable filthy character', and when he finished reading them he wrote to President Woodrow Wilson insisting that 'if all the facts about Casement ever become public, it will be well that our Government had nothing to do with him or his case, even indirectly!'

When John Harris, head of the Anti-Slavery Society, who had known and admired Casement for his work, was shown the diary extracts he nearly fainted. Although the information in the diaries was circulated privately, it was far too scandalous to be allowed to reach the press. Still, they could not simply be kept in the dark as to why Casement's support was disappearing like dust in a high wind. If they were not told something, they would start snooping around on their own and the results could be disastrous for the Foreign Office's reputation. Fortunately, when apprised of the situation, the press agreed. The editor of the *Times* simply said that releasing the information would be 'irrelevant [to the case], improper and un-English'. The pro-Irish *New York Times* agreed; a 24 May editorial stated that while Casement might, or might not, be a traitor, he was certainly a man with 'a screw loose'.

Blissfully unaware that everyone, particularly his staunchly conservative Irish Catholic comrades were deserting him like rats from a sinking ship, as late as 14 June Roger Casement stated in a letter, 'The British Government dare not hang me (they don't want to either – as individuals, I think). They simply dare not. . . . They know quite well what the world would say.' He was right. The government knew exactly what the scandalised world was going to say. It would say nothing.

Following his conviction Roger Casement was transferred from the Tower to London's Pentonville prison to await execution. During his incarceration there he requested the prison chaplain, Father Carey, to arrange his acceptance into the Catholic Church. The archbishop agreed to the request, but stated that Casement would have to confess his regret 'for any scandal he might have caused by his acts, public or private'. Shocked and distressed, Casement wrote to his cousin, 'They are trying to make me betray my soul.' Whether he, or the archbishop, was referring to his treasonable acts against Great Britain, or his private life, remains open to question. In either case, Casement refused. It was only when Father Carey discovered that Casement's parents had baptised him both in his mother's Catholic religion, as well as in his father's Protestant faith, that the conversion was allowed without Casement's confession.

On 3 August 1916 the disgraced Roger Casement, last of the plotters in the disastrous Easter Sunday Rising, was led to the scaffold at Pentonville. To the end, Casement denied the right of an English court to condemn an Irishman. In a speech from the scaffold he stated that, 'Since in the acts which have led to this trial it was the people of Ireland I sought to serve – and them alone – I leave my judgement and my sentence in their hands.' It was almost the same ploy Mary Queen of Scots had used three centuries earlier when she insisted no English court had jurisdiction over a foreign monarch. It had not worked for Mary then, and it did not work for Casement now.

Accompanying him to the scaffold was Father Carey. Deeply impressed with the way Casement conducted himself in his last minutes, Carey later wrote, 'He feared not death . . . he marched to the scaffold with the dignity of a prince.' The hangman, Mr Ellis, had a similar reaction, saying, 'Mr Casement was the bravest man it [ever] fell my unhappy lot to execute'.

It was inevitable that the execution of a man who had undergone such a sensational trial and dramatic fall from grace would make headlines. On the day of his execution the *Irish Times* wrote, 'Roger Casement's death is a miserable end to a life which, for the most part of its course, was honourable and distinguished.' Germany's Foreign Minister, Arthur von Zimmerman, wrote that he had never known, 'a man of loftier mind, of higher honour, of more burning love of home. It was a matter of personal grief to me when I heard he had made up his mind to accompany the [Irish] expedition. . . . So I urged him . . . to remain with us and to do work among the prisoners. . . . But he only shook his head, saying "I must go, I must be with the boys".'

Nearly ninety years after Roger Casement's execution, his tragic story still raises eyebrows and arguments by historians, politicians and Irish Republicans in Ireland, Britain and the US. Since word of the Black Diaries first leaked out, and even more so since their publication in the late 1950s, the argument has raged as to their authenticity. Many, particularly the Irish, insist they were clever forgeries, concocted by the British government in an effort to discredit a man whose life had become a rallying point for the spirit of Irish Republicanism. What is certain is that only days before he went to the gallows, Casement wrote a letter to an ex-lover referred to in the diaries only as 'Millar'. Years later, the man was identified as Joseph Millar Gordon, a Belfast bank clerk. What all this says about Roger Casement is left to the judgement of history.

Fifteen

THE WEATHERMAN

Josef Jakobs
1941

By the twentieth century, the Tower of London had long since given up any real military role. Beyond its capacity as a well-guarded storehouse for the Crown Jewels, it served primarily as a museum dedicated to displaying a massive collection of ancient arms and armour that had seen action centuries earlier. The one important role it did maintain, however, was that of an enduring symbol of the monarchy and the British Empire. Even during the darkest days of the Second World War, when German bombs threatened to destroy London, King George VI and the government agreed that the Tower would remain open to the public as long as it remained safe and intact. The Tower, like the British people, would stand defiant in the face of the Nazi onslaught.

Much of London was reduced to ruins during months of incessant bombing, and during these raids the Tower was struck no less than fifteen times, killing twenty-three people and two ravens. But, almost miraculously, little serious damage was done to the medieval fabric of the building. As one of the few public places which was never forced to close its doors, the ancient grey walls saw more tourists than ever flock through its gates, including millions of American GIs, all gaping in wonder at the lurid stories of medieval torture and death on the 'block', with which the tower warders regaled the tour groups.

There were always rumours that Hitler's number one henchman, Rudolf Hess, was stashed safely away somewhere in the vast Tower complex, but no one knew for certain where he was, or even if the stories were true – and the government had no intention of making the whereabouts of their most important prisoner public knowledge.

Of course, Hess was there for a short period and he would have probably remained the last prisoner of the world's oldest and most venerable fortress, except for one curious incident; and this came and went so quickly that only a handful of people even knew it had taken place. At least, almost no one knew, or remembered, until one day during the summer of 1991 the Tower was once again reminded of the official role it has played throughout history and even within living memory.

It was the height of the tourist season and the tower warders were working double shifts to cater to the massive crowds of tourists flocking daily through the ancient prison doors. As they had done for nearly two centuries, the once fierce Beefeaters were now mostly retired army officers who guided the crowds from one site to another, entertaining them with an endless string of long-ago tales of murder and mayhem. 'Here is where the young princes were held before they disappeared; probably murdered by their uncle, Richard III' . . . 'Here is where Anne Boleyn was beheaded; and they say that her ghost still roams the walkways of the tower, holding her head under her arm. . . .' It was the same routine every day, but both the Beefeaters and the crowds loved it.

It was during the height of this busy season when one of the warders was leading a tour group from Canada through the ancient, blood-soaked alleys of the Tower. Having finished showing them the site where the headsman's block had once stood, he was about to gather them up and move on to the next stop on the tour, when a middle-aged woman touched him on the arm and whispered apologetically, 'Excuse me, but . . . can you show me the place where they shot my father?' Dumbfounded, the warder could only stare open-mouthed at the woman. He had no idea what she was talking about. When she told the old soldier her father's name was Josef Jakobs, all the colour drained from his face. Now he knew – the Tower remembered.

Turning the tour group over to one of his colleagues, the guide led the woman to the office of Head Warden Major-General Chris Tyler, and asked her to repeat what she had told him. Again, the woman explained that her father had been Josef Jakobs and that she understood he had been executed in the Tower as a Nazi spy some time during the Second World War. General Tyler assured the woman that he would personally show her the spot and asked her to wait in his office for just a minute. When he returned, he handed her a pair of old-fashioned, wire-rimmed glasses and a small Bible, explaining that the glasses had been her father's and that he had requested a Bible the day before he was shot. They were hers if she wanted them.

Clutching the only surviving mementoes of her father, the woman followed General Tyler across Tower Green towards a car park. During the war a corrugated metal shed had stood in this area, and it was here that Josef Jakobs was executed by firing squad. As they walked, Tyler told her everything he knew about her father – the last man to be executed in the Tower of London.

An integral part of Nazi Germany's plan to bring Great Britain to its knees without mounting an actual invasion of the island depended on massive waves of aerial bombardment carried out both by day and night. The notoriously unpredictable English weather, however, made it imperative that updates on weather conditions be broadcast to the German air force, the Luftwaffe, almost continually. To supply this stream of information dozens of spies were smuggled into England, each equipped with a radio transmitter, a code book and a basic knowledge of meteorology.

But spying has always been dangerous work, and in the razor-edged atmosphere of the Second World War any suspicious activity could lead to instant arrest. Consequently, spies were considered nearly as expendable as bullets; pawns in an endless and violent game of power politics and war.

Exactly how Josef Jakobs was recruited as a spy for Nazi Germany remains a mystery. What we do know is that by the time he was drafted into the German army in 1940, he was already forty-two years old and had been a dentist all of his working life – hardly a likely candidate for the high-risk job of espionage.

In July of that year Corporal Jakobs was sent to a training camp run by the German Meteorological Service in occupied Holland, to which he had been assigned. There he underwent three weeks of training sessions in radio communications and meteorology. There seem to have been no special training in espionage techniques, or how to carry out such activities without raising suspicion. This probably did not concern Jakobs too much, however; after all, as far as he knew he was just a weather reporter.

By the end of the year Jakobs was deemed ready to begin his life as a spy. He was issued with a long-range radio transmitter cleverly hidden inside a briefcase, road maps of eastern central England with RAF bases at Upton and Warboys clearly marked so he could avoid getting too close to the military, a false set of identity papers, an ample quantity of counterfeit British money and a Mauser pistol. With these few tools, Jakobs was ordered to parachute into England and establish a clandestine weather station – radioing regular weather reports to German Headquarters in occupied France.

During the night of 31 January 1941, Josef Jakobs parachuted out of a German plane into the cold, quiet countryside of Ramsey Hollow in rural Huntingdonshire. Having no more experience as a paratrooper than he had as a spy, Jakobs' poor landing in a roughly ploughed field left him with a shattered left ankle. Exhausted, freezing cold and racked by wave after wave of searing pain, Jakobs lapsed into unconsciousness only minutes after pulling the parachute over him in an attempt to keep warm. When he awoke in the cold, grey light of morning Jakobs realised immediately just how desperate his situation was. There was no way he could walk, or even stand, but if he didn't get help very soon he could very well die of exposure. In a desperate attempt to attract help, he fumbled through the briefcase for the pistol and fired two shots into the air, hoping the noise would attract some attention. It did.

Two farmers out for an early morning stroll with their dogs walked towards the source of the two sharp reports. To their amazement they found a slim, balding man in a business suit and glasses lying unconscious, pistol in hand, nearly covered by a camouflage-patterned parachute, in the middle of a frozen field. While one of the men stayed behind to guard the curious visitor the other went to the nearby town of Ramsey for the police and an ambulance. As a precaution, the local constable asked several members of the Territorial Army to accompany him to the site. As they extricated the semi-conscious Jakobs from his parachute, the soldiers uncovered his briefcase with its radio transmitter, maps and a fistful of banknotes. Obviously, something was very wrong.

After being taken to the local hospital where his shattered ankle was set and put into a cast, the man was subjected to routine questioning by local authorities. Jakobs constantly denied he was working for the Germans, insisting he had only parachuted into England to escape the Nazis. Certain they had captured a spy, the authorities turned the case, and their prisoner, over to the military authorities who moved Jakobs to Brixton prison where he was officially charged as a spy and sent to appear before a military court martial under strict secrecy. Because of the war, everyone accused of espionage was tried in secret to ensure the enemy never knew which of their agents had been captured and which were still roaming free.

Under intense questioning Jakobs held to his story, insisting that he was not even German; he was a citizen of Luxembourg who had spent his life in Germany working as a dentist. He even claimed that he was half-Jewish – he couldn't be a Nazi. As his story unfolded, Jakobs claimed that he had helped other Jews escape from Germany after the Nazis had come to power, and had been arrested and thrown into a concentration camp when his activities were discovered. Although he admitted he had joined the German army, he said he had only done so as a means of escaping almost certain death in the camps and had agreed to become a spy only as a means of escaping the Nazis. All he wanted was to join the anti-Nazi resistance and fight to free his native Luxembourg from German occupation. It was a good story, but the military judges knew that German spies routinely said they were only trying to escape Nazi-occupied Europe. No final decision would be made on the case until there were more facts to go on.

It didn't take long for the truth to come out – and it was a strange mixture of Jakobs' own story and a mountain of far more damning evidence. Josef Jakobs had, indeed, been born a citizen of Luxembourg, but had renounced his citizenship to serve in the Imperial German Army during the First World War. Then, from Switzerland came court records showing that Jakobs had been arrested in 1924 for selling counterfeit gold. And finally came evidence that Jakobs had, indeed helped Jews escape from Germany, but he had charged them extortionate fees for his services. Josef Jakobs was not a victim of Nazi oppression; he was a convicted criminal, an extortionist and a Nazi spy and saboteur. The sentence was death by hanging.

The problem was, that to be hanged, the condemned had to stand on the scaffold long enough for the trap to be opened – but because of his shattered ankle, Josef Jakobs could not stand at all. Reluctantly, the military court decided Jakobs would face a firing squad; unfortunately, because Brixton prison did not have an active military contingent on duty, there was no way to assemble a firing squad on site. Jakobs would have to be moved elsewhere; and the only place where there were both unused, secure cells and an active military presence was the Tower of London, a contingent of the Scots Guards having been assigned there to guard Rudolf Hess and carry out routine military duties for the duration of the war. Josef Jakobs was duly loaded on to a stretcher, placed in the back of an army lorry and driven from Brixton prison to the Waterloo Block of the Tower. Two days later, on 15 August 1941, he was bundled back on to a stretcher and lifted into the back of an open lorry with two guards. But this time the journey would be much shorter. In his hand was the small Bible which Jakobs had requested from the warden when he first arrived at the Tower.

As the dark green truck wound its way through the early morning maze of alleyways and lanes inside the Tower complex, one of the guards pinned a small patch of black cloth to the front of Jakobs shirt, just beneath his left breast; it had been cut roughly into the shape of a heart. In front of a long, low building of corrugated metal the truck rolled to a stop. Carefully helping Jakobs off the stretcher and resting him on the tailgate of the lorry, the guards could hear men at the far end of the shed grunting and shuffling something heavy.

The long, low shed was the rifle range used by the Scots Guards for routine target practice and the men inside were moving bales of hay into position against the rear wall. It was hard work in the August heat, and it was all the more difficult because the ceiling was barely 5 feet high at the end of the shed where the target normally stood. But the target had been removed. In its place was a simple wooden chair. It was towards this chair that the two guards slowly moved the crippled Corporal Josef Jakobs. The nearer they got to the low end of the building, the slower their progress became. Finally they managed to help Jakobs bend forward and turn round so he could sit in the chair facing the open end of the shed.

Once seated, the officer in charge approached Jakobs and asked him to remove his spectacles. Fumbling with the Bible, his hands shaking, Jakobs complied, handing over his glasses. As the officer gently placed a black hood over Jakobs' head, eight members of the Scots Guards filed across the open end of the shed. One of the Springfield rifles they carried held a blank cartridge, so there was always the chance that any given man had not fired a fatal shot.

When the officer of the day walked out of the shed, the eight men threw the bolts in their rifles, loading a shell into the chamber, and took aim at the small black patch on Jakobs' shirt. At 7.12 a.m. on 15 August 1941, Josef Jakobs became the last man to be executed at the Tower of London in a bloody history stretching back more than nine centuries.

After his execution, Jakobs was quietly buried at Kensal Rise Cemetery in north-west London. The bullet-riddled chair on which he had sat during his last moments was placed in storage where it remained, almost forgotten – at least it remained nearly forgotten until the summer of 1991.

As General Chris Tyler led Josef Jakobs' daughter across the car park near Tower Green, he explained that the old rifle range had been pulled down during the 1960s but he knew approximately where it had been. Leading his charge to the spot, Tyler returned to his office, leaving her to contemplate the fate of a father she had never known. He may have wondered whether he should have told her about the chair.

In 1997 the Royal Armouries collection was preparing to move from its long-time home in the Tower to a new, modern building in Leeds. In the final special exhibit before the move, a glass case appeared among the objects on display. Inside the case was a simple wooden chair, riddled with small, round holes, each surrounded by a dark brown stain. When questioned if it was appropriate to have put Josef Jakobs' death chair on display, especially since Jakobs still had living relatives, the Tower's assistant registrar Robert Chester answered: 'It was a difficult decision, but in the end we decided to go ahead. It is, after all, part of the Tower's history.'

BIBLIOGRAPHY

General Reference

Abbott, G., *Great Escapes from the Tower of London*, Heinemann, London, 1982

——, *The Tower of London As It Was*, Hendon Publishing, 1988

Arnold, T. (ed.), *The History of the English by Henry, Archdeacon of Huntingdon*, Rolls Series, 1879

The Book of Prisoners, <http://www.tower-of-london.com/exec/book.html>

Butler, Sir Thomas, *Her Majesty's Tower of London*, Pitkin Pictorials, London, 1972

Carey, John (ed.), *Eyewitness to History*, Avon Books, New York, 1987

Carkeet-James, Colonel E.H., *Her Majesty's Tower of London*, Staples Press, London, 1953

Catholic Encyclopedia, <http://www.newadvent.org>

Chamberlin, Russell, *The Tower of London: An Illustrated History*, Webb & Bower, London, 1989

Davey, R., *The Tower of London*, no publisher given, 1919

Foxe, John, *The Acts and Monuments of John Foxe*, Vol. VIII, Seeley, Burnside & Seeley, London, 1843–9

Handbook of British Chronology, 3rd edn, 1986

Harper, Charles G., *The Tower of London*, Chapman & Hall, London, 1909

Hassall, W.O. (ed.), *They Saw It Happen 55 BC–1485*, Basil Blackwell, Oxford, 1963

Headley, Olwen, *Prisoners in the Tower*, York Minster Library, York, 1979

Hibbert, Christopher, *Tower of London*, Reader's Digest, London, 1971

Hudson, M.E. and Clark, Mary, *Crown of a Thousand Years*, Crown Publishers, New York, 1978

Impey, Edward, and Parnell, Geoffrey, *The Tower of London: The Official Illustrated History*, Merrill Publishers, London, 2000

Lewis, Jon E. (ed.), *The Mammoth Book of How It Happened*, Robinson Publishing, London, 2001

Macaulay, T.B., *History of England*,
<http//www.mindspring.com/~strecorsoc/ macaulay/m05a.html>

Mears, Kenneth J., *The Tower of London, 900 Years of English History*, Phaidon, Oxford, 1988

Minney, R.J., *The Tower of London*, Prentice Hall, Upper Saddle River, NJ, 1970

Parnell, Geoffrey, *English Heritage Book of the Tower of London*, Batsford, London, 1993

Rowse, A.L., *The Tower of London in the History of the Nation*, Book Club Associates, London, 1972

Shuttleworth, Dorothy, *The Tower of London*, Bailey Bros and Swinfen, Folkestone, 1972

Treasures of the Tower: Inscriptions, no author listed, HMSO, London, 1976

Wilson, Derek, *The Tower – 1078–1978*, Book Club Associates, London, 1978

Wilson, Mary, *Stories of the Tower*, Cassell, London, 1896

Chapter Sources
The Axe, the Arrow and the Wailing Monk: William the Conqueror

The Anglo-Saxon Chronicle, Everyman Press, London, 1912

Douglas, David C., *William the Conqueror: The Norman Impact upon England*, University of California Press, Berkeley, 1964

Heworth, David, *1066: The Year of the Conquest*, Penguin, New York, 1981

McLynn, Frank, *1066: The Year of Three Battles*, Random House, London, 1999

Dangerous Liaisons: Wat Tyler and the Peasants' Revolt

Dean, James M. (ed.), *Literature of Richard II's Reign and the Peasants' Revolt*,
<http://128.151.244.128/camelot/teams/richint.htm>

Froissart, Jean, *The Chronicles*, Viking, New York, 1978

Oman, C. (tr.), *The Great Revolt of 1381*, Stackpole, Harrisburg, PA, 1989

Account of the Insurrection of Walter Tyler and of his death at the hands of William Walworth, the Mayor, Geoffrey Chaucer,
<http://icg.fas. harvard.edu/~chaucer/special/varia/life_of_Ch/wattyler.html>

Conflagration: The Peasants' Revolt (parts 1, 2, 3 & 4),
<http://historymedren.about.com/education/historymedren/library/weekly/a a072498.htm>

Medieval Source book; Anonimalle Chronicle: English Peasants' Revolt 1381,
<http://www.fordham.edu/halsall/source/anon1381.html>

VillageNet Local History (Peasants' Revolt 1381)
<http://www.villagenet. co.uk/history/peasantrevolt.html>

A Family Affair: The Princes in the Tower

Clive, Mary, *The Sun of York: A Biography of Edward IV*, Sphere, London, 1975

Dockray, Keith, *Richard III: A Sourcebook*, Sutton Publishing, Stroud, 1997

Hallam, Elizabeth (ed.), *Chronicles of the Wars of the Roses*, Markham, Penguin Books Canada, 1988

Weir, Alison, *The Princes in the Tower*, Pimlico, London, 1993

The Warder, the Wolf and the Woman: John Wolfe and Alice Tankerville.

All the notes have been taken from the general reference books listed above.

Treason in the Bedroom: Katherine Howard

Erikson, Carolly, *Great Harry*, St Martin's Press, New York, 1997

Fraser, Antonia, *The Wives of Henry VIII*, Vintage Books, Vancouver & Washington, USA, 1994

Weir, Alison, *Six Wives of Henry VIII*, Grove Press, Berkeley, California, 2000

<http://www.englishhistory.net/tudor/letter13.html>

<http://www.suite101.com/article.cfm/tudor_england/20530>

<http://gen.culpeper.com/historical/howard/part1.htm>

<http://www.datasync.com/~davidg59/henry8.html>

Nine Days a Queen: Lady Jane Grey

Plowden, Alison, *Lady Jane Grey and the House of Suffolk*, Franklin Watts, New York, 1986

Correspondence of Lady Jane Grey,

<http://ladyjane.iinet.net.au/ correspondence.html>

Lady Jane Grey The Nine Days Queen,

<http://www.castleland.webprovider. com/ladyjanegrey.html>

Lady Jane Grey [Nine Days], [Correspondence], [Jane the Queen], [Execution],

<http://ladyjane.iinet.au/nine_days.html>

Lady Jane Grey, Marriage, Early Life,

<htttp://www.geocities.com/Athens/ Parthenon/index.html>

Lady Jane Grey, The Nine Days Queen,

<http://www.casteland.webprovider. com/ladyjanegrey.html>

List of State Papers of Queen Jane, Proclamations of the Accession of Queen Jane and Queen Mary, Accession of Queen Jane, Chronicle of Queen Jane, Will of Edward VI, Notes,

<http://tudor.simplenet.com/primary/janemary/app3.html>

List of State Papers of the Reign of Queen Jane,
    <http://tudor.simplenet.com /primary/janemary/app3.html>
Proclamations of the Accession of Queen Jane and of Queen Mary,
    <http://tudor.simplenet.com/primary/janemary/app3.html>

The Devil's Dancing Bear: Bishop Edmund Bonner

Alexander, Gina, *Bonner and the Marian Persecutions*, Kidbrooke School,
    London, 1975
Burnet, Gilbert and Pocock, N. (eds), *History of the Reformation of the Church
    of England*, London, 1891
Catholic Encyclopedia online: <http://www.newadvent.com>
Dickens, A.G., *The English Reformation*, Pennsylvania State University Press,
    Pennsylvania, 1964
Dixon, R.W., *History of the Church of England*, 1891
Foxe, John, *Foxe's Book of Martyrs*, Whitaker House, Pittsburgh, Pennsylvania,
    1985
Foxe, John, *Acts & Monuments of John Foxe*, Vol. VIII, Seeley, Burnside &
    Seeley, London, 1843–9

The Spymaster: Francis Walsingham and Anthony Babington

Hibbert, Christopher, *Elizabeth I: The Virgin Queen*, Guild Publishing, London,
    1990
Jenkins, Elizabeth, *Elizabeth the Great*, Coward-McCann, New York, 1959
Mary Queen of Scots and the Babington Plot,
    <http://ccat.sas.upenn.edu/~jmcgill/project.html>
Queen Mary's Letters to Babington/Babington's Letter to Mary Queen of Scots,
    <http://ccat.sas.upenn.edu/~jmcgill/marysletter.html>
Williams, Neville, *The Life and Times of Elizabeth I*, Weidenfeld and Nicolson,
    London, 1972

Gunpowder, Treason and Plot: Guy 'Guido' Fawkes

Caraman, Fr Philip (tr.), *The Autobiography of a Hunted Priest, Fr. John Gerard*,
    Four Faces Press, Springfield, Virginia, 2000
Fraser, Antonia, *Faith and Treason – the Story of the Gunpowder Plot*,
    Doubleday, New York, 1996
Gardiner, Samuel Rawson, *What the Gunpowder Plot Was*, London, 1897
Jardine, David, *A Narrative of the Gunpowder Plot*, London, 1857

Simons, Eric N., *The Devil of the Vault*, Frederick Muller, London, 1963
<http://www.armitstead.com/gunpowder/considerations_6.html>

A Right Royal Heist: Colonel Thomas Blood
Thomas Blood, Generally Called Colonel Blood, G. Smeeton, London, 1817
Strong, Roy, *Lost Treasures of Britain: Five Centuries of Creation and Destruction*,
   Guild Publishing, London, 1990
<http://tarlton.law.utexas.edu/lpop/etext/newgate/blood.htm>

The Bloody Assizes: The Duke of Monmouth and Judge Jeffreys
Historical Account of the Life and Magnanimous Acts of the Most Illustrious
   Protestant Prince James, Duke of Monmouth, 1683 (from the collection of
   York Minster Library)
Macaulay, T.B., *History of England*, Ch V, online at
<http://www.mind spring.com/~strecorsoc/macaulay/m05a.html>
<http://shepton.mallet.ukonline.co.uk/history/history_jeffreys_bio.html>

The King Over the Water: William, Lord Maxwell
Bland, Elizabeth (ed.), *Exciting Escape Stories*, Octopus, London, 1980
Burke's Peerage, Scotland online at
<http://www.burkes-scotland.com/ sites/scotland/esnews/es0202b2.asp>
Fraser, Paul, *Book of Caerlareroch*, Edinburgh, 1873
The Highlander: Magazine of Scottish Heritage, September/October 1992, pp. 52–5
Scott, Maxwell, *The Making of Abbotsford and Incidents in Scottish History*,
   London, 1897
The Scots Peerage, Edinburgh, 1909

The American (P)Resident: Henry Laurens
Age of Revolution, Henry Laurens,
<http://www.npg.si.edu/col/age/ laurens.htm>
American Revolutionary War in the South, Pt II, by Paul R. Sarrett, Jr, 1991,
   <http://members.aol.com/esarrett/sc/arw_hst2.htm>
'Capture of Henry Laurens', from *The Annual Register, or A View of the History,
   Politics and Literature, for the Year 1781*, Pall-Mall, London, 1782
   <http://home.ptd.net/~revwar/Laurens1.html>
*A Narrative of the Capture of Henry Laurens, of his Confinement in the Tower of
   London*, Henry Laurens, South Carolina Historical Society, 1857

Papers of Henry Laurens,
<http://mep.cla.sc.edu/dynaweb/MEP/hl/ @Generic_BookTextView/35>
Papers of Henry Laurens, Model Editions Partnerships, 1999,
<http://mep. cla.sc.edu/dynaweb/MEP/hl@Generic_BookTextView/35>

The Black Book: Sir Roger Casement
Inglis, Brian, *Roger Casement*, Coronet, London, 1974
The Crime Against Europe, Roger Casement, C.J. Fallon, Dublin, 1958
'Outcry as secret gay life of Irish hero is "proved"', *Guardian*, 25 July 1999
Rebellion in Mexico, China and Ireland,
<http://www.eurekanet.com/~ fesmitha/h2/ch06.htm>
Sir Roger Casement,
<http://www.ulst.ac.uk/thisisland/modules/ww1/caseintro.html>

The Weatherman: Josef Jakobs
Josef Jakobs file, Public Record Office
Sellers, Leonard, *Shot in the Tower*, Leo Cooper, London, 1997
Wasserstein, Bernard, 'Hitler's Jewish Agents', *Jerusalem Post*, 9 April 1999

INDEX